# The Entrepreneurial Edge

# The Entrepreneurial Edge

## CANADA'S TOP ENTREPRENEURS
## REVEAL THE SECRETS OF THEIR SUCCESS

### DONALD RUMBALL

KEY PORTER·BOOKS

Canadian Cataloguing in Publication Data

Rumball, Donald
   The entrepreneurial edge

   ISBN 1-55013-145-1          65826

   1. Entrepreneurship - Canada.   I. Title.

   HB615.R85 1989      658.4'2'0926      C89-094085-1

Typesetting:   Pixel Graphics Inc.
Printed and bound in Canada

Key Porter Books Limited
70 The Esplanade
Toronto, Ontario
Canada  M5E 1R2

89 90 91 92 93 5 4 3 2 1

# CONTENTS

*For Natalie and Jill*

# ACKNOWLEDGEMENTS

This book would not have been written without the gentle encouragement of Nick Harris, who knew just when to push and when to wait, and whose frank comments kept me on the straight and narrow. Rena Blatt's encouragement and encyclopaedic knowledge of academic research on entrepreneurs were much appreciated. My editor, Laurie Coulter, improved the book significantly—you can't ask for more than that. All the people at Key Porter have been both helpful and encouraging.

This book grew out of my happy years as editor of *Small Business Magazine*, where I discovered the world of entrepreneurship. I would like to thank Maclean Hunter for giving me first-hand experience with some key aspects of entrepreneurship during the rocky launch of this now successful magazine. In the five years I was with *Small Business Magazine*, I met many wonderful people who shared my enthusiasm for entrepreneurs and entrepreneurship; they have been enormously helpful over the years in helping me understand the many aspects of this fascinating occupation. I would particularly like to thank those who gave me all their best leads when I compiled my initial list of 600 entrepreneurs. Finally, I would like to thank the 100 entrepreneurs who contributed their time so generously in the long interviews I conducted with them. Their inspiration made the three years flash by. They all seem like friends now.

Last but not least, my wife, Jill, gave me practical and emotional support when I needed it most. And I can never thank enough my irrepressible eight-year-old daughter, Natalie, whose interruptions always made my day.

# INTRODUCTION

It is a rare privilege to travel this country from coast to coast interviewing the extraordinary men and women who lead our entrepreneurial businesses. They have the panache, the directness and the joie de vivre that flows from a total commitment to an obsession they relish. They are open and they love to talk about their businesses. As characters, they encompass every conceivable personality type, if only because one of their common traits is a resolute resistance to conformity. Nevertheless, there are patterns in their behaviour, just as there are a number of techniques which many of them have found to work well in entrepreneurial firms. This book is both a tribute to these fascinating men and women and an exploration of the principal techniques that contribute to their success.

The intense interest in entrepreneurs is a relatively recent phenomenon. Only a decade has passed since politicians discovered that entrepreneurs are responsible for creating about 80% of all new jobs. This has set in train a gradual shift in government policies to accommodate the interests of entrepreneurial firms. The general public, however, still has only a fuzzy idea of who entrepreneurs are and what they do, so their reputation is still less than satisfactory, even if it is much improved. There has, though, been an enormous surge in appreciation for the potential of entrepreneurship in the executive suites of big business. These firms, many of them groaning under the weight of growing bureaucracies, have learned that entrepreneurship holds the key to attributes that are in short supply in their own organizations—inventiveness, flexibility and the ability to use resources economically.

Big businesses have come to understand that small firms are not big firms that haven't grown big yet. They are completely different economic animals. They are breeding grounds for highly desirable attributes, and they are valuable in their own right as innovators. This has unleashed a flurry of research into the attributes of entrepreneurs in an attempt to understand the phenomenon. Though welcome at first, this attention has unfortunately mythologized more than it has elucidated. The word *entrepreneurial* has acquired the status of a buzzword and has been co-opted by too many people seeking the style but not the substance, to the point where the word has lost its meaning altogether. This book aims to set the record straight.

*The Entrepreneurial Edge* paints entrepreneurs in their environment, showing how their unique approach to life and business empowers them to provide a form of economic leadership that all nations now recognize to be critical to their long-term well-being. Big businesses and governments now recognize that they need to re-create environments which stimulate similar behaviour in their organizations. They cannot become entrepreneurs, because they lack two of the critical elements of entrepreneurship—goals that are out of the reach of the resources they control and the risk of losing all their personal assets if they fail. These are two of the seven elements of entrepreneurship, and they hold the key to entrepreneurial innovation and flexibility. They are the source of their energy. They force entrepreneurs to react to change almost instantaneously. The executives in big business and governments cannot be entrepreneurs, by definition, but they can come close. Like everyone else, they now recognize the need to understand entrepreneurship.

One hundred entrepreneurs were interviewed in depth for this book. They were asked to articulate their visions, their plans, their strengths and weaknesses, their techniques of leadership, their attitudes, their successes and their failures. The interviews were deliberately left open-ended so that the entrepreneurs could say in their own words how they approach the principal tasks of entrepreneurial leadership. Their candid views of themselves, supported by many other interviews with their friends and associates, shine through in this book. All but two of the entrepreneurs had received very little publicity at the time they were interviewed, so they did not suffer from the confusion about themselves that so often afflicts well-known people who take their own media images seriously. All were reinterviewed when their circumstances changed in the course of the three years it took to research and write this book. There was little room for illusion.

The personal attributes and business techniques of the 100 have been exhaustively analyzed. The sample is large enough to capture all the significant patterns in their behaviour, but not large enough that the proportional distribution of their techniques can be said to represent the universe of entrepreneurs. Although some of the conclusions drawn are consistent with other research, there are some new conclusions, too, which I hope will serve as hypotheses for further research. Most importantly, the in-depth interviews made it possible to develop rounded pictures of how and why entrepreneurs do what they do. Each analytical conclusion is illustrated by profiles of one or more of the entrepreneurs, who embody the principle, putting flesh on the conceptual bones.

Almost all of the entrepreneurs in this book have had business failures. Most of them probably have a few more to go. Some had failures while the book was being written. Two entrepreneurs lost their businesses in scandals which preoccupied the national media for months on end. Others were kicked out of their firms because they didn't control 50% of the shares. Failures don't faze them. Almost two-thirds felt they had benefitted from them. All have achieved great things and most of them will do so again. We, too, can learn from their experiences.

# PART I

ENTREPRENEURS AND
ENTREPRENEURSHIP

# CHAPTER 1

# VANISHING STEREOTYPES

*"The successful entrepreneurs I know have one thing — and only one thing — in common: they are not risk-takers."*
— Peter Drucker in *Innovation and Entrepreneurship*

*"I do my best when my back's right against the wall. That's when I see things most clearly. When things are running smoothly, I look for ways to dig myself into a hole. I deliberately take a massive risk. I'm confident I can work my way out of it."*
— Peter Oliver of Oliver's

In the first quarter of 1982, Roderick Bryden's personal net worth sank by $150 million. At the beginning of the year, he had been sitting comfortably on top of an $80-million fortune, based on the value of the shares he owned in his subsidiaries. He was leveraged to the hilt, having borrowed enormous sums of money from the banks to buy those shares. Then it all collapsed when the market value of the shares in one of the companies he controlled tumbled 93%, dragging down his net worth to a deficit of $72 million. The company in question, SHL Systemhouse, had made a huge gamble and lost.

Yet Bryden insists he's risk averse. It's a bizarre viewpoint, especially in such an unusually bold entrepreneur, but it's an attitude toward risk-taking that is widely shared by entrepreneurs. When they assess risk, their perception is moulded more by their own tolerance for risk than by any objective measure of the risk. It's true they don't usually go out of their way to court risks, but they don't avoid them either, because risk is an integral part of entrepreneurship. When they take a risk, entrepreneurs don't dwell on the downside, they make themselves comfortable with it. Sometimes they have supreme confidence in their own ability to overcome all potential obstacles, sometimes they trivialize the potential loss ("it's only money"), sometimes they work so hard at covering every conceivable angle that they reduce their chances of failing to minimal levels. Whichever technique they use, they minimize the risk in their own minds and wind up seeing themselves as risk averse.

This has created considerable confusion in the army of researchers who have been plumbing the depths of the entrepreneur's psyche. Too many have taken what entrepreneurs say about themselves at face value, even to the point of sending them multiple-choice questionnaires with questions like, "Do you like to run red lights?" Inevitably, they draw the conclusion that entrepreneurs are risk averse or, at best, moderate risk-takers. Peter Drucker writes emphatically in *Innovation and Entrepreneurship* that "the successful entrepreneurs I know have one thing—and only one thing—in common: they are not risk-takers." The leading academics have concluded that entrepreneurs take no more risks than managers in large corporations, thereby submerging, against all the lay evidence of independent observers, the paradigm of the entrepreneur as a risk-taker.

There is a fundamental flaw in this argument. Ownership does make a difference. A manager and an entrepreneur, faced with the same business situation, may indeed make the same decision, taking the same degree of risk. However, whereas the manager can reasonably expect understanding, shared blame and forgiveness if the venture should fail, the entrepreneur can expect personal financial ruin. If the willingness to take risks is measured by the risk-taker's perception of the probability of failure, as has been the case in many of the studies that conclude entrepreneurs are not risk-takers, there is indeed no difference between entrepreneurs and managers. But if willingness to take risks is measured by the ability to tolerate the potential for significant *personal* financial loss, the entrepreneur is a greater risk-taker by several orders of magnitude. As in other traits attributed to entrepreneurs, fiction has overpowered the facts.

Rod Bryden's meteoric rise to the heights from which he fell so precipitously in 1982 was as impressive as it was doomed. In 1974, when he was 34, he started Systemhouse in Ottawa with $200,000 in capital, a quarter of it subscribed by the employees, the rest out of his own pocket. It was an instant success and soon became a high-tech flyer and darling of the stock market. It didn't stop accelerating until 1981, when its sales hit $29 million and its profits $2 million. Despite its explosive growth—and even at that size, its sales were growing at almost 60% a year, its profits at 90%—it was well managed, having met budget for 28 consecutive quarters. Its success was founded on the talent of its programmers, who developed custom software for large organizations trying to hitch their particular needs to the power of computers.

Systemhouse's clients, however, had been sending out warning signals. They had been saying that custom software was very expensive, and many of them didn't mind adapting their systems to accommodate cheaper off-the-shelf programs. Also, good programmers were hard to find and harder to train, so Bryden's team decided to multiply the applications of each programmer's work by developing standard software that could be sold off the shelf to hundreds of customers. Called proprietary application software (PAS to the initiated), this business is radically different from custom software. When a software firm takes on a custom project, it completes the work in 90 days, on average, and then sends out its invoice. With PAS, before a single dollar of sales revenue makes it into the bank account, the firm has to develop the software, making sure it is flexible enough to be relevant to a large number of potential users, and then build a distribution network to sell the package. "It's all up front," Bryden says. "You can't borrow against it. You take hard cash and convert it into non-financeable assets. You have to build the asset. The only test of how you're doing is if you're on budget."

At the time, Bryden owned half of Systemhouse, the key employees the other half, and the switch to PAS cost too much money for them to finance it on their own. So Bryden took Systemhouse public in 1980 in a fanfare of excitement and great expectations. Work started on several PAS systems and appeared to be going according to plan, leading smoothly up to the launch date. "Then," Bryden says, with just the slightest catch in his voice, "you open the door. Oh shit! No customers. It's a true equity investment. Unfortunately we lost our money." The share price of Systemhouse on the Toronto Stock Exchange plummeted to 85¢ from $13. Many other custom houses, it seems, had come to the same conclusion as Bryden and had poured hundreds of millions of dollars into software all around the world, flooding Systemhouse's niche and drowning its product. The company had to write off all the development work for the PAS, including the sales organization.

The custom side of Systemhouse was still making money, but the company now had a massive capital deficit, subsequently declaring a loss for 1982 of almost $30 million. Although the creditors of Systemhouse might reasonably have been expected to shunt Bryden aside at that point, they decided their best hope was to leave him at the helm. He prepared a complete plan, laying out the strategies for a return to profitability, and they accepted it. Bryden put in $10 million of his own money, the public $15 million and the Bank of Montreal $20 million. As Chairman, Bryden had concentrated on raising finance, leaving day-to-day management to the team headed by Jack Davies. He now took full control of the company, slashing its work force by 40% and refocussing the business.

Bryden had already formulated his goal at that time to build a group with annual revenues of $3 billion. It may have seemed pretentious then, but no one doubts he'll make it now. His boundless ambition gives him a sense of urgency that is only partly camouflaged by the enormous pleasure he derives from his business. He talks and moves with a tightly controlled exuberance, crisply decisive and resolutely determined. Yet he retains a curious idealism, joking that he's "notorious in the company for being somewhat theoretical and philosophical."

He believes in the power of positive thinking. "A person who can identify shortcomings in everyone is generally not trusted," he says. But he's also demanding of the people with whom he works and won't tolerate poor performance: "In large organizations, they build around people who aren't performing. That's terribly counterproductive." As for himself, he knows what he has to offer the world. He knows which of his many skills are commonplace, which are rare, and he disciplines himself to focus on the activities that draw on his rarer skills.

In 1982-84, it was his remarkable approach to risk that, more than anything else, was the basis of the turnaround of System-house. He makes a clear distinction between owning and running a company. A business is a machine that makes money as long as it's properly managed; the owner's job is to preserve the financial strength that will free the business to do what it does well. If the business needs more funds to finance its growth, the owner's job is to provide those funds without disturbing its ratio of debt to equity. When owners themselves need help in financing their businesses, they should reduce their ownership level by bringing in new shareholders, or they should borrow the money to make the necessary investments themselves.

He believes in apportioning the risk among stakeholders so that each bears a fair share. Employees can't take risk. Custom-ers can't. Management can't take capital risk. Suppliers should have no risk—unless they have such a large account, they stand to benefit from their customer's growth. "Always be sure the party who takes the risk does it knowingly and benefits from the success of the activity for which the risk is taken. At the capital structure level, if it's an uncertain situation, capital has to be venture capital, where risk and return are high. If the company is predictable, shareholder risk lies in broad eco-nomic trends, so you can bring in the public shareholder."

He also believes banking risk should be strictly limited. "Banks should take no risk except for major broad-based eco-nomic changes, when they can fall back on assets. Many entrepreneurs don't understand this. If Systemhouse has some spare cash, we don't expect them to be taking equity risks with that money or we'd invest it ourselves."

Bryden has followed these tenets religiously. His ownership of his stable of companies is leveraged to a degree that would terrify most people. Nevertheless, the companies themselves are conservatively financed. If anything goes wrong, he may be replaced as owner, but the underlying asset is not overloaded with debt and therefore remains viable. From the very begin-ning in 1974, Systemhouse did not take on huge debts to finance its headlong expansion. It grew on the equity pumped in by Bryden's wholly owned holding company, Kinburn Corp. Kinburn was, in turn, financed largely by bank loans and other debt. "I always position myself to be the ultimate source of risk," he says. "I bet the company all the time, but I can only put myself at risk. I bet my ownership."

In the next breath, he says, "I'm less of a risk-taker than you think. I'm not a gambler." The rest of us may be forgiven for withholding judgement on that until the benefit of hindsight removed all doubt about his strategic acuity. But in the turmoil of Systemhouse's return from the living dead in 1982-84, most would have judged Bryden to have lost his marbles had they heard him claim he is not a risk-taker. For him, however, there was never any doubt. "I would not intentionally enter into a transaction where I didn't believe I would succeed. A third party, with the information available to them, might perceive it as risky because they don't have my perception of the value I can add. I'm making a judgement about my ability to control the outcome. On that basis, I should take the risk."

His solution to the PAS debacle ran true to form. He immediately isolated the custom side of the firm, along with a few viable PAS programs, and made them the core of the new Systemhouse. This slimmed-down business turned profitable in two years, by which time its value had risen to $17 million, according to Bryden. He then took what was left after salvaging the most viable parts of the old company, and sold them. He still thought they had great potential, so he offered them to the shareholders as a separate business. They declined and Bryden bought them himself for $14 million. Five years later, Bryden still wasn't sure he would ever recover his investment in them. They hadn't done as well as he had hoped, and he ruefully admitted that, although he had done the right thing by taking them out of Systemhouse, the price he had paid Systemhouse shareholders for them was rather optimistic.

While all this was going on at Systemhouse, Bryden had kept just as busy in the other leg of his empire, Paperboard Industries,which uses recycled paper to manufacture the boxboard and linerboard that goes into corrugated cardboard. He had first bought into the company in 1979, when its owner, Hugh Campbell, a second cousin, found he couldn't find markets for the extra production from his plant in Trenton, Ontario, after he had tripled its capacity. He had had several offers to buy his business but had declined them because he was convinced the prospective buyers would close the mill down, a prospect he refused to countenance for Trenton. He would sell to his cousin, though, so Bryden put up $500,000 for 60% of the equity and some preferred shares.

He wasted no time implementing a typically bold strategy. After several technical adjustments to improve efficiency, he spent $22 million buying five of the company's customers. Paperboard Industries was a residual supplier to its customers, and its sales fell dramatically whenever there was a downturn in the market. Buying the five companies solved that problem, although they were all losing money, because they gave Paperboard direct access to their 1,500 customers. He turned around all but one of the five companies in short order (the fifth just took a couple of years longer) and cranked up the mill to operate at full capacity.

When Bryden finally dug himself out of his $72-million hole in 1986, he started going aggressively after acquisitions. He heard that year that Morris Belkin had had two heart attacks and figured he might be interested in selling his forest products company, Belkin Inc. Bryden approached him and found a receptive audience. With annual sales of almost $400 million, Belkin was somewhat larger than Paperboard, which Bryden had by then yanked up to sales of $130 million from $35 million in 1979. Typically, Bryden had no fear. He bought Belkin for $235 million, most of which he raised in private placements. Three years later, sales in his forest products group were approaching $700 million.

In all, Bryden raised $900 million in debt and equity in 1987, before the October 19 collapse of the stock markets. He invested even more than that, however. The balance of the financing for the breakneck growth of Systemhouse and the string of acquisitions had to come from Bryden's holding company, Kinburn Corp., which was, in turn, borrowing from the banks. Even Bryden was beginning to feel a little uncomfortable with his massive bank loan with its floating interest rate geared to prime rate.

In August and September of 1987, Bryden decided to pour

some equity into Kinburn Corp., but he ran into a brick wall. Although his subsidiary companies' stocks were trading at high levels, no investors wanted to pay the logical price for a holding company in high-tech industries. They didn't believe the high earnings multiples, or those of the market in general, were sustainable. So Bryden switched to Plan B. He went looking for long-term debt to replace his daunting floating-rate bank loans. Because he didn't want to do it through a bank, and a public underwriting didn't seem feasible, he sought out large corporations with huge cash reserves. He settled on BCE, the holding company for Bell Canada, Northern Telecom, TransCanada PipeLines and many other assorted companies. BCE ultimately lent him more than $300 million.

While he was negotiating to refinance his holding company, the stock market crash hit, and Systemhouse stock dropped by a half to about $15, before climbing back to $20 by year end. It was not comforting for potential lenders, but BCE stayed the course, closing the deal in January, 1988. By then, Bryden had decided to use some of the proceeds to buy back stock in his two main companies. The crash had reduced their prices far below the levels at which they had been sold to the public, so Bryden could restore his control position profitably. The purchase gave him 100% control of Paperboard and 50.5% of Systemhouse. He used the rest of the BCE money to pay down bank debt and to buy a couple of companies that BCE owned itself, including the holding company for ComputerLand Canada stores.

As part of the deal with BCE, Bryden issued warrants to buy 49% of Kinburn's stock after five years. If BCE doesn't exercise the warrants, Bryden has to repay its loans between 1993 and 1995. As always, Bryden had figured out all the angles in his megadeal. "If I lose out on the deal and cannot support the loan, the worst that can happen is that I give Bell the shares I purchase with their loan. I would be in no different a position than I am in now, but I will have cleaned up the market. The best that could happen in this scenario [that he cannot support the loan] is that I get another investor to take out Bell."

Needless to say, he doesn't expect to be in a position where he cannot support the loan, but life with Bryden is never predictable. A scant few months after he had settled all the details of his arrangement with BCE, Systemhouse developed a couple of small problems. In the systems integration business, it can be enormously expensive to bid on a contract, because the system has to be half built just to submit a bid. A company growing as fast as Systemhouse spends huge amounts of money on bids relative to its revenues, so Systemhouse decided to write off its bidding expenses over two years instead of immediately. The analysts didn't like that. Bryden accepted their verdict and wrote off $9 million, mostly in deferred bidding costs, in the summer of 1988.

At about the same time, Systemhouse's Washington branch ran into trouble. This office, which did almost half the company's business in the U.S., was heavily concentrated in the defense industry. Bryden acknowledges, typically, that he didn't react fast enough to a deteriorating situation. He didn't pay close enough attention to the flow of information that was signalling trouble as overhead expenses got out of control. The company had thrown its hat into too many rings and drained its cash flow. The Washington office was also hit by a 40-day freeze on spending at the Pentagon. Overall, the branch lost $1.7 million in 1988 compared to an expected profit of $500,000. Bryden estimates the temporary lax controls on the branches at Systemhouse cost the company about $10 million, without impairing in any way the company's ability to earn future profits.

The stock market's judgement on these problems was dramatic. It dumped the company's shares, dropping them $15, for a total paper loss of $390 million. Bryden, looking a little more harassed by then, but still in complete control and confident of his ability to overcome all obstacles, was resigned to the short-sightedness of the market. "The shares weren't worth $30 before the crash, and they weren't worth $10 after the Washington problem. They were probably worth $20 before the crash, and they're worth about the same now."

Despite his equanimity, the ride has taken its toll. In 1988, he separated from his wife of 28 years. Like so many successful entrepreneurs, he worked too hard to spend enough time nurturing his family relationships. "If I had spent more time on my marriage," he said later, "I would have advanced one-third the way in twice the time." There was no animosity, just a recognition that his family couldn't take the pace at which he lived. "I worked hard, constantly not knowing what I was going to do until I was doing it, or even until I had done it. It was as if we were driving along a twisting, dangerous road, in beautiful scenery, at breakneck speed. It was wonderful for me, lots of fun, but it was too fast for my family. They weren't driving and they couldn't control the pace of unrelenting change."

Bryden sees his career as having accomplished in 15 years what most families take three generations to achieve. "In a normal evolution, I would have progressed from a small farm to a solid academic career as the dean of a law school or even the president of a small university. Then my children would have followed me and maybe one would have started a business and built it into something important in a region. Then his children might have built it into a national business of some size." It's all said without any hubris, just a calm statement of the bald facts.

It took Bryden almost five years from the Systemhouse collapse to work his way back into the black. His acquisition binge raised sales for his whole group from $240 million in 1986 to $900 million in 1988. In the five years from 1983, his group's sales doubled four times. At the end of this spurt, he owed his creditors more than half a billion dollars. His annual interest payments in early 1989 were more than $60 million. Even Bryden seemed a little awestruck.

Not bad for a man who started from scratch in 1974 with one employee and a good reputation from his five-year stint in and around the federal government. Despite the audacious leaps of faith he's taken along the way to turn around hopeless situations, he gives no sense of the tycoon. He has made some concessions to his prominence, however. His new offices in Ottawa's Metropolitan Life tower bear all the signs of a trendy designer's work—mahogany furniture everywhere, with brass fittings set against a grey background, highlighted with mauve. As he sits at his desk, he has a spectacular bird's-eye view of Parliament Hill.

By mid-1989, he had achieved relative stability with a net worth of several million dollars and two main operating companies that were financially sound and building significant asset value for their owner. With sales for 1989 on course to pass $1.5 billion, his goal of a $3-billion group didn't seem far off. "The next five years will generate real value for me," he said in the spring of 1989. "Not a lot has to go back down into the operating companies. I'm not very rich now, but I control a machine in good working order. I was very, very exposed, but as the balance begins to come, the increments will be considerable."

Few entrepreneurs actually enjoy taking risks; most do so only because it comes with the territory. They take risks only occasionally and in carefully chosen circumstances. They need to have a prize that is out of proportion to the risk, and it must not be a straightforward gamble—the outcome must be susceptible to the influence of the entrepreneur's particular set of skills. But when they do take risks, the risks are often larger than anything that could be tolerated by most people. There can be no entrepreneurship without a willingness to act when an opportunity arises that calls for the assumption of significant risks.

Bill Pattison is perhaps closer to this model of risk-taking than Bryden. He co-founded the first Delta Hotel in British Columbia in 1962, then went on to build it into a highly successful chain as president and 10%-owner. In 1988, when the majority shareholders (Canadian Imperial Bank of Commerce and Great-West Life) sold their interests to another group, Pattison bowed out. At 56, the respected and undisputed master of his business, he didn't want to sell, but his partners wanted out. They weren't comfortable with their controlling interest in a volatile business run by a man who, despite his unquestioned skills and energy, represented a risk to them because he had had a quadruple bypass operation two years before.

Pattison, like Bryden, has seen the spectre of failure, but it convinced him he never wanted to repeat the experience. The hotel business is a risky business, involving large sums of money and volatile markets. Pattison didn't choose the industry; he fell into it as a young man and it became his "milk cow." He has the mentality of people who grew up on farms during the Depression. "The milk cow is what enables you to keep body and soul together. It gives you the base that enables you to move." Although he wonders now if the hotel industry is an ideal milk cow, he's made it work for him. It certainly began well. His first hotel, started with several silent partners, was an instant success. His partners provided most of the money, but he took the credit as the man in charge. The early success precipitated a second hotel five years later; however, this time he got burned, because he over-leveraged his investment. The business couldn't support the lease of the property. "We nearly lost everything," he says, "so I became very conservative. Bankruptcy's something that's not supposed to happen." All his subsequent lease agreements contained a stop-loss clause that breaks the lease if the loss exceeds $5 million.

Pattison really is what most entrepreneurs only say they are. He's risk averse. Bryden's approach would put Pattison on the fast track to a nervous breakdown. He nails down risk to within an inch of its life. He measures it, shares it around, limits it, avoids it. He has paid for his strategy by growing a lot slower than he might have—and certainly a lot slower than other hotel chains—but he has nevertheless built a chain of hotels that is among the best managed in the country and large by any standards, with 5,500 rooms and annual sales of about $200 million in 1988. "We manage about $1 billion in property, although we own very little of it," he said shortly before he left the company.

Despite his vows never to repeat his experience with his second hotel, he still got burned two or three times by over-leveraging in building his empire. His original partners sold out in the late 1960s to recoup their capital gains before a capital gains tax was instituted, and the new owners expanded very quickly. These were the go-go years when conglomerates of wildly disparate businesses were sloppily stitched together, and Delta's new owners, Driver Developments, soon fell on hard times when the stock market crashed. Pattison became head of the whole conglomerate and sold off all the poor performers, salvaging the Delta chain by bringing in the CIBC and Great-West Life as investors. In full charge once more, he soon expanded to dominate the B.C. market, then expanded into a national chain in the mid-1970s, when he realized how vulnerable B.C. was to downturns in the markets for natural resources.

Pattison is a gruff man, who loves the art of business. He

knows he has to be a good manager of people, but that's a job. His passion is talking strategy. He has invested personally in many other entrepreneurs, and he has collected an impressive list of current and former partners, particularly among the Japanese, who have provided large amounts of money for Delta. Although he deals in very large amounts, rapid growth has not been one of his goals, nor has it been, one suspects, for his investors. He is acutely conscious of the need to tread the fine line between taking a manageable risk and risking everything on a major growth spurt to acquire economies of scale. "When I started, there was enough for everyone, so we could bite off less. It's not so easy now, especially in this business, which is high capital- and labour-intensive. The person who wants to win big has trouble."

Pattison still risks, of course, but he controls his level of risk as much as it is humanly possible to control it. He is almost in awe of the risks and rewards of entrepreneuring. "The use of leverage is probably the most sophisticated tool an entrepreneur can have. But it's very dangerous. The gamble is part of doing business, but you must always be able to survive if you lose everything on a gamble. You never know. You could lose it all. There's a euphoria that says there's just no way. But as you mature in business, as you build an organization, you become very conscious of not losing the farm. You might lose a herd, but not the whole farm."

Not all entrepreneurs dislike risk. If Pattison represents one extreme in his attitude toward risk, then Peter Oliver represents the other. He takes risks for the thrill of it. He owns three of Toronto's better restaurants—Oliver's (his first, of course), a French bistro/bakery/delicatessen; Bofinger Brasserie, an authentic reproduction of a Parisian brasserie; and the Auberge du Pommier, an enchantingly rustic reproduction of a French country inn in north Toronto. He's in a business that is not popular with investors and lenders. The banks rate restaurants as among the riskiest businesses around, especially in the fiercely competitive Toronto market, which has hundreds of good restaurants. Not only do they face enormous odds against surviving their launch, but even when they have made a name for themselves, they can go under in a matter of months if the fickle dining public loses interest. Canada has more than 50,000 restaurants, and more than 80% of them fail within their first three years. Oliver's could have gone the same way after a rocky launch in 1978, but its owner is rightly proud of his "stick-to-it-iveness." He kept improving it and turned it into one of the city's best, and best-attended, restaurants.

Oliver had been in commercial real estate when he first started Oliver's as a sideline in 1972, when he was 30. It was then a simple bakery, and his objective was to make an extra $25,000 a year, plus deliver a product of superb quality. But its sales did not meet its owner's expectations, so he quit the real estate business to concentrate on building the business. Oliver is a man of limitless determination, who was quite unfazed by his total lack of experience in the retail food business. A quick study on the job, he soon saw opportunities for expansion and a year later bought the building next door. He planned to join the two buildings, expand the bakery to include a 65-seat cafeteria-style delicatessen and create a new bistro upstairs.

It was a giant leap. He had started his bakery with an $85,000 investment, half of it borrowed, and worked his debt down to $24,000 in his first two years. He figured the purchase of the second building and the renovations would cost him $870,000, which the bank agreed to advance to him. Unfortunately, he overspent on the expansion, ending up with an addition of $1.1 million to his debt load. Interest rates had meanwhile shot up to 24%, and he was paying $600 a day in interest charges. His total revenues from the pre-expansion business were $800 a day. "I give banks heart failure," he says. They give him heart failure too; his bank pulled its loan, even though Oliver had never missed a payment. He was livid, but he recovered, later calling it a "learning experience," and persuaded the Mercantile Bank to pick up his account.

The new Oliver's was a great success. At first, the food didn't live up to the owner's high expectations, but the restaurant met a pressing need because it was in an area underserved by quality restaurants. (He had been eyeing the location for several years before he bought it, and it was initially the secret of his success.) Oliver knew what he wanted, however. He worked hard perfecting his management systems. He tried delegating, without success. He compiled a manual of comprehensive instructions on how a restaurant should be run, down to how many earrings a waiter or waitress could wear. As he steadily improved his operation, the money came flowing in, reducing his debt to $750,000 from $1.2 million.

Then he started getting bored. He looked at sites in Markham and Mississauga, just north and west of Toronto, for starting new restaurants, but both deals fell through. Finally, in 1985, he was approached by George Mann of Unicorp, who was trying to sell a building near the corner of St. Clair and Yonge in mid-town Toronto, a kilometre south of Oliver's. He jumped at it, but Mann sold it to someone else in a surprise deal which still rankles Oliver. However, when the new owner offered him a 20-year lease on the ground floor, he signed on, and Bofinger Brasserie was born.

Within weeks, Cadillac Fairview approached Oliver with another offer, this time for a 21-year lease in a development it was completing just south of Highway 401 on Yonge Street, in North York, the most northerly of Metropolitan Toronto's component cities. Height restrictions compelled them to have a one-storey building on the site, and the people at Cadillac Fairview could think of nothing better than a restaurant run by Oliver to fill that requirement. But Oliver was preoccupied with Bofinger's and turned them down. Twice. Cadillac Fairview persisted. "Each time I said no, they tried harder," Oliver said later. "I'm a romantic, and they tempted me with slides of flowers dripping with dew. Finally, I said 'What the hell, you only live once,' and I agreed." So began the Auberge du Pommier.

He was no longer bored. Starting two completely new and completely different restaurants simultaneously qualifies for contention as bona fide masochism. He toured the brasseries of Paris, examining their decor and planning their adaptation to Toronto. The result is a magnificent room, seating more than 200 people, all done up in mahogany and brass, with tiled floors and marble fireplaces, crowned with a stained glass dome. Bofinger's food, unfortunately, was not a roaring success. Joanne Kates, the food critic at the *Globe and Mail*, sniffed that the taste was all on the walls.

For Oliver, it was another learning experience, and he set to work perfecting the cuisine. Although he has made all the necessary changes in staff and menu design, it will still be a long battle to make that location work to his satisfaction. At St. Clair and Yonge, everyone eats lunch between noon and one o'clock. Outside those hours, the restaurants are empty. In the evening, the room is too big to provide an intimate setting, so it can be intimidating if it's not full. Two years later, the restaurant was breaking even, but in the early months, instead of providing some support for the launch of the Auberge du Pommier, Bofinger's was draining $50,000 a month from Oliver's coffers. "All of a sudden," he said later, somewhat ruefully, "I needed another $1 million." He was once again facing a staggering debt load. The Bank of Australia and New Zealand had agreed to finance his acquisitions to the tune of $2.6 million. When his expenses came in $700,000 more than he had forecast, the bank stood by him, raising its loan to $3.2 million. Oliver can't say enough for his new bankers. "Based on the results I've given them in the past six months," he said shortly before the Auberge opened in 1986, "I wouldn't lend the extra money to me."

The academics call people like Oliver sensation-seekers. It's a good name. Oliver is in the business of persuading people to pay for sensations that make them feel good. A big man, he has the hard body of a former lock forward at rugby and a soft, fleshy face which hints at the self-indulgence he controls almost all the time with his iron self-discipline. When he was researching the concept for Auberge du Pommier, Oliver took his wife, Maureen, on a tour of French country inns. In Pontchartrain, 40 kilometres outside Paris, they found the perfect prototype, the Auberge de la Dauberie. "It's perfect. That's why I like the food business. I just get so carried away. It has a perfect setting. Good wine. After two appetizers and the main course, I asked the chef to make me another main course. I was in seventh heaven!" Oliver is an avid jogger out of necessity, one suspects.

He carries the enthusiasm into his business in Toronto. "Creating a new restaurant is the most sophisticated art form. You're not just dealing with one medium, like an artist or a musician. You're dealing with smell, sound (the music, voices and laughter), sight (the decor, the garden outside, the look of the food) and taste. It's a psychological experience going out for dinner. Before they even enter the door, you want to start sending messages to their brain, preparing them for the experience. Plants just watered and still dripping, a wine rack. It's a real challenge."

His attitude toward risk reflects his sensuality. "I do my best when my back's right against the wall. That's when I see things most clearly. When things are running smoothly, I look for ways to dig myself into a hole. I deliberately take a massive risk. I'm confident I can work my way out of it. . . . I've been in so many situations where I've been scared shitless and succeeded that I now believe the one goes with the other. The moment I get blasé about a particular problem, I know I'll come short."

Taking risks makes him come alive. The possibility of eventual failure is inconceivable to him, although he admits having wondered a few times if he hadn't finally gone too far. "It would shatter me if I failed," he says. Yet he cannot endure the thought of not pushing himself to the absolute limit of his capabilities. "If I sit in a rocking chair and say to myself, 'Is that all I did?', I'll be shattered."

Bryden, Pattison and Oliver have all built significant businesses and have shown themselves to be prepared to take enormous risks to achieve their goals. But whereas Pattison and Oliver see the enormity of their risk with brutal clarity, Bryden serenely says the risks he faces don't bother him at all. Oliver and Bryden have complete confidence in their ability to surmount all obstacles, but Pattison sees the potential to be crushed by naive competitors who overbuild in a market or by economic events that turn hotel patterns on their head. Pattison has specific and clear limits to just how much risk he'll take on, Bryden accepts whatever level of risk is necessary to the achievement of his goals, and Oliver seeks out risk for the stimulation it provides to his adrenal glands.

Entrepreneurs have puzzled researchers in more areas than their attitude toward risk. There are other traits that have been attributed to entrepreneurs and then questioned or dismissed as definitive measures of entrepreneurial characters. Successful entrepreneurs have been found to have, apart from many other traits:

- a strong belief that they are responsible for whatever happens to them in their lives;
- an abiding conviction of the importance of perseverance
  and hard work;
- a powerful need to achieve or will to win;
- a strong creative bent;
- an innate ability to recognize opportunities.

These traits are true of many entrepreneurs, if not all of them, but detailed analyses of entrepreneurs against other groups of people, particularly managers in large organizations, have shown that these traits are not unique in entrepreneurs. Most successful leaders in any field have a powerful need to win and feel they alone are responsible for what happens to them. And creativity is critical to success in many, many fields.

The search for common personality traits also suffers from the overwhelming anecdotal evidence of the enormous differences in the personalities of entrepreneurs. Some are offensive, others defensive; some are outgoing, others introverted; some are aggressive, others timid; some are sure of themselves, others are desperately insecure. It goes on and on.

In the end, most researchers have given up, saying that the search for common personality traits is a hopeless task, and that it's far more productive to seek patterns of entrepreneurial behaviour. The focus for research is shifting from entrepreneurs to entrepreneurship. There is much to be said for this shift. What sets entrepreneurs apart is the environment in which they operate. The critical comparisons do not lie in how entrepreneurs compare with other people; they lie in how successful entrepreneurs differ in the way they apply their skills to the situations they face.

# CHAPTER 2

# THE ESSENCE OF ENTREPRENEURSHIP

**S**trangely enough, one of the most enduring descriptions of entrepreneurship was also the first. It was made only in the first half of the eighteenth century, despite the existence of entrepreneurs from time immemorial, by the French economist, Richard Cantillon. He first used the word *entrepreneur* in about 1730 when he made the distinction between landowners, wage earners and "undertakers" (the literal translation of the French word *entrepreneur*, now abandoned for reasons not difficult to divine). He observed three key elements of entrepreneurship: the undertakers operated in an uncertain or unstable environment; they faced certain ruin unless they possessed considerable business competence; and they provided their own capital.

Although Cantillon noted that most provided their own capital, he did acknowledge that some undertakers went into business without capital, notably those who sold only their labour, such as artisans. He later added: "It may perhaps be urged that undertakers seek to snatch all they can in their calling and to get the better of their customers, but this is outside my subject."

In the following two and a half centuries, the definitions multiplied, culminating in the quiet finality of the third edition of the *Columbia Encyclopedia* (1967 version): "The entrepreneur's functions and importance have declined since the rise of the corporation." That dismissal of entrepreneurship was, of course, shortlived, if not a fantasy, and the debate has resumed on what exactly is the essence of entrepreneurship. Before unveiling the light that the entrepreneurs in this book shed on the subject, however, it may be useful to outline what entrepreneurship is not.

## Myth #1
*Creativity and innovation are
indispensable elements of
entrepreneurship*

Most entrepreneurs are creative, but creativity is not an essential quality in entrepreneurs. Innovation is often a result of entrepreneurship, but it is not necessarily part of it and it is not always even a result.

Michael Potter sits at the top of a company that's grown just about as fast as a company can grow without being blown apart by centrifugal force. Under his leadership, annual sales of Cognos raced from $7 million to $108 million in the seven years to February, 1989. The engine of this growth is a powerful software program called Powerhouse, which is now being used by computer programmers in 48 countries. Potter is widely credited by industry insiders as the driving force behind the success of Cognos, but he disclaims any notion that he is its creative force, even though the company lives or dies by its creativity.

The first impression of Potter is deceiving. He looks like a handsome, shy, hesitant middle manager. He comes to life, however, when he starts to explore ideas and talk about his company. Even then, he's understated. His intensity and interest show only in his tightly strung body and in the questioning eyes set deep in a face that will turn craggy with age. He's quiet-spoken, almost diffident, searching always for the precise articulation of what he's trying to communicate. It's a skill he's had to develop at Cognos, because he has had to deal with colleagues whose credentials are quite different from his own. Trained as a physicist and a mathematician, he brings no technical expertise to the software programmers at Cognos. Deprived of the major strength of most high-tech entrepreneurs, who generally embody the technology of the firms they own, he has had to learn to lead, instead, by giving his employees and partners the framework within which they can give full rein to their own creativity.

His impeccable credentials as an entrepreneur make his view of creativity at least cause for reflection among those who put creativity at the heart of entrepreneurship: "The sign of a good decision-making model," he says, "is no one can say whose idea it was." Potter's style is to stir up debate, to get people talking informally, in the hallways and over lunch. After a while a consensus emerges. He avoids any formality of structure or planned process, because he says no good ideas or opportunities arise out of these situations. "We have a group who know they have the freedom to be creative," he says, acknowledging that he can never be "the prime seed sower," because that job is widely shared. He encourages people to develop the mentality of a skunk works, playing with ideas informally. The board of directors deliberately stays out of some projects while the researchers take them through their early stages of development.

Potter joined Cognos, then called Quasar, in 1972, when it was three years old and employed less than ten people who wrote custom software. He quickly became a partner as he helped expand the business, but in 1977 he and some of his original partners disagreed on the best strategy for the company. Like Rod Bryden, Potter wanted to move into proprietary application software, which involves much bigger risks and rewards than custom software. He bought out the other shareholders and distributed 25% of the shares to the firm's 86 employees in the following year. Quasar was then doing about $5 million a year. The cost of developing PAS can be enormous and the resulting sales tenuous, as Bryden discovered at Systemhouse. Nevertheless, Potter saw a golden opportunity in a program developed by one of his programmers. Later called Quiz, this program became the report-writer component of Powerhouse, which gives programmers easy access to application software when they write their own custom programs.

Powerhouse proved to be a hit and Cognos grew very quickly. However, it grew on the base of one lonely idea, designed to run on machines made by Digital Equipment, Hewlett-Packard and Data General. Without IBM compatibility and no successor products, Potter knew he had to broaden his base. He didn't hedge his bets, however, by retaining the custom-software side of the business, which provided a good revenue base. He recognized that the PAS side had all the glamour, which would demoralize the custom programmers, so he dropped the custom business over a year and a half at the beginning of the 1980s. Cognos became one of the few software companies to switch successfully from a custom base to proprietary application software.

The transition was not without its moments. Profit margins shrank and, Potter says, "the banks got mad at us." Cognos survived that crisis, then grew at more than 50% a year over the five years to February, 1987. That kind of growth inevitably wrought its own damage, and the concepts that had worked for a small company began to come apart at the seams. Potter's style of bouncing ideas around, allowing a consensus to form gradually, often over several months, was becoming too cumbersome. So he offered his job of president to Tom Csathy, then the chief executive officer of Burroughs Canada. Csathy accepted and soon mixed some of his discipline with Potter's entrepreneurial flair. "Tom will contract our eight-month discussion to eight weeks," Potter said at the time. (See also chapter 10 on leadership styles.)

Csathy's arrival built orderliness into Cognos and, after a brief hiccough in 1987, when profits dropped sharply, the company resumed its meteoric growth rate. Potter remains chairman and chief executive officer, still filling the role he has always played. "I consider myself the glue that holds some talented people together," he says, "to enable them to be talented."

This doesn't mean Potter isn't creative. His creativity is applied to the way he manages people, which is a vital skill he has brought to his company. But it is not an essential part of the entrepreneuring that has made Cognos succeed. His most important entrepreneurial contribution was recognizing the potential of Quiz and yanking Quasar out of custom software into PAS. This skill is perhaps the foremost element of entrepreneurship — the orientation toward opportunity in the context of a scarcity of resources. When Potter's partners decided to leave him in 1977, they were being sensible. The risks of switching into PAS are enormous, and Quasar didn't have the resources to do it. But Potter not only saw the opportunity, he also knew how it could be done. "We bootstrapped this company," he says. "When we started selling internationally, we didn't have a big plan. We took a couple of knowledgeable people and gave them a hell of a travel budget. When the business started flowing, we hung our shingle out."

Many of the entrepreneurs in this book do not consider themselves creative, because they get most of their ideas for opportunities from other employees or external sources. By the same token, although millions of people who are not entrepreneurs are creative, they don't use their creativity to perceive opportunities where no one else can see them. The skill to pick viable opportunities from among the thousands that float around every day is often not based on creativity, but on an obsessive commitment to the business. This commitment enables entrepreneurs to understand all facets of their businesses so thoroughly that they can recognize before anyone else the patterns that create opportunities.

Innovation is an entirely different matter. It lies at the other end of the entrepreneuring spectrum from creativity, but it, too, is not part of entrepreneurship. The first academic to focus on innovation as a central function of entrepreneurs was Joseph Schumpeter. Early this century, in *The Theory of Economic Development*, he invented the perception of entrepreneurs as a critical component in a successful economy. He emigrated to the U.S. at age 49, to become a Harvard professor, after a distinguished career in Germany and Austria, including a spell as minister of finance in Austria. He turned a lot of heads with his view that the entrepreneur is the primary agent in economic change. He zeroed in on innovation as the critical element in entrepreneurship, perhaps because he recognized the importance of innovation and saw that entrepreneurs seemed to be most adept at it. In his enthusiasm for this capability, however, all other elements of entrepreneurship fell by the wayside. Anyone who created new combinations of the means of production was classified as an entrepreneur. Anyone who didn't innovate was a manager or a capitalist, but not an entrepreneur.

His work was much later picked up by fellow Austrian Peter Drucker, who used the words *entrepreneurship* and *innovation* interchangeably in his book, *Innovation and Entrepreneurship.* He disembodies entrepreneurship, systemizes it and defines it as "purposeful innovation." He dismisses the idea that innovation is natural, creative or spontaneous. "It is work. Entrepreneurial businesses treat entrepreneurship [read 'innovation'] as a duty."

Schumpeter's innovation is joyous, Drucker's is severe, but

both perspectives define entrepreneurship by going beyond the behaviour of entrepreneurs to focus on the results of entrepreneurship. This is where their perspective runs into trouble. Innovation is not one of the essential elements of entrepreneurship, because it is a result of combining two of its essential elements—opportunity orientation and the competence to implement it successfully. Innovation is common to most entrepreneurial acts, but it is not in the fission reaction. It is the energy that the reaction produces.

Most entrepreneurs may be innovators, but few innovators are entrepreneurs. There are marvellous innovators in public institutions, for example, although it's just plain fanciful to call them entrepreneurs. Artists innovate, politicians innovate, waiters innovate, yet no one tries to call them entrepreneurs. For all these people, as much as for entrepreneurs, innovation for its own sake is worse than useless; there has to be a market for it before they can claim they're innovative. Very few entrepreneurs innovate simply because they love change. Most innovate because they see an opportunity and they have to change to exploit the opportunity. Their entrepreneurship consists of identifying the opportunity, risking their resources in the attempt to exploit the opportunity and then having the managerial competence to fashion the necessary innovation to fit the exigencies of the opportunity. The goal is not innovation, it is the exploitation of the opportunity. Innovation is not an input, it is an output of successful people.

Innovation is also not the same thing as invention. It is the implementation of invention. Unlike innovators, inventors change because they love change. Researchers fix their sights on making significant changes to the worlds they live in. Some entrepreneurs are inventors but that is a rare coincidence. Most inventors are dreadful entrepreneurs, because they cannot implement their own inventions at a profit.

Innovation is not a discrete event, either. It is untidy, in a constant state of evolution. It may be made up of dozens of smaller innovations, each an output of a particular group that may or may not be aware of parallel innovations. It is a continuum, an enduring phenomenon with people who identify opportunities, whether they be entrepreneurs, managers, bureaucrats or artists. And, while it may be tempting to copy entrepreneurial techniques of innovation, it is simply incorrect to use *entrepreneurship* as a synonym for *innovation.*

## Myth #2

*Entrepreneurship is found only in small businesses*

Many small businesses are not entrepreneurial. There are thousands of small businesses that will never grow big, because their owners want them to stay small. They can earn a good living selling their own time and skills, without having to cope with employees or the headaches of rapid growth. Their businesses are an extension of themselves, their self-employment a lifestyle decision. They are not entrepreneurs.

However, small firms in general, and new ventures in particular, are much more fertile ground for entrepreneurship than large firms. This is the source of the myth. Few large firms can avoid acquiring layers of bureaucracy that limit their ability to be entrepreneurial, because it's so difficult to run large organizations without creating manuals full of rules and regulations. But it can be done. Entrepreneurship can flourish in big firms. Jimmy Pattison runs his empire of 40-odd businesses (it varies from time to time, depending on what he has bought and sold recently) with a corporate head office of less than ten people. The odds of anyone building a bureaucracy inside one of his businesses are slim (see page 184). The dealer who fired the car salesman with the lowest production every month does not look kindly on people who don't pull their weight.

Pattison started small and built his empire on his own. Not every entrepreneur has the same skill. It is widely believed, particularly among venture capitalists, that entrepreneurship can survive only in small firms, because no entrepreneurs have the skills to run big ones. They can't adapt to the managerial discipline needed to steer large numbers of people in the same direction. There are, unfortunately, enough examples of success breeding failure that the conventional wisdom remains in vogue. These companies fail or they are taken over and lose their entrepreneurial steam. But there are enough exceptions to discount the rule. Apart from Pattison, people like Frank Stronach of Magna International, Marcel Dutil of Canam

Manac, and Rod Bryden of Kinburn are vibrant proof that entrepreneurs who start small can survive and prosper as their firms become large.

Nonetheless, entrepreneurs who want to grow their firms into major corporations usually find it best to buy a going concern rather than build something from scratch. Almost half of the owners of the large and medium-sized firms in this book inherited or bought into their first business, compared with only one-eighth of the owners of small firms.

Some researchers claim that the only real entrepreneurs are the ones who start their own businesses from scratch. However, although start-ups exact entrepreneurship in its purest form, they do not define it. There is entrepreneurship after start-up. The major question is whether entrepreneurial skills can be exercised only by people who have learned them in a start-up. This is almost certainly untrue. Among the 100 entrepreneurs in the study done for this book, 32 had either bought their companies or inherited them. All but two of them could not, by any stretch of the imagination, be described as lacking in entrepreneurial characteristics.

There is an important caveat in saying that people who buy companies can be as entrepreneurial as start-ups. Sometimes, the managers of a division in a large company buy their division from their employer when it no longer wants to own it. Normally, these managers would pay for their new company with a leveraged buyout, often becoming, in the process, one-shot entrepreneurs. They take one big risk, make the company more efficient so they can pay down their debt and then retire (strategically, if not in fact) with their large profits. These people are more managers than entrepreneurs. However, leveraged buyouts by people who have no connection with the company can be just as entrepreneurial as start-ups.

### Myth #3
*There is such a thing as*
*"corporate entrepreneurship"*

The power of entrepreneurship has inevitably created the desire among large corporations to become entrepreneurial. It makes a lot of sense for them to aim for the lower overhead expenses and the innovative flexibility associated with entrepreneurs. But even if they achieve those objectives, their managers cannot be called entrepreneurial. The environment in large corporations is quite simply not susceptible to entrepreneurship unless the meaning of the word is broadened to such a degree that it no longer means anything.

In her book, *The Change Masters*, Rosabeth Moss Kanter has provided the most impressive analysis to date of the process of innovation in large organizations. She, too, uses *entrepreneurship* as a synonym for *innovation*, but her concepts speak louder than her words. Her analysis of the process of innovation provides an excellent framework for understanding the elements of entrepreneurship as well as what is called "corporate entrepreneurship." It soon becomes apparent that the two are very different beasts.

She describes corporate innovators as people who "test limits and create new possibilities for organizational action by pushing and directing the innovation process. These new entrepreneurs do not start companies, they improve them."

Kanter's entrepreneurs are adept at moving outside the formal bounds of their jobs, manoeuvring through and around the organization in novel ways. They are rarely self-starting, preferring to exercise their genius on tasks assigned by superiors. But they are often self-directed visionaries, capable of perceiving situations in broad terms, identifying patterns and making connections. They have the courage of their own convictions, the ability to tolerate the uncertainty that inevitably accompanies innovation. They do not need instant feedback on their projects but have a long time horizon. These people are leaders who can persuade others to share their vision and build it.

Corporate innovators do not have the creative genius to invent new ideas, and they need the support system of a large organization to operate effectively. They are not risk-takers, beyond exposing their credibility to ridicule by backing untried ideas. When they do fail, it is usually because they didn't build a coalition of supporters for the concept. And when they succeed, they have to cede their leadership as well as the credit for their success to those who will carry on the innovative process.

Kanter's model for innovation is a close approximation of the innovation process in individual entrepreneurship, but it is extraordinarily complex. It works only with an elaborate system engineered to create controlled chaos that precipitates genuine communication between all the parts of the organization. Only then can the connections be made to create hundreds of microchanges which will boil up into macrochange. "Creativity does not derive from order," she writes, "but from the attempt to impose order where it does not exist, to make new connections." The subtle complexity of this model makes it only too clear why innovation is so much easier in smaller companies, where size limits the scope for complexity.

There are major differences between corporate innovators and entrepreneurs beyond those evident from the preceding comments. Kanter makes it clear that an indispensable ingredient in corporate innovation is security of employment. There is deliberate instability within the corporate structure, but not for the innovators themselves. By contrast, the equally unstable environments in which individual entrepreneurs operate exposes them to a daily diet of personal insecurity. They depend heavily on often fickle external resources. They have no "superiors" whom they can harness to the task of winning co-operation from the owners of the resources that they need. Small shifts in the economy or their client base can devastate them. Their innovation is forged in the heat of intense pressure to avoid mistakes.

Individual entrepreneurs are also invariably starved of resources. If they weren't, there would be no need to be entrepreneurial. Corporate innovators have to compete for resources, too, but their need for resources outside their control is much smaller, and they compete for those resources with people whom they are encouraged to regard as members of the same team. Kanter found that, when resources are scarce, innovation in large corporations is less common.

There are enough significant differences in the worlds occupied by corporate innovators and individual entrepreneurs that it doesn't make sense to lump them together as generic entrepreneurs. Corporate innovators may be innovative and creative, and they may be different animals from their less adventurous counterparts who administer the status quo, but their behaviour cannot be reasonably described as entrepreneurial without debasing the coinage of the word itself. They are vital players in the economy, but they are not entrepreneurs-with-a-prefix; they are, in Kanter's pointed phrase, change masters.

I don't mean to imply, however, that corporate innovators and entrepreneurs have little to learn from one another. Change masters could use some of the entrepreneurs' ability to create value without the aid of adequate resources. Even innovative large organizations still carry huge overheads. Change masters also need to learn how to make their innovations stick. All too often, their receptivity to change makes it just as easy to remove an innovation as it is to create one, particularly when ownership of an innovation has to be passed from one manager to another several times before it matures.

Big organizations realize they need a whiff of the entrepreneurial spirit to keep their operations flexible. People like Kanter can show them how to be innovative, but they have not yet found the key to unlocking the entrepreneurial genie that can leverage their resources into achievements beyond the normal reach of those resources. To do that, they have to understand the dynamics of individual entrepreneurship better and not settle for adopting the parts that are easiest to translate into big-company systems.

Entrepreneurs have just as much to learn from large corporations, of course. Entrepreneurs operate largely on intuition, so they lack the discipline of the change masters, the necessary cognitive understanding of the mechanisms of change. They often lack the discipline of superior planning and preparation, which are essential to corporate change masters. In many cases, they also lack the skills to build teams composed of people who work for them. These gaps all corrode solidity, just as the change masters' gaps corrode flexibility and sensitivity.

## Myth #4
*Ownership is not a factor in*
*entrepreneurship*

This myth is linked with myth #3. Anyone who believes in the concept of corporate entrepreneurship cannot, of course, also believe in the idea that ownership is an important part of entrepreneurship. The guru behind both ideas was the re-

doubtable Joseph Schumpeter, who disassociated the entrepreneur from ownership of the business, saying that capitalists
bore all the risk and should not be confused with entrepreneurs. Entrepreneurs per se, he said, bore no risk. Presumably
a person could be an entrepreneur and a capitalist, but the
capitalist role was incidental, no more important to the performance of entrepreneurial functions than, say, stamp collecting. The entrepreneur's challenge in Schumpeter's world is,
unequivocally, to find and use new ideas.

Once again, his disciple (in entrepreneurship, at any rate)
was Peter Drucker, who wrote that entrepreneurs are not capitalists or investors. They are often not even employers, and
they are by no means confined to economic institutions.

This view is entirely consistent with the idea that entrepreneurship is the same as innovation. Ownership is not a critical
factor in innovation. However, if it's accepted that innovation
and entrepreneurship are not the same thing, then the importance of ownership becomes clear. Ownership is a critical part
of entrepreneurship, because it bears so heavily on the entrepreneur's attitude toward risk.

If managers do not have a significant shareholding in their
firm, the risks and rewards they can expect from a venture
almost never reflect the corporation's real upside or downside
for the venture. This is inevitable, because it is extremely
difficult for large organizations to measure performance accu-
rately. The innovators share responsibility, and therefore credit,
with many other people, and their tenures in any one job are
much shorter than the life cycles of their innovations. Their
rewards and risks therefore come to them through the political
process of promotion, with the accompanying bonuses and
salary increases, rather than through the recognition of innovative performance or direct sharing in its results.

Owner-entrepreneurs face rewards and penalties of a different order of magnitude. Failure can mean loss of all personal
assets. Success can mean great wealth. This affects them in two
ways. They have to have far greater tolerance of risk for the
same objective risk, because their personal risk is so much
greater. And success or failure has a dramatic impact on their
personal finances, which forces them to accept personal responsibility for their decisions.

Even firms with profit sharing usually avoid giving their managers a stake that is a substitute for ownership, which would mean a permanent, fixed percentage of the profits from the part of the business for which they are entirely responsible. Instead, the managers share in the profits of units much larger than their own, and their share of profits is negotiated with a view to keeping their income relatively stable.

Many of the riskiest ventures of non-owner managers have nothing to do with the corporation's business at all. Ambitious managers know that the real competition in most large corporations is oriented toward corporate politics, not business. The risk/reward equation for people who are not significant owners is seldom focussed solely on the venture they are currently responsible for. It is at least partly focussed on their career or their superiors' state of mind.

This is completely different from owner-entrepreneurs, who focus more tightly on the venture itself and are prepared to commit their time and energy to a far greater degree because of the much higher stakes involved. Without ownership as one of its critical elements, entrepreneurship does not fully encompass people who own and operate their own businesses.

The other side of the coin is that, although entrepreneurs must be owners, owners are not necessarily entrepreneurs. Investors are not entrepreneurs unless they participate in the other vital elements of entrepreneurship.

## THE SEVEN ELEMENTS OF ENTREPRENEURSHIP

There are seven essential elements of entrepreneurship:

1. An orientation toward opportunity in the context of currently available resources that are inadequate for the opportunities.
2. A willingness to take risks.
3. Competence as a business manager.
4. Ownership of a significant part of the business.
5. An unstable environment.
6. The need to succeed.
7. Leadership skills.

The core sequence of three elements of entrepreneurship is:

Opportunity orientation  
in an environment of } ⟶ Risk ⟶ Competence  
resource scarcity

The other four factors—two relating to the entrepreneur and two to the environment—are critical in defining the nature of the three basic elements. Without these four elements, the core sequence would not reflect entrepreneurship, so they are included as a bank of influences bearing on the core sequence.

## ENVIRONMENTAL INFLUENCES

Instability  
Ownership

Opportunity orientation  
in an environment of } ⟶ Risk ⟶ Competence  
relatively inadequate  
resources

Need to succeed  
Leadership

## ENTREPRENEURIAL TRAITS

Take away the ability to see opportunities in the context of inadequate resources, and the challenge becomes one of only competence and planning, without the imagination and daring that sets entrepreneurs apart.

Take away risk and entrepreneurs turn into trustees. Risk is the bridge between identifying an unaffordable opportunity and exploiting it. It is the leap of faith which alone can take someone from the creative act of identifying an opportunity to the competent act of implementing the innovation as running a business. It is the bridge between where they are and where they want to be. Because entrepreneurs risk their own assets, their ownership, it is the ultimate demand on entrepreneurs. It's what forces them to stretch themselves beyond their normal limits.

Take away competence and the entrepreneurship disappears. In a volatile world, incompetence in entrepreneurial firms quickly brings its retribution. Dead firms cannot be vehicles for entrepreneurship.

Take away instability and the environment becomes predictable. That opens the door for managers of powerful resources to perform well. They are not flexible and cannot easily see opportunities, but they are thoroughly competent. Too competent for entrepreneurs, who have no competitive advantage in stable environments, because they can't apply their skill at leveraging inadequate resources to achieve their goals.

For entrepreneurs to overcome the multiple obstacles in their ambitious paths, they need to have a powerful motivation (see Chapter 7). Among the entrepreneurs in the study done for this book, that motivation is overwhelmingly (for almost 90%) the need to succeed. The need for success affects all three elements in the entrepreneurship equation. It is a vital influence on entrepreneurs' tolerance of risk. The more they want success, the more risk they will bear. The need for success also has an impact on opportunity orientation — it determines the reach of people's dreams. And it gives them the determination to learn what they need to be competent.

Finally, without leadership, there can be no achievement beyond what individuals can achieve on their own. Gamblers, for example, have a need to succeed and they are risk-takers, but they don't have leadership qualities. Leadership is the talent which leverages a person's skills to achievements far beyond his or her capacity as an individual, by enlisting the support of many others who will add their muscle to the entrepreneur's will. Leadership is the talent which permits entrepreneurs to surround themselves with people who are strong where they are weak. It is the talent through which they transmit their vision and persuade their employees to make it their own. It is the talent that glues inadequate resources to opportunity, to make it happen. There can be no entrepreneurship without it.

The absence of any one of these seven elements would eliminate the possibility of successful entrepreneurship.

# CHAPTER 3

# CAPITALIZING ON INSTABILITY

*"The real key to entrepreneuring is agility. The only way to stay alive is to change very quickly. To do that, entrepreneurs have to have their money in the game."*
— Rob Peters of Peters & Co.

**T**om Vincent of ETA Executive Travel Apartments hung out his shingle in the travel business in 1973, at age 25. Much later, after he'd made a success of another business, he said, "Anyone who goes into that business is crazy. A good return is 1% to 2% of sales." The travel business is a volatile industry which soon sinks any of its practitioners who don't keep their eyes on the ball. Vincent's first business was marketing English bed-and-breakfasts to Canadians, and it took off. A year later, he expanded the concept and started assembling a selection of villas in the Caribbean, which he rented out to vacationing Canadians. He soon had a range of 15,000 villas in the Caribbean, Mexico, Hawaii and Europe and started chartering Air Canada planes to fly his customers there.

It didn't work. Rioting erupted in Jamaica, his most important destination. The market was shifting to Sun Tours and other mass marketers, and travel agents weren't sure he had what it took to survive. He couldn't fill his planes, so he emptied his pockets, losing $150,000. Seven years after he had started it, he closed the company down. "Talk about sinking feelings," he said later. "Walking in to the staff and telling them was the worst day of my life." Shortly afterwards, he repeated the experience when his business selling time-sharing in vacation properties also folded. It was traumatic, but it was what he needed. "I ran two businesses that failed. It was poor planning and bad cash management." When he raised funds for his next project, the loans officers at Federal Business Development Bank said it was one of the better business plans they had seen.

Vincent is a tall man, with thinning hair and a beard that make him look much older than he is. His face offers a clue that he's packed more than most into his first 40 years, but he wears it easily. He's very friendly and remarkably frank about himself. He relishes his success, living the life of a successful entrepreneur with an almost boyish enthusiasm. He can still laugh at how he let his ego get out of control for three years while he drove a Mercedes-Benz he couldn't afford. More importantly, he has a clear view of his own strengths and weaknesses as a businessman.

After the villa business failed, Vincent decided to concentrate on a sideline his father had been running for him. He had leased five apartments in Toronto, furnished them and was renting them out to businesses that didn't want to pay hotel prices when they had employees from out of town staying in Toronto for several weeks. Three years before that, he had tried a similar idea with Air Canada, which wanted to persuade vacationers to spend their time inside Canada, but that didn't work. No one wanted to cook on their vacation. When he marketed the idea to businesses, however, it did work, and ETA Executive Travel Apartments was on its way. In a changing and fickle market, he had slowly honed his new concept through several incarnations that might have succeeded but didn't, until he found a niche he could hold onto. From sales of $250,000 in 1981, ETA grew to $5 million in 1987, and Vincent was projecting $15 million in 1990, when his major building program would be completed.

His apartments are fully equipped, have maid service and cost about half of what an equivalent hotel would charge. To his 350 suites in Toronto and Ottawa, he's added marketing services for similar businesses in the U.S. and Europe. The average stay in his suites is five to six weeks in the luxury suites, about half that in the less expensive ones, and his occupancy rate is more than 80%. His island of stability looks particularly good in the volatile hotel industry. Bill Pattison of Delta Hotels says, "It used to be that on February 1, you had 40% of March's business on your books and 70% by the end of February. Now, on a Monday night you might have only 50% of the rooms committed." Vincent says he escapes that problem. "Our business is not like hotels. If you're going to stay a few weeks in another town, you plan in advance. The travel industry has created an expectation that there's always a deal, so everyone leaves it to the last minute. The whole psyche in vacation booking has rolled off onto the business traveller."

Now Vincent's mining his niche, as he expands into rental search for corporate executives and even seeking suitable houses for executives who are transferred. He doubled his business to almost $10 million a year between 1987 and 1989, but he still doesn't know what the hotels will do if his concept becomes too popular.

The instability of the market for Vincent's apartments offers him his greatest opportunities as well as his greatest risks. It is one of the two environmental elements that shape the entrepreneurial process, the other being ownership.

## UNSTABLE ENVIRONMENTS

Instability is an opportunity as well as a risk, as Vincent knows only too well. It brings unpredictable gaps in the marketplace that only the nimble can move fast enough to exploit. Instability also places enormous demands on the competence of anyone implementing an innovation. Dealing with instability requires a high tolerance for uncertainty and ambiguity, talents which are abundant in entrepreneurs.

The ever-present threat of imminent disaster in entrepreneurial firms has a profound effect on their owners, both positive and negative. They take little for granted and have a legendary ability to adapt to changing circumstances, capitalizing on opportunities and escaping sinkholes. But they also often do not commit themselves fully to a chosen course of action, because they have no confidence the favourable circumstances will last. The key skill is strategic flexibility, which alone can contain costs in a new or expanding venture, where the plan changes as the venture unfolds. The entrepreneurial facility for committing human and financial resources incrementally, adjusting to the conditions at each tiny step along the way, spending only as much as is absolutely necessary at that time, can cut costs in half in an unstable industry.

Stable environments, by contrast, are better suited to big, resource-rich organizations, which are very good at managing repetitive operations that don't change much. They have the discipline and control to nail costs down to the floor and make a good profit. Their marketing power can steamroller smaller competitors when the market doesn't change too suddenly. Their inflexibility is not a disadvantage.

This is changing in some areas, however. As the shift to a service economy continues, more entrepreneurial firms benefit because they can adjust more easily to changes in their fickle customers. The extraordinarily rapid growth of applications for computers is also turning economies of scale on their head, enabling smaller firms to approach the number-crunching power of big firms. And markets are changing ever more rapidly as new products and services are introduced at an accelerating rate. It's a time when the flexibility of entrepreneurs is looking better every day.

Michael Cowpland of Corel Systems can talk with authority about the kind of flexibility entrepreneurs need to compete in the unstable markets where they function most effectively. He's better known for his earlier incarnation as co-founder of Canada's one-time high-tech wunderkind, Mitel, a manufacturer of telecommunications equipment. Cowpland and Terry Matthews invested $20,000 in Mitel and built it into a $350-million company, employing 5,000 people, before it all fell apart (see page 95). British Telecom bought control of the company for $320 million in 1985, and Cowpland stepped down as chairman, although he is still a member of the board of directors. Then he started all over again.

Tall and lean, Cowpland can cut a dashing figure when he's out on the town, clad in a leather jacket and cruising in his Corvette. He's restless and speaks very fast, as if there's just not enough time to do everything he wants to do. Like many entrepreneurs, he lives life to the full, travelling down many roads, never distraught if a venture doesn't work out and always ready to try something new. Although he approaches his businesses with dedication and skill, he doesn't take himself too seriously. He has used the personal wealth he created at Mitel to encourage many other entrepreneurs, often investing in their companies and helping them through his connections. Not all of them have worked out, and some of them have risen and fallen with the same abruptness as his investment in Mitel, so, by 1988, he was beginning to extricate himself from most of them. But he does it all with remarkable equanimity. He has an attractive openness about him and a great sense of fun, to which people respond quickly and enthusiastically. His parties are legendary.

At the time the debacle at Mitel was unravelling, laser printers were just starting to become popular, so Cowpland thought he would pick one promising market for them and go after it. He knew that there were 30,000 users of the word-processing hardware made by AES-MICOM, the major Canadian manufacturer of word-processing hardware. "If we could get 5% of that market, we were laughing," he said later. When the day came to sell his printers, however, he discovered that the owners of AES systems so disliked their systems that they refused to spend another cent upgrading them.

Undaunted, Cowpland decided to broaden his target market and sell a "dumb" laser printer, which could be hooked up to a personal computer which in turn could program the printer. Setback number two: dumb printers cannot network, and networking was just starting to become important as the personal computer revolution took off in business.

This time Cowpland hit on desktop publishing, which was still in its infancy. His strategy was twofold. He would stay away from manufacture, so he could keep his overheads low. Instead, he would study the available products, assemble the best package of equipment from all the suppliers and put it all together for the client, offering full service and maintenance. Secondly, he had learned at Mitel to be wary of dealer networks. Mitel's dealers had placed large orders for its innovative products when they first came out, but they couldn't gauge customer acceptance for at least six months. By then, Mitel had geared its manufacturing schedules to the early orders from the dealers. When the products didn't work out, the company wound up with unmanageable inventories. The carrying costs of these inventories soon put the company into financial difficulties. With Corel, Cowpland decided to market the systems through his own dealer network so that he could be sure of fast customer feedback. With all his systems in place, he took his package to the big computer trade shows and won approval from the experts. He was set to expand in an exploding market.

He had also bought 20% of a small Toronto-based firm that had spent three years developing desktop publishing technology. He estimates that if he had hit on the right questions immediately, it would have cost him $200,000 to develop the technology he needed for his systems. However, like every pioneering effort, his engineers answered a lot of irrelevant questions first, and he spent $2 million in development costs. Cowpland understands the dangers and opportunities of instability. "You always throw out your first attempt at a product when you start a new company," he says. Apple II was the first successful Apple computer and the Macintosh succeeded on the strength of the failed Lisa. "But you never tell the employees. They are all working flat out on a product that will almost certainly be canned in its entirety. Only the top guy must know that." His ten engineers focused on Ventura and PageMaker, the major desktop publishing programs and designed enhancements to them, which Corel now sells for $100 to $200 through dealership channels. "With software, once you've developed it, it's all gravy," he says, provided, of course, it's developed cheaply enough to recover the development costs.

His new strategy meant sales of the hardware in 1987 came in at $5 million instead of the $12 million he had originally expected, while software brought in another $1 million. However, the margins are much better on software than they are on wholesale hardware, so Cowpland expects his hybrid software-wholesale business to deliver the same bottom line on half the revenues he had forecast when he was going to concentrate entirely on desktop publishing systems.

Cowpland also found out later that managing a large number of company-owned dealers would put too big a strain on the organization, particularly since the major players in the desktop publishing market already had well-developed distribution channels. He decided to abandon the plan to market the desktop publishing system throughout North America. Instead, he has company outlets in Toronto and Ottawa (so that he can be sure he's getting prompt feedback from the customer) and works with Honeywell-Bull for the rest of the markets.

In the course of preparing Corel for the big growth spurt in desktop publishing, one of Cowpland's engineers made a fascinating discovery. He was working on an optical disk called a WORM (Write Once, Read Many). These disks have huge memories of 800 megabytes or more, but information cannot be removed from them once it has been stored on the disk. The engineer found a way of tricking the disk. He programmed the computer to recognize when information was changed, to skip the first entry and read the second. Although this sounds like a roundabout way of doing things, the enormous memories of WORM disks are far greater than anything available in erasable disks. It turned out that the Japanese manufacturers of optical disk drives couldn't develop the software to go with it, so Corel has supplied its software to the Japanese, who are bundling it with their hardware. Sales started to take off for these items in 1988, resulting in a sideline quite unexpectedly becoming an important product.

The WORM disks started Cowpland off on another strategy. He saw a market niche to develop software that would give IBM-compatible computers the same user-friendly graphics capability as the popular Macintosh computers made by Apple. Over a period of 18 months, his engineers developed Corel Draw, which was rated in 1989 as the Editor's Choice by *PC Magazine*, the industry bible. Within three months of launching Corel Draw, Cowpland was selling the software in 17 countries and sales leaped from $7 million in 1988 to $17 million in 1989. He has finally found his strategy. The desktop publishing systems accounted for half his sales in 1989, and they force Corel to keep in close touch with the hardware marketplace; however, he makes his real money on the software, which accounted for the other half of his sales and which has gross profit margins of 85%. Sales were growing at 50% a year for the desktop publishing systems and at 150% a year for the software.

## OWNERSHIP

The second environmental element in the process of entrepreneurship is ownership. Among the 100 entrepreneurs in this book, there was every imaginable variation in the degree of control they exercised over their companies. For the sake of simplicity, however, they can be grouped in four categories. Some have majority control (more than 50% of the voting shares, often 100%). Others control the company with a partner (both have less than 50% of the votes, but together they own more than 50%). The third category is people who do not have a voting majority, but who control the company because there are no other large blocks of shares and the shareholders are happy to leave effective control with the entrepreneurs. Finally, there are the entrepreneurs who have no voting shares at all. These are the exceptions who prove the rule!

The attitudes of these people toward their investment in their companies differed sharply depending upon ownership category. Most people who control their businesses, with or without a partner, have all their personal assets invested in the business. The people who do not have voting control of their business are far less likely to commit a significant portion of their personal assets to the business (see Appendix C, Table 3.1).

It doesn't take a study to demonstrate the main point. For the people who do not have ownership control, business failure would not be financially catastrophic. That changes the risk factor dramatically. Rob Peters of Peters & Co. has invested in many entrepreneurs and has had many people invest in some of his own ventures, including his entrepreneurial firm of stockbrokers (see page 240). He has no doubts about the importance of ownership. "The real key to entrepreneuring is agility. The only way to stay alive is to change very quickly. To do that, entrepreneurs have to have their money in the game. I never back a guy on his first venture. If he's any good, he should have some net worth."

Although he doesn't say it, Peters is focussing on a common phenomenon, which is very important to investors. Entrepreneurs who have little at risk are more cavalier with their businesses. As soon as they acquire some real wealth, their attitudes invariably change. They become more careful. There are some exceptions, like Rod Bryden, who seem to carry on with their high-risk strategies regardless of how much is at stake. But most become more conservative when failure means significant financial losses for them.

Alan Perlmutter of Micro Cooking Centres has looked over the edge of the precipice several times and lived to tell the tale. In 1987, he doubled the number of stores in his chain selling microwave ovens to 120 and tripled his sales. He said in the middle of his expansion, "I'm terrified. If all the pieces don't come together, I'll lose the whole company and all my assets. That would be disastrous. Working for someone else would destroy me."

Small and delicate, almost timid, that statement was nonetheless extraordinary coming from him, because Perlmutter is an intrepid entrepreneur. He started his first business when he was at college and wanted to go to England, but didn't have enough money. He placed a block booking with an airline, long before it became fashionable, and resold the seats to his fellow students. The organizer, of course, was given a free seat. That soon turned into a thriving business and he was hooked. He dabbled in several other businesses but hit on microwave ovens when he was 25 and saw his mother's enthusiastic reaction when he gave her one.

He expanded quickly, growing from one store in 1977 to six in 1979, when he first took on some debt, and then doubled every three or four years from then on. This last expansion was different, however. "This time, the dollars are really huge. It represents my biggest commitment by far. I went over the cliff. In all my previous expansions, I bet the company, but this time I'm terrified for two reasons. The numbers are so big. Plus I have a wife and two small children." He also had a lot more to lose. Playing double or quits every three years can mount up quickly.

He was right to be concerned. In the middle of his expansion plans, the Koreans jumped into the microwave market at prices one-third lower than those of the Japanese, whom Perlmutter was representing. The public also stopped buying, perhaps expecting prices to fall even further, and Perlmutter suddenly saw his revenues cut in half. He tried frantically to switch product lines, but the shopping malls exercised their power to refuse their tenants permission to change the nature of their stores. He had no choice but to declare bankruptcy, which overrules the clauses in the malls' leases, so he could sell his outstanding leases (valued at $2 million) and recoup all his assets. Within a week of declaring bankruptcy, he had formed a new company, Dermal Therapy, which markets therapeutic cosmetics that are as elegant as regular cosmetics. "It was financially OK, but emotionally tough," he said a year later, in 1989. "For six months I was functionally inactive, but I forced myself to go through the paces. Fortunately, I didn't make too many mistakes, and this business is now going really well. We're better than breakeven already and doubling sales every month."

Entrepreneurship can, in rare cases, exist without ownership. These are situations where a founder of a business so embodies the organization that he or she has a strong sense of ownership, which is accepted by the employees and customers. Abram Dyck has no shares in Saskatoon Fresh Pack, because he has preferred to put all the shares in his family's name since he went bankrupt some years ago (see page 86). But there's no question he runs it. He provides the entrepreneurial flair. A second example is Walter Hachborn.

Hachborn runs Home Hardware Stores from a gigantic cement warehouse, a monolith covering 20 acres, squatting awkwardly in the tiny village of St. Jacobs in southwestern Ontario. The chain is owned entirely by its 1,000-plus dealers, all of whom bought 100 voting shares for $15 each when they first joined the group. No matter how many stores individual dealers may add, that remains the extent of their holding of voting shares. In addition, dealers pay the central organization 1.9% of their purchases from head office, which is used to buy non-voting shares at $1 each. These accumulate over the years until they reach 20% of purchases, at which point the levy stops. The chain had equity of more than $96 million in 1988, on wholesale revenues of $760 million, which translates into $1.4 billion at the retail level.

It's all the vision of Hachborn, who owned the store that started the chain. He's a tiny man who must have stopped growing very soon after passing five feet. He was 65 in 1987 but he has the energy and lively step of a 45-year-old. He's unremittingly cheerful and radiates a positive attitude toward his huge family. He loves to sport the red jacket his dealers wear and tops it off with one of his omnipresent bow ties (navy blue with red spots in the picture that adorns his business card).

He started the chain in 1963, when he sold his company in St. Jacobs to a group of 108 handpicked, independent dealers in Ontario. At the time, independent hardware stores were in deep trouble because mass merchandisers were invading their market. Canadian Tire was starting to blossom and chains like Woolco and K-Mart were cleaning up on the independents. They purchased in bulk and kept profit margins paper-thin, enabling them to deliver rock-bottom prices. The independent stores had been marking up 100% on goods that the whole-salers had already marked up 25%. It was no contest. In the ten years to 1965, more than 1,000 hardware stores closed their doors in Canada.

Hachborn, from the vantage of his solitary store in a remote village, saw that something had to be done. In 1957, he had travelled widely in the U.S. and Europe, where he had seen dealer co-operatives growing in response to the same challenges. When he first proposed this idea to his partners, they weren't interested, but one of his partners died in 1962 and he got agreement from the other one to go ahead. Because he was already well known in the province—his company published a 250-page annual catalogue called *The Bulletin*, which had become the industry bible—he was able to call a meeting of 75 dealers to pursue the idea. They agreed to buy Hachborn's company and turn it into their head office. Another 33 dealers joined in and the new co-op paid Hachborn $500,000 for the inventory and $122,000 for the buildings, financed by the $1,500 levy on each of the 108 dealers who signed up, plus promissory notes for the balance.

Hachborn was elected to be president. He had not intended to expand outside Ontario, but that limitation didn't last. Two years after the co-op was started, he had signed up dealers in the Atlantic provinces and formed a buying group with three-hardware chains in Montreal, Winnipeg and Calgary. The St. Jacobs's warehouse was expanded seven times in the following 16 years. A second distribution centre was added in the Maritimes in 1979, followed five years later by another just south of Edmonton. By 1981, Hachborn had amalgamated with the Calgary chain's 400 stores, and sales really started to take off.

Not bad for a man who did sales of $450,000 when he first bought a hardware store in 1950. The original store had been started in the last century as a blacksmith, then been converted into a farm implement store at the turn of the century and later into a hardware store. Hachborn joined the store as a young man of 17, its fourth employee, in 1938. The manager had recently branched out into wholesaling through *The Bulletin*, but Canadian manufacturers wouldn't sell to the little outfit in St. Jacobs, so they sourced in the U.S. That turned out to be a blessing, because Hachborn got to know the chains and dealers in the U.S. and picked up most of the trends in the industry from them. His days as an employee ended soon after the owner died in 1948, his family sold it to Hachborn and his two partners for $125,000, financed 100% by the bank.

In the heart of Mennonite country, St. Jacobs has values that haven't changed since the first store was opened—and likely won't change for the next 50 years. Hachborn draws on that strength and serves, in return, as a pillar of the community. He's been on the planning board for 15 years, is chairman of various committees and serves on the executive of the Lutheran church, among many other activities. As the dominant employer in the area, he also takes care to stay close to the people who work with him. Every Sunday night, he drops in to talk to the workers on the week's first shift in his giant 800,000-square-foot warehouse (that's 20 acres of storage). "If I don't come, they remind me," he says. "I talk to everyone at all levels. They all call me by my first name and that's the way I want it." Hachborn makes it his business to cement relations with the Home Hardware dealers, crisscrossing the country continuously to keep in touch with them, many of whom he knows personally. "I do a tremendous pile of travelling. It can be lonely, but it's interesting."

Hachborn is unquestionably the dynamo who has driven Home Hardware in its explosive growth. He's brought in sophisticated computer systems, diversified into building materials, furniture and general merchandise (work clothing and safety equipment) and experimented with home centre supermarkets. "Our industry has gone through many changes," he says drily. "You've got to be alert. I've got more ideas and more things I'd like to do than you can imagine." Initially he worked for no salary, and even after his dealers insisted he accept a contract, he doesn't always take what his contract allows him. His plain, cramped office, with its linoleum floor and pictures of the store at various stages in its history, gives no hint of a man running a billion-dollar enterprise. Hachborn may not own Home Hardware, but he is an entrepreneur. "I was the catalyst. We were only a small distributor in the village."

## THE TOP TEN ENTREPRENEURIAL CHARACTERISTICS

The exigencies of an unstable environment and the responsibility of ownership create awesome demands on entrepreneurs. They have to be familiar with every aspect of their businesses. They should know as much about financial ratios as they do about quality control; as much about sales techniques as they do about personnel policies; as much about purchasing as they do about the competition's prices and policies. Because they lack adequate resources, most of them cannot rely on others to master the nuances of each of the many disciplines that make up a business. They also can't make do with a vague general knowledge.

The resulting tenacity in pursuing details in every corner of their business is a distinguishing feature of entrepreneurs. Even when they grow their firms into large businesses, they often retain that eye for detail, in a way that is not feasible for a big company executive who has risen to the top through specialist departments. The experience of having to do everything oneself leaves an indelible mark.

Entrepreneurs are also all alone in the world, isolated by their independence. That's the way they like it, of course, but it takes enormous strength of character to survive under those conditions. They may not have to put up with individual bosses they dislike, but they still have to deal effectively with a lot of customers, associates and suppliers who do not necessarily have the entrepreneurs' best interests at heart. They also don't have the support systems that can rescue employees who go through rough periods. The rigour of the bottom line offers few escape hatches. If they fail, they quickly find themselves alone. They operate on a high wire with no safety net. Their friendships and alliances are often contingent on their continued success. The people who help them usually do so out of self-interest. Entrepreneurs do not perceive this as a disadvantage; they know the rules of the game and know how to make the rules work for them. However, it demands an extraordinary mix of characteristics.

They need intuition to recognize opportunity, and cold logic to implement their strategies competently. They need to be immovably persistent sometimes and flexible enough to change direction in a flash in others. They have to be relentlessly dissatisfied with the way things are, so they can maintain the constant improvement in their products that alone will ensure survival; yet they also have to be boosters of the way things are to keep everyone associated with them motivated and enthusiastic.

The paragons who can meet the awesome demands of the entrepreneurial process are few and far between. Indeed, many entrepreneurs, including successful ones, do not have the necessary skills and attributes to meet all the demands of their vocation. Instead, they have an 'X' factor, some indefinable special skill which enables them to operate effectively without possessing all the skills necessary for their undertaking. That's a fundamental reality of an entrepreneurial existence, the element that accounts for their miraculous achievements as well as their devastating failures.

This environment has a profound effect on what kinds of people dare to be entrepreneurs, or on what they soon become if they plunge into their own businesses without understanding what it entails. The folklore of entrepreneurship is overflowing with stories of people who turned their first deals at six years of age, who saw opportunities when their peers could see only diversions. Many of these people grew up to be successful entrepreneurs, but many more did not. Successful entrepreneurs need discipline even more than they need natural entrepreneurial inclination.

Only half the entrepreneurs in this book consider themselves to be born entrepreneurs. The biggest single influence pushing young minds toward entrepreneurship is having a parent who is an entrepreneur. A third of the people in this book were following in their fathers' or mothers' footsteps, which is a much higher proportion than in the general population. However, whether the skills are acquired at the family dinner table or in the trenches as an adult, they are learned, usually consciously and often painfully.

I asked the people in this book what they felt were their strengths, the characteristics they possess that account for their success. These are not personality traits. They are patterns of behaviour which the entropreneurs find important in achieving their goals. Most of tl m were able to answer comprehensively and articulatel and their answers were checked against their descriptions of s cific events in their businesses. Inevitably, some didn't cover all of their strengths, and some perceived themselves as having strengths which the people who worked with them disputed hotly. However, it does give an accurate reading of what they see as their priorities in running their businesses.

The ranking of the top ten strengths of successful entrepreneurs was as follows:

| Entrepreneurial characteristic | Percent of entrepreneurs claiming to have the characteristic |
|---|---|
| 1. Inner power | 44% |
| 2. Business judgement | 44 |
| 3. Perseverance | 36 |
| 4. Motivation skills | 34 |
| 5. Idea generator | 24 |
| 6. Technical skills | 20 |
| 7. Personal values | 19 |
| 8. Marketing skills | 17 |
| 9. Decisiveness | 17 |
| 10. Empathy | 15 |

*Inner power* is a term that captures the response of many entrepreneurs to their isolation. It encompasses the inner strength that enables them to carry on through the toughest patches and the ability to set goals that attract adherents to their cause. It is the extreme manifestation of charismatic leadership and is discussed fully in Chapter 9.

Overall, the study identified 20 characteristics, which can be classified as skills in three main categories — leadership, competence and people-management skills (see Appendix C, Table 3.2). All but 3% of the entrepreneurs felt they had some form of leadership skill. Two-thirds felt they had something special to offer in the way of competence. That leaves a remarkably high proportion of one-third who don't feel they possess great competence, although all of these people said they had leadership skills and half of them thought they had good skills in motivating people. Finally, about half said they lacked skills to motivate their employees, but most of them felt they made up for it with good leadership skills and competence.

Very few entrepreneurs mentioned their ability to judge risks, that vital strength of successful entrepreneurs. This is because they see risk as something that goes with the territory, a task that is not usually pleasant but has to be performed. There is another common characteristic that was not articulated by the entrepreneurs I interviewed, but which has been identified by others and is obvious even to casual observers: high energy. Energy is the common ingredient in practically every achievement. Maintaining the status quo absorbs all the energy that most people have, so people who want to commit themselves to a major initiative must, at the very least, be able to count on an unusual supply of energy. Some are born with excess energy and some acquire it. Many find it in deep inner conflicts or traumatic setbacks, which can unleash tremendous surges of energy, which they channel into productive activities.

Ramona Beauchamp built a thriving fashion agency and modelling school, Ramona Beauchamp International. That's not easy to do in Canada, but it's next to impossible in Vancouver, which is not exactly on the doorstep of the world's great centres of haute couture. Beauchamp succeeded with a raw courage and determination that few entrepreneurs can match. She's a slight woman, with a gentle, almost quavering voice, and the mild manners of a person who has led a sheltered life. Nothing could be further from the truth. She is indeed gentle, radiating a sense of assurance which gives confidence to her pupils, but she is very, very tough. She has an iron will and prodigious energy. She succeeded in business because she refused to compromise her principles, and she put herself in a position where she had no alternative but to succeed.

The source of that energy was a personal tragedy on a scale experienced by few people. "Twenty-three years ago," she said in 1987, "I had a child who was supposed to be a vegetable." Beauchamp contracted German measles when she was pregnant with Lisa, who was born with severe brain damage. Her doctors and her husband told her to put the infant in an institution because she would never learn anything. But as Lisa began to respond to her, Beauchamp decided she would not let anyone else raise her.

It was an expensive decision, but she had been prepared for it by an equally tragic childhood. Her mother had spent most of the first 18 years of her life bedridden with rheumatic fever, then married shortly after she became mobile. Jobs were scarce, so she and her husband left Quebec almost immediately for Vancouver, where her husband worked in a sawmill while she raised a family. When Ramona was six, her father was killed in an accident at the mill. "My mother was left destitute. She had never worked and had no job experience. So she did the only thing she knew—she sewed clothes out of jute bags." To her surprise, there was a market for them. Eventually, she expanded into all kinds of fashion and made a lot of money. But it didn't rub off on her daughter, at least not just then.

Beauchamp went on to become a "talent" or a model. She had the looks and the figure but not the approval of her family. "A talent was almost like being a whore," she said much later. She persisted, and then Lisa came. Her husband, desperate to recapture his wife from her obsession with their child, tried to commit the infant to an institution behind Ramona's back. She came back to their home as her child was being taken away. After stopping this attempt to institutionalize Lisa, she set out to teach her daughter how to live a normal life with truly remarkable patience, determination and courage. She spent interminable hours patiently teaching Lisa the basics of human interaction. At enormous emotional and financial cost to herself, she painstakingly taught her child to use the undamaged parts of her brain to function as an independent person.

It was too much for her husband, who "left home because he couldn't handle it." Even her mother didn't understand. Although Beauchamp never compromised her goals for Lisa, she did give in to her family's pressure to leave her career as a model. She went to work for a lawyer, who turned out to be a wonderful boss, and settled into a groove. Some time later, she came home one night and her daughter asked her why she was unhappy. "I told her I was happy," she says. "Then I realized I wasn't, so I quit and went back into the talent business."

This time she had her own business, a fashion agency that rapidly turned into a training school for models and then children and finally businesspeople. "Through Lisa, I learned to teach," she says. "And I learned how to fight. Before that I went along with the breeze. When I wasn't aggressive, she paid for it." At 23, Lisa has her own apartment, a job and an education to Grade 8. She is an accomplished horse rider and lives a life unimaginable to those who saw her at birth. And her mother acquired an indomitable will along with the energy to move mountains.

CHAPTER 4

# IDENTIFYING
# OPPORTUNITIES

*"I'm very conscious of idea gathering. If I have a
project I want to get involved with, I become very
conscious of everything around me—books, newspapers, how people talk and act. I have files full of
ideas.... It forms a pool of creativity that may cross-
fertilize with other pools."*
— Helmut Eppich of Ebco Industries

**T**he genesis of entrepreneurship is recognizing opportunities
beyond the reach of resources currently available to the entrepreneur. If adequate resources were available, there would be
no need for entrepreneurship, because good managers could do
the job. The unique appeal of entrepreneurs is based on how
they identify opportunities and how they multiply the effectiveness of their scarce resources in exploiting the opportunities they see.

## IDEAS AND OPPORTUNITIES

All opportunities come from ideas, but most ideas are not
opportunities. An opportunity is an idea that can be exploited
profitably in the marketplace, whereas many ideas can never
be gainfully exploited, because someone else has already thought
of them or they are not viable. This distinction is important,
because the skills needed to come up with ideas are quite
different from those needed to identify opportunities. Recognizing an opportunity may demand intuition, but long before
that, it demands a comprehensive awareness of the business
environment of the opportunity.

Entrepreneurs can identify opportunities best when they

immerse themselves so completely in their business that each fibre of their body is attuned to the industry's every nook and cranny, every twist, every skeleton in the closet. This comprehensive awareness of the environment, washing over the mind time after time, in a repetitive and arduous exposure to the minutiae of the business, builds the all-important sense of patterns. It builds an understanding of what lies behind the multitude of interactions among all the players in the industry, thereby laying the groundwork for an intuitive sense of what lies ahead. The more the patterns are changing, the harder it is to read them and the greater are the opportunities.

There is no shortcut, even for the most intuitive people, to acquiring a comprehensive awareness of the environment. Only hard work and perseverance can deliver that. Market surveys are also of limited value in identifying new opportunities. They can measure reaction to a range of concrete choices, but they cannot divine what the choices should be in the first place.

The entrepreneurs in this book were asked to describe where all the ideas for their business opportunities came from. In this case, the source of the ideas is not the person who articulates them, but the person who places ideas for the strategic direction of a firm in the context of a concrete opportunity. An idea that doesn't fly is not counted as an idea. By the same token, the decision to pursue an identified opportunity does not represent a source of ideas. This last distinction is subtle for many, because two-thirds of the entrepreneurs in this book are both the main source of ideas and the prime decision-maker. Still, 17% of them drew their ideas from their employees, and another 12% generated ideas in tandem with their employees. Sources entirely outside the firm provided all the ideas to 5% of these entrepreneurs.

Ron Hume of Hume Publishing is not a spontaneous man. With his greying hair and a big frame that somehow always seems ill at ease in his well-cut suits, he is the picture of a conservative Bay Street moneyman. He talks slowly and thoughtfully, delivering his opinions with deliberation and emphasis. Yet the thing he prides himself on most is his entrepreneurial ability, particularly his ability to find, nurture and develop good ideas.

Not surprisingly, Hume builds ideas methodically. Not for him the cut and thrust of competitive creativity; he prefers to seclude himself every Friday morning, away from the bustle of day-to-day business, and think. He may stay there for an hour or he may keep going well into the weekend, but he stays there until he has taken his subject for the week as far as he can go with it. "I like brilliant people who keep their heads down and work," he says. "But they don't think. Very few people take disciplined time to think. They've got it all backwards."

He says that 15-minute think-ins don't work, because he never really gets into it quickly enough. He decides on his subject for the think-in early in the week and gathers information for it during the week. "It's usually something that's been bugging me for a while and I just can't wait to get at it. The think-in is the opportunity to grab it and deal with it. Many of my ideas would never surface if I didn't have that discipline." On the other hand, sometimes he just sits down and wonders what he should think about: "You can't legislate creativity." He thinks the world is turning right when he spends 80% of his think sessions on opportunities and 20% on problems: "If that ratio gets out of whack, you've got problems."

Hume has made his fortune on home-study courses on personal investing. His newsletter, *The MoneyLetter*, has a circulation of 100,000 in North America, and he has added four more courses to his original personal investing course: Successful Real Estate Investing; Successful Business Management; Success over 50; and The Superinvestor File. In 1989, after 17 years in business, his sales topped $70 million.

He first identified the opportunity of home-study courses when he was a vice president at McGraw-Hill Canada and was asked by the parent company to market two home-study courses in electronics in Canada. He reacted strongly against the idea but went to Washington, under protest, to check out the idea. "My head was turned around," he says now. "But I thought they were missing a good bet, because they were too narrow. So I looked for mass appeal and came up with investing." He promoted the idea enthusiastically to his colleagues at McGraw-Hill (he was already taking Friday mornings off to think). When they said they weren't interested, he quit. He now has 300,000 people a year taking his personal investing course.

In 1973, one year into his new venture, which was going well in Canada, Hume decided to go for the brass ring in the U.S. He met with a rude surprise. "We made a horrible error," he says. "We blew our brains out. We assumed what worked in Canada would work in the U.S. We didn't test." In Canada, he had run full-page advertisements in the *Financial Post* and the *Financial Times of Canada*, and taken aim at doctors and dentists through a major direct-mail campaign. It worked like a charm, so Hume ran full-page advertisements in the *Wall Street Journal* and rolled out a full direct-mail campaign "right off the bat." The response to the direct-mail campaign was 2% in Canada, 0.1% in New York. "It was ghastly," he says now. "All our assumptions were wrong. We should have tested 10,000 mailings."

It nearly put the company under, but he managed to reschedule the loans and worked his way back to profitability. There was nothing wrong with the idea, however, because he made it work when he returned some years later to the U.S. market. "The majority of people try to find out why an idea won't work," he says. "Ideas are like seeds. You have to nurture, feed, water them. There are always enough ways of finding out why ideas fail, in the normal course of market analysis."

Nonetheless, Hume has his own obstacle course through which he puts all his ideas before he lets them loose on the operating people at Hume Publishing. In the course of his think sessions, he hones an idea until he's ready to bounce it off experts in the field. Once he's satisfied they think it's viable, he works on it until he can write down a concept statement in less than two pages. While he's doing this, the only Hume executive he shares his idea with is Don Marshall, his financial man, who is chief operating officer of his holding company. "And he," says Hume, "thinks I'm nuts." Then he takes his concept statement to the executive committee and, if it agrees to the concept, it is folded into the five-year plan. The three major innovations in the Hume Group during 1988-89 all matured as ideas through this process—health letters, language training and parenting.

Unlike Hume, Helmut Eppich of Ebco and Epic Data is an inventor, although, unlike most inventors, he makes money at it. He does so because he possesses a remarkable combination of skills. His head is bursting with ideas that encompass a wide range of interests and disciplines; he is an accomplished manager who knows how to motivate and lead his employees; and he has a determination that just doesn't know when to quit.

Intense, with no sense of time when he's absorbed in what he's doing, Eppich is built like a pocket battleship, with a mind to match. Born Austrian in a town that is now Yugoslavian, he moved to Germany in 1938. His education thus "interrupted," he had to wait until after the war to get his tool-and-die maker's certificate and come to Canada. Once here, he went to night school for 36 years to learn whatever he needed to know to run his business successfully. His thirst for ideas and knowledge is insatiable.

Eppich started Ebco in Vancouver in 1956 as a tool-and-die maker. By 1988, the company's sales had grown to $81 million, and it had diversified into metal fabricating of all kinds, including automotive and aerospace, as well as furniture manufacturing. The company's most recent new venture is a contract from the Atomic Energy Commission of Canada to design and manufacture an atomic cyclotron, or particle accelerator, using basic technology developed by the University of British Columbia. Ebco also has one other subsidiary, Epic Data, which designs and manufactures electronic data collection systems.

The story of Epic Data is itself an epic saga. When Ebco was expanding rapidly in the 1960s, Eppich began finding it hard to keep track of everything at his plant, so he started searching for a control system. Most people would have gone into the marketplace to find what was available, but not Eppich. He had an idea of what he wanted and he decided to design it himself. It was not a chore. Any conversation with Eppich is peppered with quietly passionate little outbursts, as when he says with his earnest sincerity, "I just *love* systems." In 1966, he came up with a concept that suited him perfectly.

The concept was based on digital theory, which was then being applied at the leading edge of computer science, but which was not well known outside academia and the leading research laboratories. Eppich had never even heard of it. All he knew was that it would work for Ebco, and if it worked for him, it would work for other manufacturers. He decided to develop it for the market, based on his estimate that he could develop a prototype for $135,000. He took the concept to some consultants, who were not impressed. "Some people right out laughed when they saw my drawing," he said much later. "I saw it from the logic point of view, they saw it from the electrical point of view." They said it would cost $1.8 million to develop a prototype.

He didn't listen to the consultants and went ahead anyway. It was to prove a far braver decision than he could ever have imagined. First he had to go back to school. Although he never bothered to get a degree, he learned all about digital theory, electrical and electronic circuits, computer theory, logic. "I thought our experts knew it, but they were only good in their own specialty area." Eppich and his engineers ran into one problem after another, but Eppich kept going. "It would not stop gripping me." He battled and resolved, in turn, chips and chip organizations, electronic standards, telecommunications systems, power supply, mechanical designs, tooling, pricing. He was hypnotized, a man possessed. The system eventually cost him $20 million before it started turning a profit more than 10 years later. It was an extraordinary triumph. Lockheed's engineers said it was the best system in the world, beating out all the blue-chip majors. "They had to fight their own top management, who didn't want to deal with a dinky-rink B.C. company. Their jobs were on the line, but our system makes them look good."

Epic Data went public in 1986 when its sales were $18 million. When he brought new investors into the firm, he had to take all its debt into Ebco, so the company could finance its own continuing R&D. By 1988, Epic's sales were $31 million, and the firm had added security systems to its product line. Eppich is proud of his idea and the way it has grown to independence, but the experience has left him exhausted. He is no longer running Epic Data, although he still retains 80% ownership. "I could never do that again," he says, remembering the bottom of the pit, when his obsession nearly sank his whole business. Ebco's debt peaked at $28 million in 1981, when interest rates were 25% and the company's annual sales were only $38 million. For a while, the man who always had a smile for everyone never laughed. He says he's got his sense of fun back now, though, and he's built a file so full of ideas that "it would take me 1,000 man years to do them all."

Eppich is the ultimate idea man. "Ideas come from all over. If I have to design anything, whether it's data collection systems or finding out how to talk to people effectively, it requires a lot of thought and experimentation. It's like a hobby." When he designs a circuit board, he imagines himself to be a tiny, tiny part with all of the other big components around him. Then he figures out the best way to make them work together. He redesigned a 21-part card-reading slot system to a 1-part system. It's a one-millimetre piece, and he shrank himself down so that the card reader was as big as his study. He says Einstein's imagination worked the same way.

"I'm very conscious of idea gathering. If I have a project I want to get involved with, I become very conscious of everything around me—books, newspapers, how people talk and act. If there's anything that contributes to solving that problem, I keep it in my head. Then, when I'm ready, I write them all down and take those that are most useful and use them as a means of designing something. I have files full of ideas. It forms a pool of creativity that may cross-fertilize with other pools."

His projects are all over the map. He's looking at storage systems, shaving kits, toy robots to do Punch and Judy shows, plus many other more ambitious projects. "It's beautiful," he says. "Nobody challenges me. Nobody fights." However, he's no idle dreamer. "The real world is more demanding. Whatever we do, there's some cost attached to it."

Not all entrepreneurs see themselves as the main source of ideas. Mike Potter of Cognos doesn't, nor does John Seltzer of GBB Associates (see page 65). Like many entrepreneurs in service industries, which rely on the initiative of their employees, Seltzer is happy to let them formulate and implement their own ideas: "I like to use people in the way they want to use themselves, rather than use them to achieve what I want. We use—or get other people to use—opportunities creatively."

Most of the entrepreneurs who consider themselves to be idea people, like Eppich, founded their own company. Founders are more likely to be their own best source of ideas. Seventy percent see themselves this way, compared to 50% of the people who bought their businesses and 17% of those who inherited theirs (see Appendix C, Table 4.1). Only 12% of the founders rely exclusively on other people for their ideas, compared to 38% of the acquirers and 83% of the inheritors.

## PERCEPTIONS OF OPPORTUNITY

There are two major perceptions of opportunity among the entrepreneurs in the study.

Opportunity creators believe they create opportunities through their own skill, effort and good organization. They believe that if they make up their mind to achieve certain goals, the opportunities will materialize when they need them. Furthermore, they often believe they won't have any trouble recognizing them, because they will have prepared themselves so thoroughly for them.

Opportunity grabbers believe that opportunities present themselves only briefly and that the talent demanded of entrepreneurs is to recognize them in the first place, then exploit them quickly and decisively, before they float away again. But they do not believe they have any part in creating them.

Some entrepreneurs find that they are a combination of the two. They believe they create their own opportunities, but they also recognize that some opportunities just fall into their laps and they have to be ready to grab them.

Jim Brickman of Brick Brewery created his own opportunity. Most of his friends thought he was mad when he decided to start a brewery. The Big Three brewing companies not only own all but a miniscule fraction of the market, but, in Ontario's archaic distribution system for beer, they also own the monopoly on retail outlets for beer. They spend hundreds of millions of dollars in advertising every year, making it a daunting challenge to have an impact on beer drinkers. It was not an opportunity staring Brickman, or anyone else, in the face.

Before starting his brewery, Brickman had a promotions and direct-mail campaign business in Toronto. With annual billings of $6 million, Brick Promotions was doing well, but Brickman was getting bored. He wanted to promote his own product. "I wanted a product with a high profile," he says, "an established product that I could approach from a different angle. Distilling is too long term. Wine is too gourmet. So I started thinking about beer. You can relate to beer."

Brickman then set out to learn the brewery business. Low-key, he stalked his prey deliberately and cautiously. He spent six years nailing down the fine points of the brewing business. He travelled the world, visiting breweries, meeting brewmasters. He drew up detailed and methodical plans and went after financing. He drew a blank 22 times, before the Royal Bank agreed to lend him some money. The other investors fell into line after that, and he raised $2 million, partly through the Small Business Development Corporation, which gives a grant to investors through the tax system.

Brickman was not, of course, trying to take on the Big Three brewers. He knew that if he ever won a market share of 1%, he would attract the ire of the three big companies, for whom a point in market share is a prize worth winning. In classic entrepreneurial style, he picked a niche that was too small for them to bother with but big enough for him to make good money. His favourite line at the time was that Labatt's spilled more beer than his total output. "The market was segmenting into special beers. The baby-boom generation was rebelling against big business. There was a preconceived idea that small companies produce better quality."

Brickman has nothing but praise for the quality of the beer brewed by the big three companies. "It's not a question of quality, it's taste," he says. "There's a sameness to them." He knew, however, that beer has an incredibly loyal following. Beer drinkers often define themselves by their brand of suds. Brickman couldn't spring up with his new brand and expect them to rush to the stores to try it out, so he looked at a completely different taste. He tried the European taste.

Brickman had found his niche. He took the plunge, buying an old building in Kitchener-Waterloo and gutting it to restore it to its former beauty. He hired a brewmaster from Carling O'Keefe Breweries and started his first vat on November 21, 1984, one day after his target date. The strong hoppy taste of European beer has not been popular in Canada, which is why the big companies have not pursued it, but there are enough aficionados to generate the revenues and profits to keep Brick Brewery in business, along with the other microbreweries that started springing up all over the country at about the same time. He also had a stroke of luck when the unions in the big breweries went on strike just as he launched his brewery.

With sales of about $4 million in 1988, his fourth year, Brick Brewery is limited mainly by capacity. He's also had problems with his bottling line, and his quality control has to be impeccable because he doesn't use preservatives. Consequently, the profits have been slow coming, but he knows his place. "I don't want to be another E. P. Taylor. The logical next move is to start a similar operation somewhere else. I haven't spent any money on that, but I've done lots of thinking."

There are two approaches among the opportunity grabbers. Some of them create an environment that attracts deals to their attention. It can be any deal, and it may or may not have any connection to directions they had considered for themselves, but if it looks good, they'll exploit it. Others have a specific kind of opportunity in mind and prepare themselves for it, so that they are equipped to exploit it when it comes to their attention. All agree, however, that they see opportunities only when they are attuned to what's going on around them; they miss all kinds of opportunities when they are immersed in a major project.

Dave Campbell is an opportunity grabber who misses very little, no matter how immersed he is. "Some people think it's a gift, but it's just natural for me," he says. "I see it all the time. They're there and I have to recognize them and capitalize on them." He has a good eye. In 1987, he sold his best idea, CMQ Communications, for US$75 million to Telerate, the U.S. company with which he teamed up in 1980. CMQ had penetrated 70% of the Canadian market by then, and it was time to embark on a massive expansion into the U.S. or sell.

CMQ provides on-line information on prices and related ratios of 56,000 securities in 22 stock exchanges in North America every second of the trading day. "If everyone asked a question at the same time, the response time would be 2.2 seconds," he says with undisguised pride. CMQ also carries the service provided by Telerate, which covers bonds from 600 institutions around the world, as well as currency exchange rates and precious metal prices. Altogether, CMQ data appear on 25,000 computer screens, including 5,000 outside North America. Its contributors and subscribers are in 40 countries and 600 cities in the U.S., communicating through dedicated telephone lines and satellite feeds.

Telerate was actually the second company to buy CMQ from Campbell. He sold it the first time to General Telephone, but bought it back in 1979. The second time around, he increased sales from $6.5 million to $36 million in eight years, an annual compound growth rate of 24%. He's very laid back about it, however. He spreads an atmosphere of calm in his office. There is free coffee and juice for his 200 employees, and if anyone gets hungry, there's also a good supply of apples. In the middle of a conversation, Campbell is liable to pick up an apple and start munching on it, slouched casually in his chair with one leg draped over an armrest. A small man, with unusually long legs, he walks with a spring in his step that belies his 66 years. His hair is white and his face thoroughly lived in, but his voice is that of a 30-year-old. Supremely self-assured, he likes to affect great humility.

His own office is dominated by a three-panelled, folding parchment screen with two-foot-high illustrations of beautiful Chinese calligraphy. They say, appropriately enough, "Always look to the future." He likes beautiful things. He has expensive art on the walls and sterling silver statuettes in the boardroom and his office. For CMQ's 25th anniversary, he commissioned a special edition of the works of Ken Danby, highlighting the two owned by CMQ. Most of all, however, he supports the Toronto Symphony Orchestra, which has benefited greatly from his enthusiasm, while he feels it has given CMQ some "stature."

This reflects, perhaps, the twilight of a career that is more notable for its agility and daring than for its refined elegance. When he first hit upon the idea that was to become CMQ, Campbell owned the leading cable TV system in Montreal. The Montreal Stock Exchange called him in to see if he could film the stock-quotation chalkboard and send it by cable to the stockbroker in the city. After he did it, he remembered an article he had read in one of the many electronic magazines to which he subscribed. It had told of an American who had left RCA Victor to develop a system that could retrieve information for stockbrokers. Campbell spent three months finding the man, then visited his company to ask for the Canadian rights to its product. They told him he was "nuts," but Campbell saw a future in the system. He bought some of their product for cash plus a royalty and took it back to his engineers at the cable TV company.

He spent $2½ million developing the technology, then solid state transistors were invented, and he had to start all over again. In 1961, when he was finally ready to sell his product to the brokerage industry, he arranged a demonstration of a hook-up to the Boston exchange. No one bought it. "We were ready to pack up," he says, "then a French guy came in. He asked me to prove my system worked. I asked him what stock price he'd like. He said Jersey Oil. I got the quote and he said, 'You see it doesn't work. I've just bought some stock and the price was different.'" Campbell asked him to phone Boston and check. He did, and his broker told him the price had changed in the few minutes since he had made his purchase. Combined Market Quotations had its first customer. "That," said Campbell, as he often does, "is the way the pickle squirts."

Campbell obtained the Canadian rights to the technology by buying shares in the American company, which sold out to General Telephone in 1969. Soon afterwards, GT approached Campbell. "I set a very interesting price, and I walked away with a lot of money." GT offered a ten-year no-competition clause to persuade him to stay on as chief executive officer. It was lucrative but not Campbell's cup of tea. "I used to come up with ideas and they weren't keen. I told them the company had to move or go backwards." GT didn't agree, so he quit in 1976 and moved from Montreal to Toronto. He told them he was going into competition with CMQ, even though only seven years had passed in his no-competition agreement. The alternative was to sell the business back to him, which is what GT eventually did, and Campbell became, once again, sole owner of CMQ in 1979.

By then he had sold all his other businesses, including the cable TV company. He had come a long way. He started his first business in 1944, when he brilliantly manoeuvred Decca and RCA Victor into supplying him with records at a time when they were as scarce as hen's teeth, because there was a shortage of shellac. Later, when the industry came out with 33⅓ rpm records, no one could get them in Canada because there were no players available. Campbell manufactured them in the basement of his Montreal home and imported the records. That was when he decided to quit his regular job at Northern Telecom. He later dabbled in appliances of all kinds, even buying the Canadian rights to All detergent for automatic washing machines.

When he was selling TV sets, soon after they first became available, he realized that people who lived on Mount Royal couldn't get U.S. signals, so he sold them antennas. That, of course, didn't solve the problem, and it wasn't long before he found the man who invented the switch that made cable TV possible. He started a cable TV company in 1952. After building it up to 800 miles of wire and 55,000 customers, he sold it in 1971 to the *Montreal Star*, which later sold it to Jean Pouliot (see page 108).

There have been many more businesses. His friends all tell Campbell he should write an autobiography. "If you want to go into business," he says, "you must identify a need. You can't be me-too. I have always expanded through new products, even though it's risky. You have to learn to bend with the wind, move very quickly." When he sold CMQ, he was almost 67. Within weeks, he had incorporated a new company and taken offices in the Royal Bank Plaza.

## THE SPUR OF INADEQUATE RESOURCES

Identifying opportunities is one thing. It's quite another to exploit them when the available resources are inadequate for the task. When John Seltzer of GBB Associates was trying to build his actuarial consulting business in the early 1970s, all he and his two colleagues could afford was a tiny room with one desk. Seltzer had no choice but to get out of the office and pound the pavement looking for business, because the business he brought in forced Barry Sutton to use the desk while he performed the requisite actuarial valuations. Then Sutton had to clear out and sell, too, so that Joanne Busyk could use the desk to type up the reports.

Over a cup of coffee one day, Seltzer was relating his frustration with the arrangement to Ted McConnell, who was then the president of the Canadian branch of the Mercantile Bank, which had offices one floor below GBB. McConnell was sympathetic and offered Seltzer the use of his office, which was large, beautifully furnished and dominated by a magnificent wooden desk. The next time Seltzer invited a client to visit him, McConnell cleared out, instructing his secretary to tell visitors that the office was GBB Associates and to introduce Seltzer, ensconced in his impressive office, as the president.

A scarcity of resources draws out the visionary aspect of entrepreneurs as well as their ingenuity. They define their limits in terms of potential rather than actual situations—their own potential and the potential of the resources they control. This is what enables entrepreneurs to dream as others can never dream. It's also the genesis of magnificent failures by entrepreneurs who overestimate their own potential. Its real importance lies in the attitude it creates in entrepreneurs toward the deployment of resources. They are positively miserly compared to large firms.

When large organizations embark on a project, they usually arm themselves with a room full of plans and studies, and a firm commitment, up front, to deploy the human and financial resources necessary to make the project a success. Entrepreneurial firms, on the other hand, parcel their projects into many small phases with options and contingencies galore. This approach is more flexible and a lot cheaper—and out of the question for a big organization, which couldn't handle the repeated demands for strategic decisions at each step along the way.

By doling out the resources in such small amounts, entrepreneurs can afford to dream of leveraging the resources they control far beyond what outsiders would consider to be their limits. This theme runs through most of the stories in this book, but none more so than in the tale of Jim Robinson of Petwa Canada.

Robinson is a big man with curly red hair and a high-pitched, effervescent giggle that bubbles out of him whenever the spirit moves him (which is often). His passion in life is cars. His office features a massive stylized portrait of a Ferrari, a car that he would buy if he ever filled his bank account full enough to match the exponentially increasing price of his dream. He'll no doubt get his way one day. As a youngster, his dream was to buy a Sunbeam Alpine, so he worked until he had saved enough to buy one for cash. The dealer had to drive him home, because he was only 15. Still, he could sit in the driver's seat and listen to the radio, waiting for the moment when he could get his licence.

Petwa is a water treatment company. It had sales in 1989 of about $7 million, earned from three main sources: drinkable water for homes and municipalities; waste water treatment for industry; and high-quality water for hospitals, which use it for dialysis and similar delicate operations. Robinson's background hardly suited him for this technical field. He was a Phys. Ed. instructor "before hunger set in." He had made a good friend in the Scout movement, however, named Al Davidson, who had a technical background that included water treatment. Robinson persuaded him to go into partnership with him, selling water conditioners for homes.

Sales had risen to the princely sum of $75,000 when Robinson heard about a water treatment machine made by a company in Milwaukee. He and Davidson flew down to see the manufacturer and asked for the rights for southern Alberta. They returned with the rights to the Prairies and the Northwest Territories. "We hardly knew what they were talking about," Robinson remembers in gales of laughter, but they figured it would be of interest to the annual convention of the Canadian Water Quality Association then taking place in Calgary. "We hired two top models, bought them great dresses and rented a hospitality suite. Nobody had ever heard of us, of course, so we pretended to be big deals. We said we hadn't sold in Canada because we were all in exports. We got our suppliers to give us samples free. It cost us $4,000."

But it worked. They sold one machine to Esso and two to Sun Oil in the first week. One other order in their first year pulled their sales up to $200,000, and they were on their way. They wound up supplying most of the water treatment equipment for drilling rigs on the Beaufort Sea with that machine.

Davidson later lost interest and left Petwa to go back to

school, but his father never left. "He was our mentor," Robinson says. "He had a lot of wisdom. He had done it the textbook way and he had done it the street way." He died some years ago and asked to be buried in the flower bed at Petwa. "He said he wanted to be with the boys," Robinson recalls. His picture still hangs in the reception area.

# CHAPTER 5

# RISKING

*"When I started, I bet the store—but that was myself. You bet the store because that's the minimum. If my father had given me $100,000, I would not have rolled it at all."*
— Steve Chepa of Dicon Systems

**E**ntrepreneurs don't go into business so that they can take risks. A few, like restaurant owner Peter Oliver, seek out risk for the thrill of it, but almost all of them regard it as a means to an end, not as a motivation. That doesn't mean they dislike taking risks. Indeed, their nervous systems could not withstand entrepreneuring if they didn't derive some satisfaction from taking risks. It is more than a necessary skill, however; it's the moment of truth, it's the essence of the game. They see it as betting on themselves.

For entrepreneurs, risk-taking is an autonomous decision to expose a valuable possession to the chance of loss, in return for the opportunity to acquire something much more valuable. This applies as much to starting a new venture as it does to deciding to stay in business with an existing firm. Many entrepreneurs fold their businesses because they no longer believe the rewards are worth the risks or the hassle.

Taking risks is a very private balancing act between the upside and the downside, but it is not an objective process. Risk-takers invent, in their own imaginations, the relative weights of the two sides of risk-taking, sometimes with only cursory reference to their objective weights in the real world. The upside can be wildly ambitious or conservative, indeed anything they want it to be. And the downside can be a mere bagatelle, no matter how much money is at risk, or it can be unthinkable.

There are three components of entrepreneurial risk-taking:

- the perception of the potential loss,
- the entrepreneur's tolerance of risk, and
- the degree to which they control their risks.

The potential loss is usually money, but it doesn't need to be. It can be reputation, credibility, time, pride, self-respect, a marriage and family, or the independence of running one's own company. The potential loss itself is far less important, though, than the entrepreneur's perception of it. If they feel comfortable with the risk they perceive in a venture, they can operate effectively. Without that comfort level, they are likely to be frozen by the fear of failure. Usually, the comfort level is a perception that there is virtually no risk involved, hence the discovery by researchers that entrepreneurs are not risk-takers. However, this perceived comfort level should not be confused with the objective risk of a venture. The perception of a risk is a combination of how they assess the objective risk and their own attitude toward the perceived risk.

An important part of risk perception is the entrepreneur's personal exposure to the potential loss. Two similar risk-takers facing comparable potential losses will react quite differently if one owns 10% of the business and the other owns 100%. Equally, a highly leveraged venture distributes the potential loss between the entrepreneur and the bank differently than a business without debt. Also, the entrepreneurs with smaller exposures to potential losses often place relatively more weight on the preservation of their own credibility as entrepreneurs in their perceptions of potential losses.

Given their perception of a risk, entrepreneurs still take risks in widely divergent ways, depending on their tolerance for risk. This also depends on two factors. They are greatly influenced by their assessment of their own competence to surmount the risks they take on. And, they may be prepared to tolerate risk that surpasses their comfort level by a margin that reflects how badly they want to achieve their goal.

Finally, risking is not a static game. Once they have settled in their own minds their perception of and tolerance for the risks, most entrepreneurs also seek to control the risks they face.

They do this by limiting their exposure, limiting the maximum possible losses or by reducing the probability of failure.

## PERCEPTION OF RISK

The entrepreneurs in this book assess an objective risk in one of three ways: some face up to their risk, fully acknowledging its extent; some ignore it; and others trivialize it, thereby making themselves invulnerable to the potential losses.

Steve Chepa of Dicon Systems has figured out most of the angles in running an entrepreneurial business, but he doesn't take himself too seriously. This detachment is part of his competence, and it's also what allows him to trivialize his potential losses. That doesn't mean he doesn't care, just that he doesn't worry about the effect failure might have on him. When ruin stared him in the face, as Dicon's fortunes reached their lowest ebb, Chepa stared it down. "It looked like I was going to lose it all. So we felt, 'We've lost it, we'll just go on fighting. There's only one way to go.'" It's easier for entrepreneurs to take that attitude when they've already lost everything, but Chepa kept his nonchalance, even after he became extremely successful.

With annual sales of about $18 million in 1988, Dicon is an exporting success story. Its smoke detectors have achieved significant market shares in all the major developed markets in the Western world. Now Chepa's diversified into security systems with a comprehensive home-intrusion system, which will monitor fires, medical emergencies, electrical power and a few other things through the telephone. He's aiming to change the market for security systems, traditionally the domain of professional installers. Dicon's product does the same job, but it's a movable appliance that can be installed without professional help.

"The talking chip is the technological breakthrough that makes it possible," he says. Chepa estimates his new system, which retails for $600 to $800, will lift Dicon sales to $100 million by the middle of the 1990s. Meanwhile, it was just like any other start-up, and Dicon was only breaking even as the stores stocked up with the first models of his home-intrusion system in 1989. Shortly before he launched it, Chepa commented drily, "The worst that can happen is we can lose a bit of money and feel bad. The downside is of little consequence."

Chepa's first job, in 1965, was at Chubb Canada, where he was something of a wonderboy, rising from chief accountant to vice president and general manager in less than five years, "because that's what you were expected to do." He made his mark selling alarm systems to high-rise building operators and other big customers, but typically declines to accept all the credit. The market leader then was ADT, which he says stood still while Chubb was busy developing new products. It couldn't last, however. Chepa says his ego was too big for the firm's chairman and when troubled times came, he was let go.

He's a small man, with a great mane of wavy silver hair, swept back in a big lick over his head and ears, and accented by bushy, pitch-black eyebrows. He has the feel of an alert, bright and mischievous person, who is constantly prodding at the edge, seeing how people react. His offices are unpretentious, with linoleum floor coverings and plain decor. An iconoclast who prefers philosophical books to management books, he loves to philosophize. He had long wanted to build his own business, so it wasn't a crushing blow to part company with Chubb, even if it did mean a year of unemployment.

While he was at Chubb, he and a partner started a small business on the side, selling false eyelashes, but it didn't work. They had a host of start-up problems. They couldn't find the right formula for the glue, lost their lead time, and then the majors came into the market. Although the company did well, it didn't reach the point where the profits became significant, and Chepa sold out to his partner. The business later took off, but the growth was too much for it and the firm slid into bankruptcy.

A year after he had parted company with Chubb, he finally found his niche when he heard that a company called Neeco was selling a subsidiary, Check Security Systems. It manufactured alarm systems for high-rise apartment buildings, so Chepa was confident he had the experience to turn it around. He persuaded John Mallory, an engineer whom he had hired at Chubb, to join him in buying the company. "I was sure I was going to succeed in business. At that time, I rolled my total fortune on it. I'd done it successfully with Chubb. Now I was going to do it again, with a different owner." As always, Chepa had no qualms about the downside. "When I started, I bet the store—but that was myself. You bet the store because that's the minimum. If my father had given me $100,000, I would not have rolled it at all."

His time had not yet come, however. Check was in terrible shape. It was so bad, they had to change its name. Even then, his touch had no magic in that marketplace. "We got killed because the big guy, Edwards, undercut us on every bid." After two years of frantic scrambling, Chepa and Mallory had lost everything. They sold out to Mirtone Industries in return for a two-year employment contract plus the rights to a residential smoke detector that Mallory had developed to prototype stage at Check. Mirtone didn't know it, but it had thrown the destitute pair a lifeline. When they left Check two years later to form Dicon, they already had an order for 20,000 smoke detectors, at $19 each, from Sunbeam.

They were on their way, but not out of the woods yet. After two successful years building their business in Canada, they assaulted the U.S. market and were badly mauled. They rescued the firm only through drastic cutbacks and a redirection of their focus to Europe. Chepa handled it all with remarkable equanimity. He gets a big kick out of what he sees going on around him. A small smile playing at the edge of his lips, he is both a doer and an observer of the human condition. He can see both sides. He is himself an investor in entrepreneurial businesses. "It's not as easy as I thought it would be. It's hard to find entrepreneurs who understand you have something at risk. Too many entrepreneurs think it's a sure thing and anything you give them is usury." He hasn't had too much luck as a passive investor, with only one winner out of all his investments. "A mutual fund would probably have given me a better return. But the process of looking at companies in trouble or starting up is a good exercise."

Chepa has been through the stage of taking on massive risks because he had nothing to lose. That stage often passes as soon as entrepreneurs succeed and acquire some wealth, as indeed has happened with Chepa. Yet, although he likes his horses and other expensive playthings, he is not owned by his possessions. "It's only money," he says with his mocking smile. He still retains a certain insouciance about the downside in his investments. He trivializes his risks.

Jim Egan of Egan Visual prefers to ignore his potential losses. He has succeeded in his business of manufacturing visual aid products, but it took ten years before he felt confident enough to deal with his downside. His main product, accounting for 80% of his $15-million annual sales, is the modern substitute for boardroom chalkboards. He makes beautiful wooden cabinets that conceal smooth white surfaces on which felt pens can be used to write easily erasable messages. He has seen more than his share of brushes with failure and prefers not to think about them. "I always chose not to consider failure. It would make you start thinking about risk."

He started Egan Visual in the early 1970s when he found out before anyone else in Canada that the Japanese had invented the material for the whiteboards that have since replaced blackboards. He brought the technology to Toronto, figuring his biggest danger was the "knock-off artists" who plague the furniture industry. These people are a menace to innovators, because they copy new designs and flood the market with them, thereby eliminating the competitive advantage of innovating. He accordingly kept a very low profile to begin with, hoping he might win a year with no competition from the knock-off artists. He didn't advertise or show his product at trade shows.

Naturally, his growth suffered, but he was as thrilled as he was surprised when his respite from the knock-off artists stretched out to 13 years. However, even after he had several competitors, he never went for rapid growth with advertising and promotion campaigns. He prefers to sell through word-of-mouth and a prodigious amount of travelling, which have still enabled him to increase annual sales to almost $20 million in 1989.

He aims his pitch mainly at the designers who buy his product as a small part of corporate contracts to redesign offices. His offices reflect that priority, decorated with the fashionable greys, off-whites and mauves that might attract designers. Smooth and handsome, Egan dresses tastefully and clearly enjoys the material benefits of his success, which include a 41-foot trawler moored in Fort Lauderdale. However, the years of keeping his head down in the hope no one would notice him have left their mark. He seldom felt secure enough to open up with people. For ten years, he allowed himself to be harassed by his bank manager, who phoned him every day of the week to find out which of his expected cheques had come in. "I don't even like to think about it," he said much later. "It would have been easier if I'd told them I was going into competition with IBM." When he finally screwed up the courage to tell his bank manager he'd had enough, he was ready to walk away from his business. "That would have been ten years of my life down the drain if he had called my bluff," he says now. "In those days, everything was in my businesses. If one went, everything went. I didn't like it."

He also had a black period when he moved his factory to Cobourg, 100 kilometres east of Toronto. He was still paranoid that the knock-off artists would find his product, so he diversified, starting a business renting out houseboats on the Trent-Severn waterway. It was a disastrous move that wound up hurting his main business. "Everything went wrong, so I escaped back to Toronto." He was worth minus $75,000, but the Ontario Development Corporation lent him some money and he never looked back. "I had periods when I was concerned we couldn't pull it off," he says now. "But I always knew we would." When he says it, however, it seems more like a remembered hope that the difficulties would just go away, than any strong conviction that he had the power to pull it off. Most people who ignore their potential losses have a strong, sometimes blind faith that they can overcome any obstacles.

The third approach to assessing potential losses is to face them squarely, as do Peter Oliver and Bill Pattison. Both are in awe, at times, of what failure would do to them, although Oliver's shudder may be more of a thrill than a fright.

The second part of risk perception is the entrepreneurs' attitude toward the risk, which also follows one of three approaches: some resolutely accept the risk as something that goes with the territory; some gauge carefully their potential loss, with the intention of keeping it within acceptable limits; and others deal with the downside by persuading themselves they have nothing to lose so they might as well go ahead and take the risk.

Walter Oster of The Whaler Group owns a string of seafood restaurants and a brand new hotel on Toronto's lakefront, the Admiral Hotel. He also owns a construction company, which he uses mainly on his own projects now. He knows exactly how big his risks are, and he accepts them without any qualms. "I had to risk everything for this hotel," he says. "I love it. I'm investing in myself. It's directly tied to a challenge." When he walked into the bank to borrow $30 million to build the Admiral, he was as nervous as when he borrowed $15,000 in 1965 to start his own business. "I have more confidence now, but the banker still has to ask, 'How do you know it's going to work?'" The big difference is that he had nothing to lose in 1965, and he knew he could always find a job selling if he failed. He was a wealthy man when he put it all on the line for his hotel, but he resolutely accepted the bigger risk as a necessary part of the game.

"I've always been in a situation where if anything went wrong, I'd lose everything. The hotel is a $36-million project, which has grown to $40-million," he said in 1987, just after the hotel opened. "When I negotiated the financing for it, interest rates were 18% or 19%, but I said in my proposal the mortgage would cost me 12.5%, because I knew they had to come down. In the end, my takedown will be 11.5%."

Shortish, with a large, balding head, Oster is irrepressibly cheerful. He starts his day at 7 a.m., walking the construction site or working on whatever is uppermost in his mind at the time. He lives his life at full throttle, in tune with one of his favourite sayings, "Life is not a dress rehearsal." Although he is the proud owner of one of only 75 Rolls-Royces produced in celebration of the 75th year of the marque, he doesn't drive it often. He prefers his small four-wheel-drive Jeep, which doesn't attract scratches in parking lots the way the Rolls does. He loves a party, and it's rare when he doesn't have plans on the go for at least one big bash. He has been known to take a large group of friends on a caviar cruise on Lake Ontario, to "taste test" a variety of champagnes. It's extravagant, but it is all done with an impish sense of spontaneous, understated humour, which makes him popular with his friends and acquaintances.

Hotels and restaurants, of course, are the scourge of cautious bankers, and Oster dove into the industry with no experience, a sure-fire way to fail. Actually, it wasn't his choice; he fell into restaurants by mistake. Eight years after he started his own construction company, a friend had leased a restaurant property, then failed to raise the financing, so Oster suggested to his two partners that they might each chip in $10,000 and see if they could make it profitable. He ran the construction company during the day and was maitre d' at night, while his wife Mary acted as the hostess at the door. Because they both enjoy cooking, it was a hobby as well as an apprenticeship. The expansion started two years later with a second restaurant, and apart from a few hiccoughs when he tried different kinds of restaurants, he never stopped growing, reaching annual sales of $24 million in 1988. By then he had 3,000 restaurant seats, the hotel, a golf course, and several apartment blocks.

Oster has never shirked risk. Nine days after he turned 16, he told his father he was fed up with school. He was in Grade 10, and his father told him, "If you quit school, you start working tomorrow." Many parents have tried that bluff, but few meet with the response that young Oster gave. The following day, he started work at Frankel Steel, producing blueprints from draftsmen's drawings. It was a messy job that no one liked to do. Oster wasn't crazy about it either, so he expressed an interest in becoming a draftsman, took an aptitude test and did well. He completed his six-month course on structural steel drafting in three months and became Frankel's first draftsman for the new-style open-web steel joists.

The people at Frankel were beginning to get a feel for Oster's limited patience with obstacles to his progress. By the time he turned 22, he had become Frankel's top salesman of structural steel, having also mastered along the way the order desk, pricing and estimating. After two years as a salesman, he left Frankel to become a partner with Iggy Kaneff, whom he decided needed a job superintendent. He was back at Frankel within two years. One year later, the entrepreneurial urge was becoming irresistible. "I was giving so much advice to a client that I decided I might as well do the job myself. So I did it, moonlighting." He formed Osin Construction, which immediately started bidding on construction projects.

This posed some conflict-of-interest problems, because he was bidding against Frankel's clients, but Oster had a quick solution. When a project came up for tender, he removed himself from the bidding process. The president of Frankel didn't quite see it that way, however, and objected to his star salesman's moonlighting. With just a hint of triumph, he asked Oster, "What makes you think we'll supply you?" Oster's comeback sealed his fate at Frankel, "What makes you think you'll get the business?" That was in 1965, and he's never looked back. He will never stop taking risks. High-risk items, he likes to say, produce a bigger profit. He's a prototype for those who face their risks and accept them resolutely.

The entrepreneurs who adopt an attitude of resolute acceptance of risk are much more likely to have committed all their personal resources to the business than are their fellow entrepreneurs who gauge carefully their potential loss. Perhaps it's because it's their money, and they feel they can take as many risks as they want with it. Certainly, people like Bill Pattison of Delta Hotels, who owned 10% of his company and who has invested in many other businesses, are more likely to adopt a cautious attitude toward the amount of risk they are prepared to consider.

The third attitude of entrepreneurs toward risk is feeling that they have nothing to lose. This is common among start-ups, often because it's true. Steve Chepa and Walter Oster both felt this way when they started their businesses. It's less common to find entrepreneurs carrying this attitude into maturing businesses, when they have accumulated significant wealth, but John Buhler of Farm King Allied is one. Although he has several million dollars to lose, he doesn't look at life in terms of acquiring or losing money.

Buhler, who comes from a poverty-stricken Mennonite family, has never translated his wealth into a fancy lifestyle. If he loses everything, he says he'll just be back where he started. "I don't need any security," he says. "I'm secure in myself. If I went broke, they can't take away my energy and talents."

His firm is based in Winnipeg, where it manufactures farm implements, an industry that was devastated by overcapacity during the 1980s as farm incomes in the West collapsed. Farm King Allied remained profitable throughout this period, while many other firms went under, but Buhler has had to be nimble. Only half his sales are in western Canada now, and he's had to pare his costs to the bone. In the litigious U.S., now an important market for him, Buhler carries liability insurance for only $150,000, to cover the "piddling" stuff. A major suit from a customer would bankrupt the U.S. subsidiary. He could buy the insurance but he won't. He won't even buy insurance for his wife's fur coat. "I say, 'Why?' If you lose it, you lose it. I carry insurance only because the bank wants me to carry it."

Five-foot-four and bouncy, Buhler has a high profile in Manitoba, because he has tried to buy several large manufacturing concerns, including Flyer Bus, White Farm Equipment and Massey-Ferguson's Canadian operation. None of these came off, but many of his other acquisitions have, and he has earned a reputation as a master turnaround artist. He enjoys his success, not for what it enables him to buy, but for the notoriety and reputation. His only concession to his wealth is his car—a Cadillac. His second wife Bonnie's car is a standard family car, which is in such great demand by her two daughters that she has agreed to let them keep it, provided they guarantee to drive her whenever she needs to go somewhere. They both like to stress that their requirements in life are very small.

Buhler has a remarkable approach to life. He is shrewd and a keen judge of people, yet he seems almost naive in his openness to new experiences and new people. He's far from naive, of course, but it's as if, having broken free of a first marriage that was mired in an unforgiving, severely religious view of life, he is making up for lost laughter. His joy is infectious. He trivializes his tribulations, joking about having to use his glasses to read anything, but his eyesight is so bad, his wife has to read the daily business papers to him every morning.

He has a marvellous gift, earned in the poverty of his childhood, of making everyone he meets feel at ease. He started life in Morden, Manitoba, a Mennonite centre, where he ran a paper route before dropping out of school at Grade 9 to bring in some money for the family. His entrepreneurial instincts eventually found an outlet when, at 24, he and his father put down $1,500 to buy a service station and auto wrecker. He made the business prosper and put his profits into real estate, which later served as his golden goose when he needed credit at the bank.

At 37, he made his first big breakthrough when his first wife's father, once the richest man in Morden, started running into trouble with his business, a plant manufacturing farm implements. He joined the business, turned it around and then bought it for $135,000. Within a year, he had more than tripled sales and had borrowed $1 million to expand. That was 1973. Several acquisitions and divestitures later, annual sales for his group reached $20 million in 1987, and Buhler is still looking for the break that will catapult him into the big leagues. Retained earnings in his company were $10 million in 1988, but he doesn't touch it. He has never taken a salary of more than $50,000. He carries only a little change in his pocket and a company credit card. He has no savings account, no bonds, no registered retirement savings plan. The company owns his car.

This doesn't mean that Buhler doesn't care about succeeding. He wants it badly. He also cares about the risks he takes, claiming categorically that he is not a risk-taker. When he was 16, he made a commitment that if he ever went broke, he'd spend the rest of his life paying off his customers. However, that hasn't stopped him from taking what any other person would consider to be some significant risks. He has taken some companies in desperate trouble and poured money into them before turning them around and selling at a handsome profit. Buhler lost no sleep over these ventures. "They were all guaranteed to succeed," he says. Guaranteed, of course, only because he knew exactly what he had to do, and he had complete faith in his own ability to pull it off. A major factor in that confidence is his deal-making ability. He has an acute, intuitive business sense, that enables him to establish a price at which he knows he can make money on a deal. Then he negotiates brilliantly without budging from that price. A lot of sellers lower their prices. The ones that don't have to find other buyers.

What gives him the security to allow his self-confidence free rein is his meagre lifestyle. It is so modest, it would barely change if he lost everything. In that sense, he has nothing to lose. Far more than making money, however, he wants to employ 1,000 people by the mid-1990s. His real downside is not money at all, it's losing his credibility. He knows that he cannot reach his goals without credibility, because that is what gives him the power to attract the resources he needs. "Thousands can do what I'm doing, but they don't have the credibility. Credibility has to be built, and once you've got it, you've got it. That's my biggest asset, and I sure don't want to blow that."

## RISK TOLERANCE

Michel Gendreau lives in St. Georges in the Beauce, the heartland of entrepreneurship in Quebec. Throughout the long period when the rest of the province accepted the priorities set for them by the concordat between the Catholic Church and nationalist provincial governments, the Beauce was resolutely entrepreneurial. While the children in the rest of Quebec entered the church, the law or the civil service, the children in the Beauce learned about risk at the dinner table. In the 1980s, however, entrepreneurs acquired star status in Quebec, and the Beauce acquired almost mythological proportions, blurring its real importance in the process. The region's strength lies in its indomitable spirit, not its competence. The Beaucerons were starved for so long of management training and emotional succour from their government that their entrepreneurship was rough and ready, plagued by setbacks, erratic in its direction, but heroic in its steadfast ambition. Only now, in the sunshine of their province's universal admiration, are Beaucerons like Michel Gendreau beginning to blossom.

Gendreau's father is an entrepreneur, who owns a hospitality centre and an old-age home with 165 beds. He needed some help in 1982, so he persuaded his son to leave stockbrokers Geoffrion, Leclerc and be his general manager. A year later, Michel Gendreau heard about the bankruptcy of a local firm called Garaga, which made garage doors. He had dreamed for a long time of building a large company that might grow into another General Motors, and he decided the time was ripe to pick a business and go for it. He bought Garaga's assets from the receiver. He knew it was badly managed and figured he could fix it. Without the benefit of a formal study of its prospects, he put in $25,000 of his own money and borrowed the rest to pay the $60,000 purchase price.

He soon realized that he needed more investors. That necessitated a written plan, so he commissioned his first study of

Garaga. The study came back with unequivocal recommendations. "It told me," he said with a wry smile three years later, "to liquidate the business and find myself a job. It said there was no market for the product, the machinery was inappropriate and the people working there were rotten." Gendreau shelved the report, did his own three-year plan, which was a lot more sanguine, and went after his investors. He didn't share the study with them. "They have to think the glass is half full," he said, still smiling.

Gendreau is a roly-poly man with a big shock of black hair and twinkling eyes. He was 27 when he bought Garaga, and in those first few years, he had the time of his life. Like all startups, he was in charge of everything, dealing with every problem imaginable from one moment to the next. His enthusiasm was so strong that he would run from one consultation to another, joyfully juggling his priorities. He's succinct, never using three words where he could use two. He also has complete confidence in himself. He knew full well he was taking an enormous risk ignoring that first study while he raised money, but he was so convinced he could make it profitable that he had no qualms whatsoever.

He duly sold the Quebec government on two or three grant programs, and he brought in as investors the National Bank and a "Sodeq" (Société de développement de l'entreprise québecoise, under which the provincial government provides investors with a 30% tax break on investments in entrepreneurs). In his first year, he persuaded the National Research Council to collaborate with him in designing new machinery to make his garage doors more efficiently. It cost him $100,000, but it did the trick. He also fired all the key people in the company and invigorated his new team with his enthusiasm. His rented plant looked as if a tornado had hit it. The floor was a mess with shavings and clutter everywhere, while his weird Rube Goldberg machine chugged away, doing its thing in one corner. With no distribution system, sales that year were only $450,000, and the company still couldn't afford to support Gendreau, who carried on running his father's old-age home.

In its second year with Gendreau at the helm, Garaga made a small profit on sales of $1 million. Meanwhile, Gendreau had bought another bankrupt company, which made polyurethane roofing insulation. More importantly, he inherited that company's engineer, who was able to take over the development of better machinery for both divisions of Garaga. The following year, sales reached almost $2 million, and Gendreau felt he could leave his father's business and work on Garaga full-time. His three-year plan for his investors in 1983-84 had proved to be too conservative, and by 1987 he was already making his second three-year plan look timid. In 1988, he had sales of $7.5 million with 50 employees and was expecting sales to reach $10 million in 1989.

By then he had built significant value into Garaga. He had invested $2.2 million in a new factory and new machinery, giving him a more workmanlike and organized plant. He had taken almost no money out of the company, in order to keep his debt load down and build up a strong line of credit. In early 1989, he was prepared to jump on the bargains he expects to come on the market when the long-awaited recession hits. Nevertheless, he says he won't take risks as big as his early ones. "I'm not interested anymore in playing double or quits every year," he says. "There's a significant amount at risk now." Although he has become more concerned with managing his risk, his self-confidence obviously hasn't diminished, and he won't stop buying companies. He said in 1986, when he was 30, that he had given up his dream of building a really large company. He may change his mind again.

Many entrepreneurs share Gendreau's powerful belief in his own ability to overcome almost any obstacle. Rod Bryden has it, as do Peter Oliver and John Buhler. However, all these entrepreneurs have avoided serious failures. They have had setbacks, in some cases awesome setbacks, but as long as they surmount them, their faith in themselves just keeps on growing. When they take on risk, their self-confidence insulates them against fear of the downside.

Others, often including those who have lived with the spectre of defeat, are less sanguine, preferring to rely on long experience to assess cold-bloodedly their chances of success and to assume an appropriate amount of risk, consistent with their personal skills. Michael Cowpland of Corel Systems believes in picking goals that entail as little risk as possible. "You have to avoid reinventing wheels," he says. "Too many people go blindly down paths of inventing a better mousetrap when it's already been invented." He's never perceived himself as taking big risks. "I always shot for a low-risk strategy. Maybe it turned out to be high-risk, but it never started like that."

The other key determinant of risk tolerance is how badly the entrepreneurs want to achieve their goals. Some entrepreneurs are highly aggressive, almost fanatical, in pursuit of their goals. They will tolerate almost any risk if that is what is required to reach them. People like Bryden, again, set themselves targets that most people simply would not consider as even remotely possible, and they drive for it with extraordinary zeal. Others carefully balance their goals against the accompanying risks. For them, the goal is worthwhile only if the risk doesn't exceed their comfort level.

Harold Duffett of Standard Manufacturing is one such entrepreneur. Like many in the Atlantic provinces, he's a canny entrepreneur with a sly sense of humour. He makes his moves with deliberation, preparing the ground carefully, thinking always of the long term. "I think things through very carefully," he says. "If we run into stormy weather, we change course. If it works, you have to give it the tender loving care to make sure it keeps on working. I have friends who say, 'If it's working, don't touch it.' But not me, I give it positive reinforcement every day to keep it working perfectly."

Duffett came from the wrong side of the tracks in St. John's, Newfoundland, but he's managed to work his way to the top of the social tree in a province where that's not easy to do. He now owns Standard Manufacturing, which manufactures paint. It is the island's only manufacturing operation that isn't based on natural resources. He bought the controlling interest in Standard in 1982 from Gordon Winter, scion of the establishment, signatory to Confederation and former Lieutenant-Governor of Newfoundland. It gave Duffett an entrée to the establishment that was beyond the wildest dreams of his parents, who had deprived themselves of creature comforts for many years to send their son to a private school. They never lived to see him when he was commodore of the Royal Newfoundland Yacht Club or when Prince Edward was a guest aboard his boat for a day.

Duffett, almost 50 when he was interviewed, is courtly in his carriage, secure in his new role, and keen to put behind him the scrambler who built a fortune with superb business acumen and timing. He is short, but walks with long, bouncy strides that contrast strongly with his almost portly body. A stranger might take him to be stuffy, except for his sandy hair and sly smile—and his reputation as a real character whose parties are legendary. His companies had annual sales of $50 million in 1988 and employ about 400 people. He's in the offshore business, producing drilling mud for offshore oil rigs and a catering service to the crews. He also has a thriving office equipment outlet and a stationery store. Plus he's the largest single property owner in downtown St. John's, a quarter of which belongs to him. Driving through the city with him is like playing a game of Monopoly as he points out all the property he owns. He accumulated it over the years, leveraging himself to buy a piece of property then paying it down as quickly as possible. None of his property has debt of more than 50% of its value and much of it is debt-free. It gives him almost limitless financing power. Yet he won't expand mindlessly. He was offered a share in a fish processing plant in Happy Adventure, a small village on Newman Sound, where he has a country home, but he turned it down. "I chat to the fishermen whenever I'm there," he says. "I want to be one of the boys there. What would happen if there was labour trouble?" Equally, he won't expand into breweries or other businesses with which he's not familiar.

Being cautious doesn't mean he's uncertain, however. Duffett has great faith in his ability to make a venture succeed. "You can drop me tomorrow in Lower Slovobia without a nickel and not speaking the language, and I'll survive. Defeat is something I don't know what you're talking about." He would take a lot more risk than he does if the potential loss were just money, but his real asset is his social position. "One of the things I want to do now is put back into the province some of the things it has given me."

## CONTROLLING RISK

There are two steps in risk-taking. The first is deciding whether it's worth taking. This revolves around the perception of the risk and assessing whether it falls within the entrepreneur's tolerance limits. The second, assuming the decision is made to take the risk, is adjusting the risk to suit the entrepreneur's tastes and capacities. These adjustments may be made before or after embarking on the venture, but entrepreneurs know in general terms how they will reduce a risk at the time they decide to take it. There are three techniques of risk adjustment:

- improving the probability of success,
- reducing exposure to the loss, and
- reducing the potential loss.

One-fifth of the entrepreneurs in this book made no attempt at all to control or adjust their risks. Two-thirds of those who do try to control their risks preferred narrowing the odds to the other methods. The least popular is limiting the potential loss, which is favoured by only a quarter of the entrepreneurs. Some people like to think of entrepreneurs as gamblers, but very few of them are. There's a world of difference between a gamble and a risk. Gamblers are betting against odds over which they have no control. Entrepreneurs usually have considerable influence over the chances of success for their businesses. They are betting on themselves. When they try to reduce the probability of failure, they are changing the odds. They can do that by thorough planning and market research. They can do it by making sure they have the necessary skills; many of the entrepreneurs in this book have taken night courses for years to gain the skills they need. They can do it through the "nibble" theory, which means testing a strategy often and in small increments, so that they can quickly abandon efforts that seem unlikely to bear fruit. They can do it, like Steve Chepa, by pre-selling their product before they start production. Or, like Abe Dyck, they can keep their costs of entering a market so low that they have a permanent built-in advantage against competitors with a much larger investment.

Abram Dyck of Saskatoon Fresh Pack Potatoes never makes plans and his strategy for hiring his key executives is simple— the eight most important positions in his business are filled by members of his family. Abe is general manager and owns no shares because he went bankrupt in the 1960s. His eldest son, Fred, is president and Fred's wife, Elise, is national sales manager. The only members of the family who don't work at

Saskatoon Fresh Pack are two daughters, one of whom is a lawyer, while the other is still at school. But if his staffing and planning are idiosyncratic, he does understand niches, and he knows how to structure the finances of a business so that it has the maximum opportunity to grow and make money, regardless of the vicissitudes. In his long career as an entrepreneur, he's also found out first hand what happens when he doesn't try to narrow the odds. With a $3-million business, he is living proof of the effectiveness of the entrepreneurial school of hard knocks.

Dyck started his first business in his early twenties when he and a brother opened an agricultural implement dealership in Rosthern, Saskatchewan. It was just after World War II, and although Dyck's German-Canadian background didn't make it easy to attract customers, he made it work anyway. Some years later, in the course of selling to potato growers, he found out that they couldn't move their produce because the local packagers preferred to buy their potatoes in Manitoba. So Dyck and some of his numerous siblings started a potato chip plant in the late 1950s, but the business collapsed in a wave of squabbles and Dyck lost his $20,000 investment. "We just didn't know enough," he says now.

That episode started a rough decade for Abe. He bought a hotel in Rosthern and sold his implement dealership to concentrate all his energies on his new venture. It bankrupted him. First of all, Rosthern didn't allow an establishment to provide "mixed drinking" unless a plebiscite of the town approved. The catch-22 was that you had to build the establishment before you could ask the town for approval. Dyck poured a lot of money into a tasteful bar where men and women could drink together, but the town didn't like it and didn't grant him his licence. A little while later his switchboard operator was having a smoke in bed (so Abe figures) and fell asleep, with results as bad as might be imagined. Worse, Abe did not have full insurance on the hotel. He was ruined.

It was 1969 and he figured it was time to leave Rosthern for Saskatoon. Dyck is a big man, with a capacity for food and drink to match. He's quiet-spoken, gentle, and affects a humble self-deprecation. But he has been toughened physically and mentally by his setbacks. He knows exactly what he wants and has enormous energy even in his late 60s. The move from Rosthern to Saskatoon was a new beginning, but it was tough, at 51 years old, in a new city, with no money. His biggest asset was a storehouse of knowledge about potatoes, so the Dyck family went into the potato business again.

They acquired a farm and planted potatoes, which they peddled from door to door in Saskatoon. It didn't take long before Dyck's restless energy took the family into new product lines. They manufactured french fries and potato chips. "We begged, borrowed and stole equipment." Unfortunately the french fries didn't work out. Refrigerating them is a puzzle that has defeated many firms, and the Dycks were no exception. They couldn't maintain the quality they needed and the exchanges from dissatisfied customers erased their profits. Dyck soldiered on. In 1976, A&W placed a large order for breaded onion rings, which rapidly became the top line for the family business, raising employment to 15 and sales to $150,000. Then a new manager came on the scene at A&W and stopped the contract after only four years, long before the new equipment could be depreciated.

A year previously, Dyck had been talking to a competitor in Winnipeg who made perogies, and he thought it might be an idea to try them out. He bought a perogie machine, which sat idle in the plant until A&W pulled the plug. It seemed only natural to get into the perogie business. Six years later, he had 37 employees, and profit was $80,000 on sales of $3 million, three-quarters of it from perogies. Dyck was beginning to think big.

Perhaps the major thing he's done to narrow his odds (even if unwittingly, because he has not always worried too much about risk control) is to buy his capital equipment at such low prices that he can make money at prices well below the market. He learned when he didn't have a nickel to his name how to make machinery work at a fraction of the price his competitors pay. "We're a bunch of do-it-yourselfers," he says. "We've cut the cost in half for this latest expansion of our freezer capacity. My sons are very good with machines." He paid $20,000 at an auction for a new boiler which would have cost $200,000 from the manufacturer. He bought a standby freezing unit from the potash mines, at $40,000 installed, that would have cost him $160,000 new.

His biggest competition is from no-name products, which have cut prices to half the level of brand names. It will hurt Dyck's competitors more than him. "I know I can outproduce no-name cost-wise. I can flatten 'em. We've got a tiger by the tail." The price war has slowed his growth, however, although he boosted sales 35% in 1989 when he started supplying Loblaws with President's Choice perogies.

The other two ways of controlling risk are to reduce the potential losses or the entrepreneur's personal exposure to those losses. Bill Pattison of Delta Hotels uses both these methods with skill. When he finances a new hotel, he puts a clause in the lease that allows him to break the lease if his operating losses exceed a specified limit. He also brings in other investors in all his investments, thereby reducing his personal exposure.

The catch with reducing personal exposure to loss is that it also reduces the share of the rewards, so many entrepreneurs prefer not to control risk this way. The entrepreneurs in this book who control their risks this way amounted to only one-eighth of those who have voting control of their firms, compared to one-half of those with minority shareholdings.

One of the most popular ways of limiting both potential losses and personal exposure is franchising a concept. Des Rice of The Weed Man has developed more imaginative financing schemes than most. A high-school drop-out at Grade 10, Rice started The Weed Man, a lawn-care business, at age 19 because he couldn't stand his job at Goodyear. Short and bubbly, with a laugh often lurking beneath his handlebar moustache, Rice loves his work. In 1970, his first year, he drove the truck and his wife Brenda took the orders as they scrambled their way to total revenues of $13,000. He expanded quickly, until he started franchising in 1976, when sales really took off. By 1989, he had almost 120 franchises across the country, producing retail sales of about $30 million.

He was intrigued when he heard about attempts to run a window-washing business for profit, surely a contradiction in terms. He figured his experience in the lawn-care business could be adapted to window washing. "Lawn care is spraying down, window washing is spraying up," he says. That greatly understates his innovation. The people who had tried it before were applying the same technology that homeowners used—squeegies and brushes. That was much too inefficient for Rice. He figured he could do a whole house in 22 minutes with sprays and charge only $39. His secret is a soap that won't streak, which he developed himself through hundreds of experiments with "my herbs and spices." His Blue Diamond trucks are equipped with their own water treatment plants which are tailored to each city's water supply to filter it to the right degree of softness and the right temperature.

By mid-1989, Rice had sold 30 Blue Diamond franchises in Ontario and three American states, but his first few were the most interesting. He didn't have a strong enough cash flow from The Weed Man to finance the R&D to develop the system for Blue Diamond, so he persuaded some people to buy franchises in the year before the company rolled out its first truck in the spring of 1987. He charged them $10,000 and guaranteed they'd get their money back by the end of September if the system didn't work out. "They were taking a risk, so they deserve to be rewarded. That's venture capital." Once the system was developed in early 1987, the price of a franchise rose to about $40,000. The early franchises didn't work out well, however. "They couldn't grow with the company," says Rice. Most of them dropped out.

Rice thinks banks are fair-weather friends, so he prefers not to rely on them. "You have to become creative. I have never had to finance except by using my customer base. When I need money, I go and tap them. I don't like risk. I gamble on things I control." It seems to pay off. He projects total upfront revenues for Blue Diamond of more than $20 million by the mid-1990s, plus annual royalties of $2 million.

At the other extreme from Rice, there's Joe Landry of Cape Bald Packers. Landry makes no attempt whatsoever to control the risks he takes. With 250 employees, he has annual sales of more than $20 million a year packing lobster and crab in a tiny plant in Cap Pelé, on the north shore of New Brunswick. His reputation extends as far as Japan, which has bought fast-frozen crab from him since 1980.

From the roadside, his plant looks ramshackle. Landry himself does nothing to dispel the image. Dressed in khaki, with rubber boots that seem to be part of his body, he works out of an office that can only be described as a mess. It is utilitarian, strictly a working space. The packing plant, on the other hand, is immaculate. He has a forlorn-looking face, sensitive and gentle, always ready with his wry smile. He mumbles a lot, switching between French and English as only New Brunswickers can, mangling both languages in the process. Landry has made it as a businessman against all the odds. It was never planned, though. "Each expansion was something that was offered to me," he says, "and I didn't back out. I'm walking on thin ice."

Landry is not the only entrepreneur in this book who doesn't try to control his risks, but the others usually measure their risks before they charge ahead. Landry can't, or won't, say no. Every time he's offered a deal, he jumps in with both feet. He prospers, even if not as much as he should, because his powerful, innate business sense gets him out of the corners he's backed himself into. The word has got around. When a styrofoam plant in the area went bankrupt in 1982, the provincial government turned to Landry to rescue it. Although he knew nothing about the business, he bought it anyway and turned an annual loss of $75,000 into a profit of $100,000 in four years. Then a federal agency gave a grant to three people to start a competing plant in the Maritimes and his profit margins collapsed.

Another time, a fish processing plant on Grand Manan Island was going bankrupt, and the banker responsible for it said he'd keep the plant's loan alive if Joe Landry came in as an investor. Landry financed its restoration and left his three partners to run it. His lawyers warned him that they were not in Landry's league. "I thought he meant they were too good for me," he said much later, "because I'm just a grammar school boy. But I found out it was the other way round." His partners took advantage of him and lost control of the business, which went bankrupt. Landry was the last investor in but lost the most—$600,000.

Landry started out as a carpenter with little education. He bought his fish plant with his brother and a third partner in 1947 (on Friday, February 13), because the previous owner kept burning down his smokehouse and Landry grew tired of repairing it. A couple of years later, he bought out one partner, then, after 11 years in business, he became the sole owner by buying the shares held by his brother, who thanked him by taking with him all the good contracts with the fishermen. Landry had used all his money to buy them out. He had no debt, but no money either. "I was so gosh-darned stubborn," he says. "Everyone laughed at me. I stammered then, and they laughed at me for that too. I proved them wrong. Every time they smiled at me, thinking I wouldn't make it, I just got mad. I don't know how to stop proving myself now."

He built an apartment in the plant that year, moved his family of eight in, and worked his way out of his hole. He worked as an electrician or engineer in the winter to make ends meet, while his plant lost money for 11 years. He eventually won back all the contracts with the fishermen, partly by becoming their chief financier, and built a top-quality processing plant. By 1970, he had expanded into the U.S. and had started making significant profits. Six years later, 16 years after he bought out his brother, he moved his family out of the plant and into a house again. Now all his children are back in the plant, this time as employees. His eldest son, Patrice, started taking on more responsibility after his father reached 65 in 1987. Several months later, Landry said that, since Patrice had stepped into his shoes, the family looked properly at investments before jumping in. Landry is still there, however, and still 100% owner. Time will tell. Three years earlier, he had said, "I'm the type of guy, I'm not happy when I'm not in a mess."

# CHAPTER 6

# MASTERING THE BUSINESS

*"Identifying your weaknesses is very important. I question myself and if I can't answer the question, I get outside advice. I believe in using people's experience."*
— Michel Lapointe of DAP Electronics

Incompetent entrepreneurs aren't entrepreneurs for long. No matter how good the idea, no matter how well calibrated the risk, if the entrepreneur cannot manage and control the implementation of a strategy, it will lead inevitably to failure. Entrepreneurship is fantasy for people who cannot master their business or find someone to master it for them.

Competence has traditionally been the Achilles' heel of entrepreneurs. The intuitive skills that make them good at identifying opportunities and at taking risks are no use at all in controlling a business, which demands linear thinking. Some entrepreneurs can combine the two sets of skills, but many cannot. The all-too-common pattern has been that, as soon as a business starts growing rapidly, expenses run out of control because of the loose controls so often associated with non-linear minds. This soon precipitates a cash crisis, which brings in new investors, who quickly set about firing the entrepreneur, who by then has lost voting control. There are two ways to circumvent this fate: learn, as one entrepreneur said, "to be what you're not"; or hire a hotshot who can deliver the linear skills. The wisdom to recognize this need is the highest order of competence.

Ron Hume showed just that kind of understanding. In January, 1987, he gave up his title of chief operating officer of the

Hume Group. "The revenues were growing like crazy, but profits weren't growing as fast. It hit me like a ton of bricks. We had become badly structured. I said to myself, 'Hume, you're a crummy manager.' So I stepped back." He hired Alan Hahn in the U.S. to run the publishing business, and he hired Don Marshall from Hees International Bancorp to run the holding company for the group. "Marshall is very good at monitoring day-to-day slippages," Hume admitted at the time. "I take a greater interest in the product and marketing. I couldn't run anything very effectively."

This is the man who had earlier looked squarely into the mirror as he prepared to launch a new business back in 1971. "I knew I was short a few ingredients. I didn't have enough background in finance and accounting." So he developed a business plan and a prospectus and enrolled in night school at the University of Toronto to study accounting, finance, marketing, business law and economics. He used his own business plan as a case study.

This is also the man whose father, a brilliant inventor, started his own business twice and went bankrupt twice, but who persuaded his young son that he had to be technical to succeed. Although Hume didn't have the aptitude, he tried anyway. He flunked out of school in Grade 12, then went to work for Lever Brothers as a lab technician. When he didn't fit in there, he quit and went to work for Bell Canada as a telephone ordering clerk. "My father was very domineering; he never listened. He told me I had to be technical, so I became a draftsman."

He worked at Bell for several years, then the chance of promotion came and the company sent him to take an aptitude test. He had to decide whether he was going to fill in the questionnaire to get the job or to find out the truth. He decided to be honest and didn't get the promotion. Bell wouldn't let him see the results, but his boss got them for him. They said he should be in advertising and publishing.

For two and a half years, Hume applied for every single job advertised in that field in Toronto. He also wrote to every single advertising agency and publishing company in the city. No luck. So he faked a portfolio. He persuaded his boss to say he was the manager of the advertising department, while some friends in the business promised they'd say he had freelanced for them. That was when he was fired from his job as a draftsman because he made a $150,000 mistake, but, as luck would have it, McGraw-Hill happened to be advertising for someone in sales promotion. "I lied and cheated my way into the job," he says. In his first year, he was promoted twice. "I was home. I knew I could do it well." Within five years he was a vice president, and he had best-sellers on his list from the day he started to publish. His father's insensitivity had been a boon for him. "My technical background came in handy, because M-H was so artsy and I had some discipline."

The discipline was not enough to run the day-to-day operations of his own $70-million publishing empire. Hume controls two-thirds of the stock in The Hume Group through a holding company owned equally by himself and Trevor Eyton, the dynamic chief executive of Brascan, the holding company for the conglomerate then controlled by Peter and Edward Bronfman. Hume understands that he can contribute entrepreneurial skill to his business, not managerial competence. "A lot of people are very good at managing things but not good at starting. Hiring Hahn wasn't courage—it would have been dumb not to. Now I'm working for someone else again. Alan Hahn is questioning everything, even my sacred cows." As he handed over the day-to-day reins to Hahn (he remained chief executive officer), he was resigned to letting his baby go five years later if it turned out he could no longer contribute. "It's a relief to be able to take a back seat while they negotiate big contracts. And I'm going to play tennis on Tuesday."

Not everyone sees the light as early as Hume. For Michael Cowpland, the boom fell when he blinked and missed the warning signal. Cowpland is now the owner of Corel Systems, for which he has ambitious plans, but he's better known as the co-founder of Mitel Corp., which he helped build into a $350-million company before he lost control and sold his shares.

The apparent reason for Mitel's failure was that it tried to develop a sophisticated new telephone switching system and grossly underestimated how long it would take to do it. That cost the firm its credibility, which cost it, in turn, a tie-in with IBM that would have assured it permanent prosperity. But the real reason lies deeper. Cowpland says now, "I took my eye off the ball. I got bored. You need different kinds of management skills to run a giant corporation." It is not Cowpland's idea of fun to spend hours orchestrating vast teams of people into waves of meetings, many of which go over the same ground again and again. His ebullient sense of fun will never allow him to fill the self-conscious leadership role required of the chairman of a large corporation. He might have the intellectual capacity to run it, but it isn't easy for him emotionally.

The result was he lost control. He listened to dealer orders when he should have been listening to customers. The prospect of a deal with IBM also didn't help the cause of those arguing caution in Mitel. "Now," says Cowpland, "I'd get better numbers in place. There's no substitute for having good scorecards. That's part of the secret of non-bureaucratic systems. You have to have a lot of flexibility for people who make decisions, as long as you can tally what's happening."

Others have made the transition to big-company leaders, including Rod Bryden of Systemhouse, Marcel Dutil of Canam Manac, Frank Stronach of Magna International and Walter Hachborn of Home Hardware. Then there is the new breed of entrepreneurs, who come to entrepreneurship after a long career in a large corporation, where they have learned to be skillful managers. They are not "natural" entrepreneurs, but acquire the necessary skills on the job. Their strength is their logic and their managerial competence; their challenge is to develop their intuitive faculties. These corporate refugees are shifting the centre of gravity in the composite of entrepreneurial skills. The entrepreneur as romantic adventurer is giving way to a blend of entrepreneurial intuition and competence, thanks in part to the computer, which gives small businesses the capability to run systems as sophisticated as those of most big businesses. The entrepreneurial elements are all intact, but there is much less tolerance for lax controls than there was in the simpler world of even 20 years ago.

Although it is extremely difficult to measure failure rates in new ventures, it would appear that the rate has not changed much in the past decade or two. The number of failures has risen dramatically only because the number of start-ups has risen just as dramatically. It would seem reasonable to conclude that entrepreneurs are acquiring the necessary skills to survive in their more demanding environment. There are, nonetheless, some who say that entrepreneurs are successful only because of an extraordinary confluence of circumstance and narrow talent, which they cannot repeat, even in the same industry. All entrepreneurs, by this theory, are doomed to flare briefly, in a firmament crowded with shooting comets, before they sputter and die, never to return again.

There are indeed many who conform to this pattern. A great many more putative entrepreneurs sputter before they even get a chance to flare—they just fail and quietly return to the relative safety of the corporate womb. Others make a lot of money in an early venture and lose it all again when they try something different. The causes of their demise range over all the key elements of entrepreneurship, but the element that sinks the most businesses is lack of competence. Most people who fail as entrepreneurs just don't have the capacity to absorb the range of skills they need. Many of those who succeed do so in part because they go back to school to learn the principles of running a business.

That's what Michel Lapointe of DAP Electronics did. When he and Robert St. Laurent bought DAP, Lapointe had no experience at all in running a business. He had been an engineer in charge of development at Select-O-Sonar, when St. Laurent tried to persuade him to leave his job to run DAP, which he wanted to buy. Lapointe refused, but St. Laurent persisted, asking him to take a look at the company and give him a verbal report on what needed to be done to turn it around. Lapointe agreed and took the day off to do his friend a favour. His report on DAP persuaded him to accept St. Laurent's offer, and he became his equal partner in the venture. That was in 1979, when DAP had eight employees and sales of $200,000. Ten years later, it had 100 employees, one-third of them in R&D, and sales of more than $10 million.

Lapointe seems almost surprised at being called an entrepreneur. His cerebral engineer's calmness doesn't fit the popular stereotype. Short and stocky, with thinning hair and classic Grecian features, he's unfailingly courteous and soft-spoken, revealing nothing of his emotions. His office is large, cool and spacious, almost empty, all done in shades of blue and grey, with light wood. It's meticulously tidy, as befits an engineer, drawing warmth and life from two beautiful paintings and a picture of his family.

In his first year at DAP, he had only one product, a backup alarm for trucks, which he sold to the auto companies. He couldn't export, however, because he had such a limited range of products, so he hired an engineer to build an R&D team to develop other products. In the second year, sales doubled and the two partners breathed more easily, as did the Royal Bank. In his third year, his R&D team developed a hand-held data collection terminal, and Lapointe commissioned a market study on it. "I'm too loyal to my product," he says, "so I get outside consultants. Sometimes the market isn't as big or small as I thought it was—sometimes there are more competitors than I expected." The market study was positive, and DAP's terminal is now used widely by Loto-Québec and Hydro-Québec. His R&D team has since developed three generations of the terminal as well as an electronic flasher for the auto market in the U.S. and Canada.

It was hard work and Lapointe, like most entrepreneurs in small companies, was involved in every detail in DAP. He kept his eye on the long term, though, demanding productivity reports even though he was so busy he didn't have time to read them. He knew he'd need them one day. He found out what kinds of other information he would need to run the firm effectively and saw that his employees delivered them. He had monthly statements from day one, although he wasn't sure how to read them. He took courses at the local CEGEP (community college) on finance, accounting, marketing and administration. Even that didn't arm him sufficiently to deal with the needs of his growing enterprise. "Identifying your weaknesses is very important," he says. "I question myself, and if I can't answer the question, I get outside advice." His partner is a financial expert, so Lapointe consults him a lot. "I believe in using people's experience."

It's clear how much importance the entrepreneurs in this book attach to their own competence from their rankings of the entrepreneurial strengths they bring to their firms. Five of the top ten characteristics are related to competence—business judgement, technical and marketing skills, motivation skills and empathy.

## BUSINESS JUDGEMENT

Few entrepreneurs can match Richard Prytula of Leigh Naviga- tion Systems in Montreal for his dispassionate, logical ap- proach to making good business decisions. "My managers believe I'll make the best decisions that will deliver the best bottom line," he says matter-of-factly. "I'm Capt. Kirk to their Spock and Dr. McCoy, both of whom are always right in their sphere. So only Kirk makes mistakes and admits it." He sees himself as closer to Spock than McCoy, because he's always a couple of steps ahead of them. "I've thought through the logic better."

LNS would test the nerves of most entrepreneurs. It manu- factures air traffic control towers, mobile towers, runway light- ing systems and radio spectrum monitoring systems, mostly for Third World governments. These clients are usually authori- tarian, and the people they send to buy Western equipment are some of the toughest negotiators in the world. But Prytula is equal to the challenge. In December, 1984, he signed his first really big contract with a prominent African government for $26 million. It was an occasion for rejoicing. Annual sales that year were $2.7 million, up almost a million from 1983, and the new contract would put LNS on a path of unstoppable growth. But it took Prytula another 18 months to clinch the deal, which had dropped to $20 million by then, because the client's economy took a turn for the worse.

The negotiations had stretched over five years and included 28 trips to Africa. In the year and a half between signing the contract and clinching the deal, LNS spent $1.4 million con- solidating and reselling the deal. With all the available re- sources of the company being poured into the big contract, however, sales to other clients fell off and cash flow shrivelled. It almost sank the firm. Prytula had to lay off half the staff as his losses mounted to $340,000. When the money eventually started flowing, LNS sales rose to $4 million in 1986, then $17 million in 1987. "It was the big breakthrough," Prytula says. "We bet

the company and almost lost because of the client's economy."
Never one to think small, Prytula's next target was the Chinese,
with whom he closed a deal in 1988 after five years of negotiations.

Prytula grew up in Saskatchewan, the oldest of nine children. His father was a teacher, and he retains, perhaps, some of his father's pedagogy as a regular guest lecturer at his alma mater, the University of Western Ontario. Tall, with a head of hair that looks as if it would spray out of control if it wasn't cropped so closely, Prytula is not suave. In a city filled with Gallic good dressers, he looks anglophone average. But he radiates intensity and focus. He can't speak fast enough to keep up with his thoughts. "I work very fast. I could burn out our management team here very quickly, so I keep busy in other things."

When the federal government opened its Pandora's box of Scientific Research Tax Credits, he decided to go into the venture capital business. He invested in more than 20 companies across Canada, building a comprehensive understanding of mergers and acquisitions. He developed standard agreements, contracts, by-laws, stock option plans, no-competition clauses and much more. He perused dozens of business plans and became intimately involved in the lives of the entrepreneurs in whom he was investing. He would never do it again, but it was an unparalleled learning experience, which has given him uncommonly good business judgement. His mind is like the customized software that was his initial specialty. He's methodical, thorough, capable of storing almost any kind of information and retrieving it very fast. "I believe I can do anything if I want to," he says. "As long as you are comfortable with your own abilities, Allah will look after you. You're playing probabilities."

It isn't surprising to learn that Prytula became bored at LNS and sold it in 1988 to the man who had been its general manager before he bought it. "The trouble with a small company is you can't use all your talents," he had said in 1986. In 1989, he launched a $30-million fund that will invest in turnarounds. "I wanted a wider variety and more diverse companies," he says. "I needed a larger company than LNS to do that."

Steve Chepa of Dicon Systems has demonstrated his own good judgement in circumstances that have tested him to the limit: "I have the skills to recognize what's necessary to succeed. It's an analytical ability, the ability to look at something that's never been done before. And when it's running, the ability to see what it needs to keep going. You've got it or you haven't." In their assessments of their own greatest strengths, the entrepreneurs in this book ranked good business judgement first, equal with inner power.

## TECHNICAL SKILLS

Basil Peters and Peter van der Gracht, chairman and president respectively of Nexus Engineering, are two whiz kids who have learned to run a business with verve and skill (see page 196). But they're still "techies" at heart. "One of our fears is we'll lose the magic," says van der Gracht. Peters adds he's "afraid of the day I won't be able to solve a technical problem. It'll happen, but I'm trying to avoid it."

Peters describes how one of his technical experts came to him with a problem which he couldn't solve on the spot, so he said he'd get back to him with a solution the next day. He collected every book he knew of on the subject and read them all that night. The next morning, he gave the person the answer, on schedule. The relief in Peters's face is transparent. "I will no longer be useful if I can't keep abreast of all the technology. Technical competence is important—you have to fight to stay at the top. We have to keep on winning. If we stop being the strongest guys, we'll be out."

Although the young men at Nexus are unusual for the way they have acquired management and leadership skills, as well as technical skills, their angst about their technological prowess is by no means uncommon. Many high-tech entrepreneurs embody their firm's technological expertise, leading by example. They often fail to notice the need to administer the business, however, and don't acquire the necessary skills, with predictable results. In fact, technical skills can often become an obstacle to effective entrepreneurship, if only because it takes so much energy just to keep abreast of new developments, there's no one left to run the business.

Jack Wilson of RSI Robotic Systems International was a boy wonder on the computer in the 1970s (see page 125). When he started his robotics firm, he was still a leading techie himself, but he has dropped technical brilliance down his priority list now that he's trying to make his business grow. "Technologically, I read all the literature, the papers, in my area of expertise," he says, "but I also need to know about fibre optics, what's happening in Japan and so on. This knowledge is an important part of leadership. So I can't get to the level of technical detail I'd like. I'm not competent as a particular technician anymore. I can't write good computer code anymore. I'd like to be chairman of the board, with the company being run by professional people. My role would be like Mao Tse-tung's permanent revolution—in the skunk works keeping the business from fossilization."

These examples are in high technology, but the principles are equally applicable in low technology. Mary Macdonald of Venture Economics (Canada) has built a thriving business collecting and disseminating information relevant to the venture capital industry. She quit a job with a prestigious firm of management consultants because she wanted the independence of being her own boss. She knew she had solid experience in a field that was, and still is, expanding rapidly. She also has "hard skills in researching and writing."

She decided that she's an information-age techie. "I used to think I was good at administration, but I'm not. I'm not good at disciplined financial planning either. I want to be recognized as the expert source in this industry. I have no visions of a grandiose corporation. I don't want to spend the bulk of my time just running the company — I want to be involved in the delivery. Management is great, but it's time-consuming."

## MARKETING SKILLS

Gail Gabel of Anderaa Instruments has a high-technology business, but she will never allow the technology to dominate the marketing. "To keep ahead, we have to obsolete ourselves," she says. Her engineers are always looking at the next generation of their product lines. "I'll break their fingers if they produce engineer-driven products." Just to keep everyone honest,

Gabel also has her own market research firm. She uses it for her own businesses, of course, but also does studies for other companies.

Gabel was born in Australia and has settled on Vancouver Island, where she has become a high-tech powerhouse. She speaks with almost no Australian accent, sounding somewhat English. Her gentle manners and feminine dress camouflage a determined entrepreneur, who pioneered high-tech companies on the island, long before they became popular, and who has become an important voice in the B.C. science community. Her principal company is Anderaa Instruments, which has annual sales of $1 million a year. Anderaa produces remote meteorological and oceanographic instruments, which measure everything from wind speed to humidity and solar radiation. Gabel runs the Canadian operation for its Norwegian owners. She did own one-third of another company called Meteor Communications, which she started, then sold to a larger company in return for shares in the company.

The idea for Meteor Communications came to Gabel when she was looking for a way to communicate the findings of Anderaa's remote sensors without having to pick them up on location. The technology she found uses the billions of meteors that penetrate the earth's atmosphere every day as a kind of galactic satellite that can bounce messages from a transmitting station to the remote sensors carrying Anderaa's instruments and back again. Gabel spent $1 million developing the technology for meteor burst communications. The pioneering for the technology was done by the National Research Council in the 1940s and 1950s, but it became economically feasible only with the arrival of electronic miniaturization.

Gabel came by her technological aptitude in a unique way. She studied law at university in Australia then joined the attorney-general's department in the federal government. The bureaucracy got a bit mixed up, however, and put her into the defense ministry, where she was put in charge of a program to refit the Australian navy's submarines. She had worked previously for a machine tool company, where she had acquired a taste for machinery, but wasn't interested in submarines. She protested and was told that she would be transferred to the right department in due course. The transfer never came and Gabel, typically, settled down to do the job and did it very well. She didn't stay with the submarines too long, leaving Australia for the reason most Australians leave—she wanted to travel. She got as far as Canada, where she met the man who subsequently became her ex-husband.

Since selling Meteor Communications, she has started another company, Intermarine, which negotiates contracts to lease time and equipment aboard the scientific oceanographic ships owned by the U.S.S.R. Intermarine then resells the time to Western researchers. The Russians started allowing government departments to deal directly with foreign companies in 1989, and Gabel has become, once again, a pioneer. Although she has become familiar with technological issues, her core skill is marketing. She does a lot of the surveying herself in her market research firm. She hires one man just to do library searches. "The public library is an incredible source," she says, "but you can't delegate your contacts with the key person who knows the market and the product."

In her own companies, her marketing is highly sophisticated. She gives Anderaa the full treatment four times a year—where the market is, the competitors, what people are prepared to pay, informal costings. When she travels, she picks up market information, then figures out if it's compatible with her products. If it is, she writes out a complete marketing plan. It's a tough discipline, and she drums it into her employees. She often takes her technicians on trips, just to make sure they understand the needs of their customers.

## MOTIVATING PEOPLE

Because their resources are limited, entrepreneurs simply have to extract superior productivity from their employees. Successful entrepreneurs are therefore often not warm people, but they usually understand what motivates people, and they apply their knowledge firmly and consistently. Few of them have any illusions about people, and all of the successful ones are thoroughly frank in their relationships with their employees. Most importantly, they give more than 100% of themselves and expect the same from their employees.

Harold Duffett of Standard Manufacturing has had his share of setbacks with employees, including the dismissal of a valued and senior manager who betrayed a trust, so he has had to learn the hard way. "My single most successful attribute in business is my commitment to people and my judgement and choice of people," he says. He will do whatever he can to engender loyalty and support. "I look for practical individuals, who can make it happen. I rarely make mistakes, but if I do, I try to change them. When we part with someone, it's no surprise because we've had enough discussions that it's clear."

Entrepreneurs in this book use two primary approaches to motivating their employees. One school subscribes to the principle of 'How are you doing?' rather than 'How do you feel?' They prefer quantitative measurement to personal development. The other school treats employees as a valuable resource, encouraging them to develop their potential in whatever direction offers the best fit between them and the firm. Chapter 12 discusses these approaches and employee motivation in the context of leadership.

## EMPATHY

A third of the entrepreneurs I interviewed rate themselves as having good motivational skills, while half that number rate themselves as having strong empathy with their employees. This means that half of the entrepreneurs in this book don't rate themselves highly on people skills. In general, the ones who pride themselves on their empathy are not hard-driving with their employees. They try to create an environment in which their employees will voluntarily motivate themselves. It can be a highly effective technique, provided the culture of the business is receptive.

Marcel Dutil of Canam Manac prides himself on his empathy (see page 119). One of the sharpest business minds in the country, he makes the personal development of his employees a priority, for human as well as commercial reasons. He believes that the way he treats people is his greatest strength. "It's simple. If I was in that position, how would I like to be treated? I've had to change company presidents who didn't do that."

Another well-known entrepreneur who prides himself on

his empathy is Frank Stronach, the strong-willed chairman of Magna International, which enjoyed an annual compound growth rate of 37% in the five years to 1988, when its sales reached $1.5 billion. "Nature has bestowed on me health, good senses, sensitivity," he says. "I'm very observant for details, people's behaviour." The casual observer may miss that aspect of Stronach, who spends more time espousing his theory of fair enterprise than listening to the people he meets (see page 110). However, he is unusually sensitive, even if only when he feels like it.

When he's on an evangelical roll about fair enterprise, even in small groups of two or three people, he can become oblivious to his audience, acting as if he were giving a speech to thousands. His concentration consumes him as he wrestles his mental models of his new society into a flood of words, illustrated by his patented pictograms of modern societies' stark options. The sensitivity of which he's so proud evaporates. He brooks no interference from his listeners, as he steamrollers the conversation, his eyes burning with the conviction and the inner power that makes him stomp from one end of Canada to the other, selling his ideas for a better society.

Then, abruptly, he'll turn it off and open his senses to his listeners. Every fibre of his body tunes in to the people he's with. His eyes bore in, watching every movement, soaking in every detail, every nuance. He sucks in every word, his questions cut through the protective wrapping, exploring the inner feelings of his listeners, who have been temporarily transformed into talkers. For a minute or ten, he doesn't miss a thing, as he absorbs their whole beings, gauging their views, their inclinations and their proclivities. Then, just as abruptly, he stops and he's off again, expounding.

"I've had tremendous exposure in so many social and economic environments," he says. Indeed, he lived under democratic, Nazi and Communist rule in Austria before he emigrated to Canada. "I've experienced life from all kinds of levels. I've worked at the lowest level. I've been hungry, I've sweated and thereby I have developed a sensitivity toward my fellow person, my surroundings. I've never forgotten it—my deeds and actions will always be, 'Would I be treated that way? Would I accept it?'"

# CHAPTER 7

# THE NEED
# TO SUCCEED

*"I have a burning need to succeed and the urgency
to do it quickly. I'm motivated by the joy of
achievement. I'm very future oriented, so once I've
achieved something, I lose interest—I'm already on
to the next mountain."*
— Richard Prytula of Leigh Navigation Systems

**S**uccessful entrepreneurs all have a special kind of fire in their
bellies. Without it, few would be able to dig deep within
themselves, to deploy talents they never knew they had, as they
fought to overcome the daunting obstacles along the paths they
have chosen for themselves. The source of that deep-seated
drive, the quintessential determination of successful entrepreneurs, is their need to succeed. This is the motivation that
seduces entrepreneurs into setting ambitious goals, far beyond
the reach of the resources they control.

The need to succeed can also push entrepreneurs to extremes. On the bright side, they will study at nights, face up to
their own shortcomings when they need help, exercise greater
self-discipline to make themselves more effective, do anything
they have to do to run the business well. But there's a dark side,
too. When entrepreneurs see their businesses in danger of
failing, they will often stop at nothing to save their dream of
success. They will resort to any action—sometimes illegal,
sometimes immoral, always distasteful—that offers even the
slimmest hope of warding off failure. Sometimes they get away
with it, sometimes they don't, but most successful entrepreneurs have dallied with the ethical dilemmas posed by near
failure.

The need to succeed is not, of course, the only motivation important to entrepreneurs; however, it is the most important. Three-quarters of the people in this study mentioned it as a prime motivator.

At a time when most successful entrepreneurs his age are thinking of winding down their business activities, Jean Pouliot embarked on an ambitious and risky project that most people would find daunting at any age. In Montreal, which was already a highly competitive media market, well served by several established TV stations, he started, from scratch, at 61, a brand new television station. To be sure, he had some advantage in owning CFCF, the CTV English-language affiliate in Montreal, but his new station, Quatre Saisons, was a French-language station and Pouliot's concept was so new that it had no models to follow in its innovative trail blazing.

But then, Pouliot likes to live life to the full. A lifelong aficionado of sports cars, he has a scale model of one of the most famous sports cars of all time, the MG, on his coffee table. His favourite was his first sports car, a Triumph TR3, although he will admit to comparable satisfaction with his purchase in 1986 of a Ferrari, a model of which has also made it to the coffee table. It seems a little out of place. This quiet, soft-spoken man with sensitive, earnest eyes behind thick glasses just doesn't look like a racing fan. He has, however, seldom turned down the chance to tilt at an opportunity. Careful without being cautious, sometimes bemused at other people's timidity, he has never stopped accepting new challenges.

His goals have never been money or fame. He doesn't seek, or even particularly like, the high profile that usually goes with being a media baron. His passion is his team. He derives his greatest satisfaction from building an organization in which individuals can stretch themselves. He built Quatre Saisons the way he did because that was the only way he could build an organization that is special, that he will be proud of, that will last.

It all started in 1984, when Francis Fox, then minister of communications, made a speech complaining that French-Canadian viewers were watching too much English-language television. He suggested another TV station in Montreal would be a good idea. That riled Pouliot, who felt he was being criticized for doing too good a job at CFCF. He decided to take up Fox's challenge. By September, 1985, he had won approval for the new station from the Canadian Radio-television and Telecommunications Commission.

One year later, in September, 1986, less than two years after Fox's speech, Quatre Saisons broadcast its first program. Pouliot's strategy was unconventional. He went after young viewers by creating an aura of youth in every aspect of the station, including the employees, who were young and inexperienced. They were less than fully professional, but they were enthusiastic. Although the industry was underwhelmed in the early days, he has succeeded in pulling his young viewers away from the established channels, while his employees are building professionalism quickly. His confidence in his strategy and in his people never wavered, even when Quatre Saisons was the butt of many cruel barbs during its chaotic first few months.

"Business is a lot like a family," he says. "Quatre Saisons is like a baby. You're helping the kid move. It's a feeling of having created something. Everyone's proud of their child—I feel the same way about Quatre Saisons. If you walk around the place, you'll find a hell of a lot of smiling people. It's the feeling you're part of it."

The theme of family and team dominates the dreams of more than a third of the entrepreneurs in this book. They want to build an organization that will last because it is well structured and well run. That might seem like a necessary condition for any entrepreneur who wants to succeed, because a powerful team has to be part of their objectives, but building a team is not necessarily an end in itself, as it is for Pouliot. There are three other motivations that represent different aspects of the need to succeed: the need for a sense of accomplishment, the need to win in business and wanting to make the world a better place to live in.

Richard Prytula of Leigh Navigation Systems, for example, works hard at building his team, and even finds it a rewarding exercise, but he is motivated by the need for a sense of accomplishment. "I have a burning need to succeed and the urgency to do it quickly," he says. "I'm motivated by the joy of achievement. I'm very future oriented, so once I've achieved something, I lose interest— I'm already on to the next mountain."

For others, accomplishment is more simply defined. "It's the fun of winning," says Normand Carpentier, the controlling shareholder of Camoplast, located in Kingsbury, Québec (see page 245). Carpentier's firm came within a hair's breadth of going under in 1982, soon after he bought it from Bombardier, where it had been a struggling division. He saved the firm, however, and has gone on to become highly successful. "If I had failed in 1982, I would not have been a winner. I would have gone off to be a clerk somewhere, a loser. If I lost everything today, I might still be a clerk, but I'd be a winning clerk. I don't need the money anymore, but I could never stop. It's what life is all about!"

The final type of motivation that reflects the need to succeed is the desire, not stereotypical for entrepreneurs, to change the world into a better place. Perhaps the most inspired is Frank Stronach, the mercurial chairman of Magna International. He wants to change the developed world's economic system on the basis of the ideas he formed while building Magna into a world-class business. He lost in his first bid to be elected a Member of Parliament in 1988. Although he may or may not run again, he has set his sights on creating, in or out of parliament, a new system of capitalism that will save the system from what he sees as its death wish.

The basic tenet of his philosophy is that political democracy cannot function effectively without individual freedom, which in turn cannot exist until there is economic democracy. He believes Karl Marx may have had a point in saying that capitalism contains the seeds of its own demise. Stronach sees that seed in the exclusion of most employees from direct ownership of shares and direct participation in profit sharing. He is convinced that as long as capitalists don't breed their own clones, the clones of the bureaucrats will dominate the voting booths and drag the democratic nations into socialism and communism.

His solution to this great flaw of the free enterprise system is "fair enterprise," which might be described as free enterprise for the masses, with everyone enjoying the individual freedom that comes from financial independence. He sees no reason why the rewards of labour should not be sufficient to enable hard-working people, who have reached the age of 55 or 60, to own a fully paid house and car with enough money in the bank to live comfortably off the interest. If that security were achieved through ownership of shares and direct participation in corporate profits, they would also appreciate the advantages of the free enterprise system and would want to keep it healthy. Stronach believes voters like these would force the political system to retreat from the stifling clutches of bureaucracy and embrace the liberating opportunities of individualism.

"I strive for fairness," he says. "Change is unavoidable. It's just a question of time before anything changes, but the change should be constructive. In history, revolutions didn't give everyone a fair slice of the pie. If a leader can implement changes in a quiet revolution, which is not destructive, especially to human life, that is preferable."

Stronach intends to be that kind of leader. "Everyone has hopes and desires for personal freedom," he says. "A lot of people are institutionalized. They are pacified with a regular job and ordinary living conditions. If you expose someone long enough to an environment that trains individual freedom out of them, you can create a very passive creature. But I don't want to live in a way that someone can tell me what to do."

He certainly lives what he preaches. No one tells Frank Stronach what to do. His thinking, behaviour and image are all his own creation. He certainly doesn't look like a multi-millionaire and leader of a two-billion-dollar company. He wears his grey hair long and unruly, and his immaculately cut double-breasted suits sometimes seem to have been made for some other body. With his tie perpetually loosened, he saunters around, unpretentious and completely comfortable in his own skin. His lifestyle is as unconventional as his looks. He loves to party and used to spend a lot of time in a nightclub called Rooney's, which he could call home because he owned it until 1989. He has been known to carouse into the small hours of the morning there and elsewhere, but he gave it up when he entered politics. He loves to ski and he travels extensively. This is not the tool-and-die maker who laboured for years on end to build an auto-parts manufacturer. Stronach today is on his second career, having dumped mechanical engineering for social engineering. Long before he ran for Parliament, he was spending a large part of his time working on his political ideas. He doesn't put in the hours at Magna he used to; he arrives at his office most mornings punctually at 10:30 a.m.

It would be wrong to characterize him as self-indulgent or hedonistic, although his behaviour often gives that impression. His extravagant recreational pursuits are an expression of his own individual freedom. He is still a driven man, as driven as he was when he started Magna in 1958. He's constantly pushing the outer boundaries of how far he can go with people and situations. Yet this sense of freedom has not made him arrogant or pretentious. Nor is he a selfish man. People who are close to him pay tribute to his extraordinary generosity. They admire his spontaneity and impulsiveness. He is never afraid to try something new or to terminate something that isn't working. He does like to exert personal dominance over other people, more, one suspects, to winnow out the people who are uninteresting because they let him walk all over them. More importantly, he seems genuinely to want everyone to enjoy the same sense of power over their own destinies that he so clearly has.

His missionary zeal for individual freedom and economic democracy is a long way from running one of the most impressive success stories in Canadian business, but it is the basis for his unique approach to running a large fast-growing business. Stronach's formula has worked for Magna, and now he wants to make it work for everyone. He has developed two charters of rights, one for the stakeholders in his corporation and the other for his employees, which he hopes will become models for other corporations in Canada and throughout the world (see page 200). A true visionary, his social and political ideas now absorb the prodigious energy and passion that once went into building Magna. He has not left Magna. Although he is giving the management at Magna the right to vote his shares as long as they respect the social structure he has erected for them, he still controls more than half the votes in the company through his Class B shares, which have 500 votes each. It is true that he has become a different kind of entrepreneur, but, true to form, his goals still far outstrip his resources.

Stronach's prescriptions are too strong medicine for some people. Many entrepreneurs like his instincts, though, even if they don't always agree with the details of his formula. The idea of contributing to a better society is a powerful source of energy to entrepreneurs who direct their businesses in a socially conscious way. There is a danger, however, of transferring the intensity that makes them successful at business to their social engineering. Too often that leads to disaster, because zealous do-gooding cannot co-habit with entrepreneurial focus. Stronach's empire will not suffer from his launch into social evolution, because he built it to a size where it had the management depth and momentum to carry on without him. George Jenkins of Process Technology Ltd. (PTL) was not so lucky; he tried to do both too soon.

Jenkins came close to creating a miracle. He built a high-tech business, coating silicon wafers for the worldwide semi-conductor industry, in the tiny town of Oromocto, near Fredericton, New Brunswick.   The competition in this industry is ferocious, and Oromocto had no trained labour force, poor connections to the centres of the computer industry in the U.S. and elsewhere, and was far from the supportive infrastructure of high-tech centres like Ottawa, Toronto, Montreal, Saskatoon or Vancouver. In the end, however, it was none of these disadvantages that killed his business. PTL went into receivership because Jenkins couldn't separate his social and business missions.

Jenkins was born in New Brunswick, and he chose Oromocto as the location of his business because he wanted to prove to central Canadians that a rural community in New Brunswick has what it takes to succeed in fierce international competition. He was profoundly disturbed by his perception of attitudes in Ontario, where he had worked for some years as a researcher with Northern Telecom. He felt that Ontarians assumed that Maritimers were good for only welfare and UIC because they weren't prepared to try. He rejected that misconception with passion, blaming the economic environment in the Maritimes on unfair trade laws which favoured the high-population areas concentrated in central Canada.

A deeply religious man, when he makes a decision, Jenkins always asks himself if the Lord would want him to do it. It's his way of knitting together all the projects he undertakes within the pattern of his overall goals. It's his litmus test for determining if a project is worthwhile. He found his Holy Grail when Northern Telecom turned down the commercial application of a technology he developed there for coating the silicon wafers used in the production of computer chips. It was, he decided after asking the Lord what he should do, his manifest destiny to use that technology to build a new industry in New Brunswick. "The secret of a successful businessperson is to acknowledge that he'll have his time and he's got to have the courage of his convictions. You've got to go beyond that and really want to do it. Failures say they can't do it or back out halfway through."

Jenkins started PTL (the acronym was not accidental) in 1982, in the middle of a recession. He became an overnight hero. Winning orders far faster than he had hoped, he drove annual sales from $650,000 in 1983 to $7.5 million in 1985. It would be normal for a new high-tech company to lose money for at least five years, but PTL moved into the black in its second and third years. Jenkins seemed to be invulnerable, possessed of a magic touch.

Perpetually tousled and tieless, brimming with conviction, Jenkins loved to talk about his beliefs while he still had a thriving business to prove his points. A visionary with a boyish face and an aura of bottled-up energy poised to propel him into action, he doesn't care much about material things. He drove a 1980 Pontiac when he was first interviewed for this book in 1986. He shared the executive suite with his two vice presidents, both of whom had immaculately tidy offices, furnished with plain but comfortable furniture. Jenkins had a utilitarian office dominated by bookshelves along two walls and a huge desk, which looked like the book-return table of a busy metropolitan library.

During the heady days when he was a guru, he was in demand all over the country. He sat on numerous boards and associations. He spent hours with journalists. His philosophies and ideas are attractive, based on respect for his fellow man and his infinite sense of possibilities. It was inspiring to listen to him.

Then he hit a brick wall. Expansion capital dried up and the firm lost its momentum, slipping quickly into receivership by early 1987. There are rarely neat, identifiable reasons for a tragedy like Jenkins's, but there are straws in the wind. His financial backers said at the time PTL went into receivership that he had become inflexible and insensitive to the needs of his investors, whom he considered far too cautious and short-sighted. His absolute faith in the long-term prospects of his business persuaded him to spend money on projects that might not have a pay-off for several years. "If you know the business, you don't have to think too long about decisions," he said in 1986. "It bothers a lot of people — 'Oh! George has jumped off the bridge again!'—but they just don't understand what we're doing." The investors understood, however. It was Jenkins who had allowed his zeal to improve the world get the better of him.

## THE MAJOR MOTIVATIONS OF ENTREPRENEURS

Almost three-quarters of the entrepreneurs in this study mentioned one or more of the four motivations that reflect a desire to succeed—building a lasting organization, a sense of accomplishment, winning in business, and making the world a better place. In all, the entrepreneurs articulated 17 different motivations. They can be grouped in six categories:

| Motivation | Percentage who said this motivates them |
|---|---|
| Need to succeed | 74% |
| Enjoyment | 57% |
| Money and recognition | 48% |
| The challenge | 27% |
| Altruism | 24% |
| Affiliation with interesting people | 9% |

Within each of these groups, there are several specific motivations mentioned by the entrepreneurs:
- **Enjoyment**. More than half the entrepreneurs said they do what they do because they enjoy it or it affords them self-fulfillment. This includes having fun, producing a quality product, and being creative and independent.
- **Money and recognition** was mentioned by almost half the entrepreneurs as a motivation. A related motivation, cited by

relatively few but a factor nonetheless, is power, or the ability to call the shots in the community, which is a form of recognition for entrepreneurs.

- **The challenge** of an entrepreneurial existence motivates some entrepreneurs, although much less than the first three categories. Related motivations are a love for solving problems and, occasionally, the need to prove a point to doubters who thought the entrepreneurs couldn't achieve what they set out to do.
- **Altruism** motivates some entrepreneurs, who love to see other people fulfill their potential. Still others do what they do to help their family or some of its members.
- **Affiliation**. Only 9% of the entrepreneurs in this book mentioned this as a motivation. This is not surprising, since a need for affiliation is an unusual companion to the fierce independence of entrepreneurs.

The top ten specific motivations are as follows:

| Motivation | Percentage who said this motivates them |
|---|---|
| 1. Having fun | 44% |
| 2. Building a lasting organization | 34% |
| 3. Money | 33% |
| 4. Winning in business | 29% |
| 5. Recognition | 26% |
| 6. Sense of accomplishment | 23% |
| 7. Seeing people fulfill their potential | 21% |
| 8. The challenge | 14% |
| 9. Improving the world in some way | 12% |
| 10. Problem solving | 10% |
| Producing a top-quality product | 10% |

Note: See Appendix C, Table 7.1 for a full list of motivations.

## ENJOYMENT

Linnvale Steel's Albert McElwee, a small, soft-spoken Scot, had done well in his structural steel business, building it to 36 employees and sales of $8 million in 1989, 13 years after he went on his own. His secret is his transparent love for his métier. In 1963, he left the depressed shipyards in Glasgow to join the Hudson's Bay Company in its northern stores division. Stationed in northern Saskatchewan, he could hardly have been farther away from the John Brown Shipyard where his father had ordered him to take his apprenticeship. He didn't stay long, moving south after a year to Saskatoon, where he returned to the machine shops with which he was so familiar.

Twelve years later, McElwee had risen from labourer to plant foreman. He took the plunge into his own business in 1976. It was the fulfillment of a dream for him, and he blesses both the country that gave him the opportunity to do it and the father who forbad him to find work outside the shipyards until he had taken his apprenticeship. "I love the smell of steel," he says. "People don't think of work as a smell, but a steel plant has a certain aroma." As he says it, the gentleness becomes passion and his eyes sparkle. When he thumbs through the annual catalogue of gigantic machines that bend and shape great slabs of steel, he looks like a child with this year's catalogue of Christmas toys. It's what makes him get up in the morning.

Carol Johnson of Pace Setter Swim & Gym Wear is another entrepreneur who loves her product, quality clothes. She believes she is successful because she never compromises on quality. "When I go to a show, I'm like a peacock," she says. "I'm driven by the love of our product. That has never changed. Poor quality is like being a liar—you're cheating yourself and the company."

Johnson had never intended to go into business. Her daughters were competitive swimmers, and when she couldn't find decent swimwear she made it herself. It was no big deal; she had been making all her family's clothes for years, as had her mother and grandmother before her. She never dreamed she could make money at it. Her daughters' swimsuits were a great hit, however, and she was encouraged to start selling her handiwork. It was a new experience for the divorced mother of two girls, who earned her living for 19 years as a social worker, while she studied at night for her masters degree in criminology. But she had all the skills she needed. "There isn't a thing in the world I haven't sewn," she says. In her first year, 1978, she sold $45,000 worth of clothes at a small profit, although she knew nothing about costing or marketing. Even when her sales topped $5 million eight years later, her top priority was still to produce the best quality clothes she could.

Then she decided to let her daughter, Ginette, take over some of the management of the operation, while she gave some thought to spending more time and money on herself. She says, with her husky laugh which is never absent for long, that her dream is to be the oldest grandmother to win an annual speedboat race off the coast of Florida. She would also love to become an expert skier and learn how to windsurf, if she can find time from her annual fly-in fishing trip to northern Manitoba. An avid boater, she keeps her 33-footer moored on the Red River in Winnipeg and dreams of the day she can buy a 54-footer and moor it somewhere where it's warm for eight months of the year.

It hasn't happened yet. After a couple of years, Ginette decided she wanted to do something else and Johnson hired an operations manager. That year, 1988, she lost money for the first time, on sales of $6 million. Her manager was used to a bigger company where managers don't have to roll up their sleeves and pitch in. He quit the following year, and Johnson had to learn how to run the company again. She worked very hard, moving people around and reorganizing, and soon realized how much she had missed the action. "I'm thrilled to be back as a hands-on owner," she says. "It's interesting to get back in and know why things are being done that way."

Johnson has a long list of new products she'd like to introduce. She has also acquired the authority of success, having overcome her hesitancy to be the "boss." Now that she enjoys the business game, her goals are starting to stretch and she now wants to be number one in Canada. She just might do it.

The last two motivations associated with pure enjoyment are the desire to be creative and independent. Since all successful entrepreneurs are already independent, most of them tend to take it for granted, so it's rarely mentioned as a motivation. It is more likely to be mentioned as a motivation by people just starting their first enterprise. Even for established entrepreneurs, however, independence is important, as virtually all of them relish the thrill of being entirely responsible for what happens to them in their lives. Creativity is also an important part of most entrepreneurs' lives, but most view it as a strength rather than a motivation.

## ALTRUISM

A fifth of the entrepreneurs in this study are motivated by their desire to see their employees fulfill their potential. Occasionally, an entrepreneur's family is the beneficiary of this noble motivation, but not often. Parents with children in the business are more likely to do battle with them than to pursue strategies that encourage the young to usurp their parents. Of the significant proportion of entrepreneurs who do derive motivation and satisfaction from the desire to help others grow, Marcel Dutil is probably one of the best examples. This talented and aggressive entrepreneur, has built a powerhouse of a company, Canam Manac, which is taking on the competition in the U.S. and triumphing. He's one of the leading role models for aspiring entrepreneurs in Quebec.

Dutil started out on his own in 1964, when he acquired voting control of the fledgling steel fabricating company his father had started four years earlier with some U.S. partners. Sales then were $200,000. Twenty-four years later, sales were almost $650 million, and Canam Manac employed more than 3,000 people all over North America. That doesn't count the 45% interest Dutil acquired in Noverco, the holding company for the natural gas distributor, Gaz Métropolitain, which had annual sales of more than $1 billion in 1988. He has taken Canam Manac public, but he still controls a majority of the voting shares. The core group now manufactures steel products (including steel joists, the basis for the company's growth in the early years), semi-trailers and furniture.

The original plant was started by his father in St. Georges, the main city in the Beauce, south of Quebec City and far from the industrial heartland of Montreal. The young Dutil worked there in the summers before he quit school to take over from the plant manager, who had resigned. He was then 20. A year or two later, he bought 51% of the shares from his father and his partners, raising his holding to 100% over the following eight years.

Dutil's stocky build and down-to-earth manner make him look ordinary, but his bluff face and bland expression hide a celebrated mind. The people who sit on boards with him are generally awestruck by his ability to absorb, with lightning speed, the nuances of complex situations and draw penetrating conclusions on the spot. He delivers his ideas with extraordinary precision and economy of words, speaking gently and unhurriedly, which belies the rapid-fire pace at which he moves through his days. Yet there is never any sense of his pushing his worldview at his listeners. His obvious dynamism isn't a tool for him to wield power over lesser personalities; it is directed at encouraging people to cut through the bafflegab and deal with situations, then move on to the next problem or opportunity. He sees himself as a mentor and guide, rather than as a charismatic leader. He feels he has an obligation to create an environment in which the people who are loyal to Canam Manac can grow to more than 100% of their capacity. That's what drives the dynamic growth of Canam Manac. If the company isn't growing fast, the managers will not have the room to grow.

Some of that growth has come through acquisitions, and a lot of it has been from internal growth, powered by his managers. He made a huge investment buying control of Noverco, which was intended mainly to provide steady earnings to counterbalance the cycles of the construction industry. And in the steel business, he has tried on several occasions to buy companies, but the asking prices were often too high for a man who likes to keep his debt at less than half his equity. Whether the companies have been bought or grown, though, Dutil has found that the key to success has been to put his own loyal people into the key spots, in plants all over North America, so that they could spread the gospel of the company's culture: "We've got people who've been here 25 years. You've got to give them space. If we plateau, we lose all those people."

## MONEY, RECOGNITION AND POWER

The attitudes entrepreneurs express toward money are complex, partly because most people find it hard to deal with wealth, whether they have it or not. The conventional wisdom is that entrepreneurs are not driven by the need for money per se, but rather that they value it as a means of keeping score of how well they are doing. For a significant proportion of entrepreneurs, that's a bit ingenuous, a reflection perhaps of their telling people what they think they want to hear or what they think they *should* say. Successful entrepreneurs more often than not like to wear their wealth on their sleeves because they figure they've earned it—and they are generally not afraid of making a statement about themselves.

"We're not in business just to say we've created jobs," says Michel Lapointe of DAP Electronics. "It's a tough, stressful job, tough on the family, so I should profit from it." His sentiments are shared by Lawrence Bloomberg of First Marathon Securities (see page 210). "I wasn't making as much money as friends who had started their own businesses," he says. "I was essentially an employee. Most of my friends are entrepreneurs. It's a hard one to sit there earning a salary. I feel sorry for all those people who don't give themselves a chance. As a significant shareholder, you're creating wealth. In seven years, we've created a company worth serious money."

A much more common attitude among entrepreneurs in this book was that they unabashedly liked money for what they could buy with it. Mary Macdonald of Venture Economics loves to travel, and she wants money to feed that hobby. She sees money in the context of time. If she can earn enough, she will be able to buy all the services she doesn't want to do for herself, such as shopping for groceries. If she makes enough money, she will also be able to reduce her workload to make more time for travel.

Although more than half the entrepreneurs who said they are motivated by money said it was because of what the money could buy for them or because they valued it as a scorecard, it's likely their justifications for wanting money are irrelevant. The people who say they are motivated by money have the same characteristics regardless of their justifications. And they are quite different from the entrepreneurs who say they are not interested in money.

Those who admit to being motivated by the prospect of a lot of money are much less interested in taking up challenges than the rest, and much more interested in winning in business and gaining recognition for their success. On the other hand, the entrepreneurs who say they are not motivated by money are much more excited at seeing people fulfill their potential and at making the world a better place to live in.

Overall, money is probably a bigger motivator than is generally recognized, particularly as many entrepreneurs are reluctant to admit to a motivation they fear might appear greedy. Almost a third (30%) of the entrepreneurs in this book said money was important to them and nearly as many (27%) said emphatically it wasn't. However, almost a third of those who said money was not important acknowledged that it had been important before they became successful. After the first couple of million, these people find the allure pales. There are only so many meals you can eat in a day, only so many cottages you can buy and use. If these people are counted as being motivated by money, even if only at one stage of their lives, then money comes very close to the top of the rankings of motivators, at 41%.

The need for recognition is a strong and related drive in entrepreneurs, a quarter of whom mentioned it. Often, the desire for recognition is muted in the early days of a business, if only because entrepreneurs know they will receive no respect at all until they have demonstrated their prowess as businesspeople. But once they succeed, the dynamics change. Pierre Boivin of Norvinca was driven by money as a young man and he made his first million before he was 30. After that, he found that becoming wealthy was no longer the goal. That's where the desire for recognition came in.

Stocky and businesslike, with immaculately groomed, short-cropped hair, Boivin is all business. His office is sparse, dominated by two magnificent pieces of Inuit art—a big soapstone plaque with a hunting scene carved on it and a foot-high carved whalebone. Beyond these two impressive works of art, there is little of Boivin himself. His passions and interests are kept elsewhere. In 1988, Norvinca had annual sales of $25 million in wholesale sports equipment, and now that it's running smoothly, he has time to shift his focus to a larger community. He has accepted a large number of invitations to join boards and associations. "It's a pain in the ass," he says, "but it's stimulating. I've done the same socially, with fund-raising for school boards and so on. I get a big kick out of the high profile. I have an ego, like everyone else. Although I don't do anything to create it, I would be very disappointed if I didn't get the aura of recognition."

Some people need more than recognition; they want power. However, only 8% of the entrepreneurs in this book mentioned power as a motivation. Many entrepreneurs view power as being healthy if it is a result of what they do, but regard it as a dubious motivation for an entrepreneur. It's possible that many more of them want to exercise power but they feel power is a pejorative word, so they decline to reveal their feelings about it. That's unlikely, however. Entrepreneurs are generally not shy about expressing their viewpoints on any issue, so it would be out of character for them to turn coy about power. Also, almost all entrepreneurs have to suffer through a period of low status in the eyes of the community before they succeed, so they have to learn to do without power. And by the time they are success-ful, they don't need the power because they have the money. There is a great deal of skepticism among researchers as to the validity of assertions that entrepreneurs are not motivated by power, but it's probably true.

## THE CHALLENGE

Most experienced entrepreneurs are happier when they are not being challenged. In the beginning, it's all very well living at the limit of your resources and stretching your talents and skills as far as they'll go, but it can be an exhausting life. The majority of entrepreneurs prefer to be in control. Steve Chepa of Dicon Systems says it best: "Challenge is a myth. Anyone who isn't smart enough to take the easiest course is a fool. I'd fire him. A guy who's looking for a challenge should be an athlete."

Like independence, the challenge of running a business is a motivation that often fades with experience. For people start-ing their first business, the challenge is paramount, because so many feel their talents have been stifled as employees. But once a business is running successfully, minimizing risk be-comes more important than accepting challenges. The thrill turns into the careful exercise of good judgement.

Some challenges don't fade, however. Many entrepreneurs find continuing pleasure in solving problems, a motivation that ranked tenth among the entrepreneurs in this book. Most of the ones who mentioned this as a motivation are quiet, thoughtful people, given more to penetrating reflection than to the exuberance that characterizes the people who love a challenge. Jim Neill's company, Metro Toronto News, distributes more then 2 million copies a week of the 2,500 magazines sold at 6,000 news-stands and bookstores in central Ontario. Quiet and courteous, he first arrived in MTN when the company was owned by Maclean Hunter and losing money badly. Neill, whose background is in data processing and computer systems, was sent in to help out with computerizing the business. He was soon named president and went to work to clean up what had become a hornet's nest of labour problems and antediluvian business practices.

He turned the company around, but by then Maclean Hunter had decided it didn't want to be in that business, so Neill bought it in a leveraged buyout shortly before interest rates began to soar toward 25%. Neill knew the business like the back of his hand, so he never doubted he could survive that difficult period. He merely worked a little harder at improving his cash flow and paid off his loan "pretty quick." His territory covers a radius of almost 250 kilometres around Toronto. With so many products, so many destinations, orders varying from fifty to thousands, and deadlines that simply cannot be missed, it's a business that demands precision and efficiency. It suits him perfectly. His mind is trained to solve problems, and he's happiest when he can devise systems to make his firm more efficient or effective. "I believe in taking the problems that I can solve and solving them. I gain a great sense of satisfaction in seeing things run well."

Like many people who enjoy solving problems, Neill doesn't find it as easy to identify new problems as he does to solve them when he finds them. He has thought of several ways of redefining his business to open up new paths for expansion, but none has led to new businesses or acquisitions yet. "We have a transportation business, but we're not in the business of coming up with new ideas. We're more into finding products where time is of the essence." Although he says he wants to expand outside physical distribution, he suffers from the malady of many managers who buy their businesses from their employers. They know their business well when they buy it, and they can see what problems have to be solved to turn it around, but they miss out on the benefits of the creative discipline of honing a fresh business idea through the examination of dozens of options.

Finally, there are the sometimes obsessive entrepreneurs who derive their inspiration from people who think they'll never succeed. They want to prove them all wrong, wrong, wrong. It's not always a healthy motivation, since it can narrow perspectives and distract attention from unrelated opportunities, but it certainly gives some people the determination to succeed (as opposed to the need to succeed).

Jack Wilson of RSI Robotics Systems International makes robots. His machines have made him well known throughout North America. It was his robot that picked the pieces of the Challenger space shuttle off the ocean floor when it crashed into the Atlantic. His robots were the spiders in the Hollywood film, *Runaway*. He is now selling robots for handling nuclear waste, servicing oil and gas wells in oceans, harvesting trees, taking photographs in the depths of the ocean, and demonstrating remote control applications in university laboratories. From his remote offices in Sidney on Vancouver Island, he defies the nay-sayers who said it couldn't be done in Canada.

Wilson is a former "techie," an intellectual hired gun who lent his youthful and hyperactive brain to some of the most prestigious organizations in North America. Born in Philadelphia, he earned his computer science degree in Colorado, then went to Washington, where, for three years, he helped the Brookings Institution create an advanced computer centre with mathematical models, "the first time-sharing model for commerce." He also worked with the President's Economic Council on mathematical modelling. He was at the nerve centre of Richard Nixon's power network, but became disillusioned at the destruction reaped by Nixon's "California cowboys." So the budding genius succumbed to the flower-child siren-song of the 1960s and took his family in a converted school bus to

Texada Island on B.C.'s Sunshine Coast. There he did odd jobs salvaging logs, selling cedar shakes, looking after an inactive logging camp and starting a tugboat business.

It didn't last. His wife left him, taking their children with her. He was devoted to the children, but the support payments left nothing over to pay for regular visits. So he did odd jobs in logging to augment his income. As anyone would know who has ever watched "The Beachcombers," it was high adventure. It was also as hard on his psyche as it was on his body. The community on Texada Island regarded log salvagers a little like cattle rustlers, and he felt like an outcast, never able to feel part of the community.

Tired of being an outsider, he decided to "drop out of dropping out." He went to Malaspina College on Vancouver Island, where the president wanted to establish a computer facility better than the comparable facility at the college's greatest rival, the University of Victoria. Wilson did it for him, but once it was set up, the president didn't want Wilson to run it. A slight man, with blonde hair and a dark moustache, Wilson is quiet, almost hesitant when he speaks. There is nothing tentative about his views, though. He has forged the disappointments of his peripatetic career into a steely deter- mination to succeed. There is no hiding the anger. "The world gave me credit for what I'd done, but nobody wanted me in the structure they'd set up."

After the Malaspina College experience, he tried consulting for the provincial government, but that didn't last long either. He didn't find the administrative programming very challeng- ing, so he soon got bored and bowed out. Just at that point, he suffered a severe back injury, which presented him with the opportunity seized by so many people who have achieved great things—an extended period of enforced inactivity. This gave him the time to reflect on himself and the possibilities for his future. It allowed him to channel his anger. He decided to focus on robots, partly because it was a new field with great oppor- tunities for his programming genius, and partly because the federal and provincial governments said it was impossible for a Canadian firm to compete with the Americans. "The govern- ments said we couldn't hack it, that we could only hope to supply the U.S. robotics industry. I'll show 'em." He did show 'em, building his business to $2 million in sales by 1988, but the anger hasn't gone. "The idealism of youth is still there. I've never had a job like other people. I've always had to entrepreneur it. I'm unhirable."

## AFFILIATION

A number of entrepreneurs will admit to enjoying the people they work with, but few count it as a motivation. One of the most methodical and ambitious entrepreneurs anywhere in Canada is Richard Prytula of Leigh Navigation Systems. He sets himself specific objectives for meeting people, as he does with every other aspect of his life and work. "Success is who you mix with in governments and institutions," he says. He has set himself the goal of becoming a director of the Royal Bank before he reaches 40. And he wants to become governor-general before he turns 50. He has no interest in becoming prime minister—"That's a thankless job."

# CHAPTER 8

# THE SEVEN TYPES
# OF ENTREPRENEURS

The conventional wisdom would have it that there are no patterns in the way entrepreneurs behave. The previous chapters have shown that this is not the case in the specific elements of entrepreneurship. Moreover, there are also patterns in their broad approach to business. This chapter identifies the seven distinctive types of entrepreneurs among the 100 interviewed for this book.

The first two types are start-up artists and deal-makers. They are everyone's favourite stereotypes, because they have the personal characteristics that most people think of when they say "entrepreneurial." The third and fourth types are generally in small- and medium-sized businesses because they prefer to stay manageably small. They are maestros and niche players. Supermanagers are the fifth type. They are the ambitious managerial entrepreneurs who usually come from a successful background in big business and want to make a lot of money on their own, so they buy existing businesses, often using a leveraged buyout. The sixth and seventh types are both organization builders, because that's the focus of their business plans. They are conglomerateurs and visionaries.

Many entrepreneurs are also active investors in other entrepreneurs. Usually they don't take an active role as operators, or they would be conglomerateurs, but their involvement can be extensive. They are seldom in these companies for the long haul; they tend to make the investments to keep themselves sharp, to make money and to have fun. There are investors in all seven types, so their investment activities were not a factor in categorizing them.

Like all attempts to categorize people, who are infinitely variable, there are entrepreneurs in any single type who do not have one or more of the skills attributed to their type. They do have most of them, however, and the tone of their characteristics is in tune with the composite profile. Also, a number of characteristics are not mentioned in each type, because that type has a distribution of those particular characteristics that is similar to the distribution for all entrepreneurs, so that it does not distinguish that type from the others.

## EVERYONE'S FAVOURITE STEREOTYPES

### Start-up artists

These entrepreneurs start a lot of enterprises but don't stay with them for long. They get their kicks out of the process of creating new ventures. They dislike management, so will not embark on the process of administering the businesses once they're up and running. They prefer to sell them off as soon as they have built value into them. Usually creative, overflowing with ideas, they are independent and rarely seek advice from others. They seldom have a board of directors and if they do, it's usually passive. They are extremely persistent and have a strong sense of their own inner power, but feel that the success of their ventures is heavily dependent on whether their timing is good when they launch a venture. They are not normally interested in people—in fact, they seek to avoid dealing with them, as they are the principal component of the administration they hate so much. They nonetheless have a keen eye in choosing partners for their fledgling enterprises.

### Deal-makers

These people love to make deals. Hot negotiators, they'll always make money because they can winkle out the best deals possible. That's where they get their kicks. They love a challenge. Deal-makers don't derive as much pleasure from running a successful company as they do from closing the deal that makes it successful. Yet, unlike the start-up artists, they often keep their successful companies, because that's what gives them their cash flow and their operating base. However, if something better comes along, they won't hesitate to sell their holdings. They usually have clear ideas of the kinds of businesses or deals they want to get into and can be long-term planners—although their goals are very personal, as opposed to organizational. They play their cards close to the chest with employees as well as outsiders and are usually hands-on managers who give their employees relatively little leeway. They seldom have boards of directors.

Deal-makers don't use a lot of leverage as a rule and are the most conservative of all the entrepreneurial types when it comes to risk. They rely on their experience to assess risks rather than having great faith in their own abilities. They face their risks squarely and pay a lot of attention to the level of potential loss they'll tolerate. They are extremely flexible and will jump on an opportunity very quickly. They don't believe they have any control over the timing of their deals, but don't think timing is particularly important anyway.

## SMALL- AND MEDIUM-SIZED BUSINESS

### Maestros

These people are experts in their fields. It could be electronics, restaurateurship, book publishing or any particular niche of expertise. They're there to exercise their technical skills, more than to make money. They are enthusiastic and love the nuts and bolts of their businesses. They have fun with their avocation and are not particularly interested in challenges or rapid growth. Prolific in generating ideas, they love to roll up their sleeves and do the job themselves. They are perfectionists about their products, but not particularly persevering in running their business, although they pride themselves on their business judgement. Like the previous two types, they like to fly solo and don't delegate easily. They tend not to consult their employees much, but like them to show initiative. Their organizations are generally unstructured, and they often dispense with a board of directors.

They rarely sell their businesses, which are product-driven as opposed to market-driven. They are usually not keen disciples of risk management, and, if they do control their risks, it's likely to be through reducing their exposure, not through controlling the potential loss or the probability of failing. They often take on huge risks (knowingly or otherwise) because the project makes sense in the context of their special expertise. The risks don't bother them; they resolutely accept the risk of failure and don't suffer anxiety attacks over the potential losses they face. They also tend not to plan in a disciplined way. They prefer to ride the tide of their skill, following the serendipitous opportunities as they identify them in the course of their vocational interest. They can grow quite big, although many fall by the wayside.

### Niche players

This is by far the most common category, as it includes more than 40% of the people in this book. These entrepreneurs pick a niche and mine it effectively for the long haul. They are essentially businesspeople, who have chosen their niche because it seemed like a good business opportunity. They are market-driven, freely changing their product lines or target markets to keep a tight fit between their products and their customers. They rarely stagnate in their niches. Of forty-two niche players, only five had not recently changed their product lines, target markets or geographical markets. Most of them (60%) had changed their product lines, while almost half had changed territories and a sixth had changed their target markets. The changes in product lines are rarely radical departures from their existing products.

Niche players strive to be competent businesspeople, acquiring solid business skills. They tend to give greater priority to profit than to growth. They like the reward of money and recognition, and they are usually conscious of the need to build an organization that can function effectively even when they are not there. They look for employees who are team players, and they share decision-making easily. They are more likely than other entrepreneurs to let their employees learn by making mistakes. They prefer to keep to a size they feel they can manage effectively. Some of them are more growth oriented, but they are not the dreamers who aspire to great heights—their growth is oriented to perceived opportunity, not dreams of high achievement.

These entrepreneurs tend to be careful planners, although they don't have elaborate strategies. They are more likely to pick a project and concentrate on it until they are ready to move on to a new project. They are careful with the risks they take. They control their risks to the greatest degree of all the types, especially through keeping a lid on the potential loss and minimizing the probability of failure. With all these risk-control measures, they have great faith in their ability to succeed and tend to ignore the possibility that they might actually suffer major losses.

## AMBITIOUS MANAGERIAL ENTREPRENEURS

### Supermanagers

These people buy companies using a lot of debt. They may or may not have their own money in the deal. They pay attention to the timing of their decisions, because their interest charges can vary so much depending on when they close a deal. They borrow large sums of money because they have enormous faith in their own abilities. Their attitude toward risk is consistent with this. They concentrate on keeping their potential losses within acceptable limits (a necessary function when they borrow large amounts of money), but then trivialize the risk.

They tend to be scientific managers, who prefer to build comprehensive strategies rather than stay flexible in order to grab unforeseen opportunities. They tend to be open to other people's ideas and look for employees who are good team players. They invite participation when they formulate their strategies, and they almost always have an active board of directors. In their leadership style, they are enthusiastic and project their personal values as an example to employees. They are perfectionists who strive to deliver outstanding products with an effective organization.

Supermanagers tend to be ambitious and strive for high growth rates. They are not particularly driven by the prospect of money or recognition, but they love to win and, in line with their scientific management, they generally try to build a smooth-functioning organization.

## ORGANIZATION BUILDERS

### Conglomerateurs

These are the quintessential businesspeople. They love the business of business. They accumulate companies, in all of which they take an active, operational role, so that they can diversify their interests, smooth out their cycles, and learn business techniques that they can apply to their other firms. To them, buying and selling is like playing a hand of cards. Sometimes the companies are completely unrelated, sometimes they are slightly related to one another. They believe that the success of their strategic moves hinges on good timing, which they believe lies within their control.

They are opportunity grabbers rather than creators. In their planning they try to create an environment that will attract opportunities rather than lay out a preferred path to their goals. They seldom have a plan for the overall business, although they usually have comprehensive plans for their individual companies. They are very profit oriented and motivated by the prospect of money, but don't like to use too much leverage, except in short bursts. They are not likely to lead by projecting their own inner power. They lead with their enthusiasm and are extremely persistent. They usually have boards of directors and listen to them.

### Visionaries

These entrepreneurs set themselves extraordinarily ambitious goals. They make comprehensive plans, and they tend to believe they create their own opportunities rather than grab whatever is passing by. They also believe they can control their own timing in terms of reaching their objectives. They have a strong belief in their own inner power and are decisive, but they are rarely good at conceptualizing their goals. They are not particularly persistent and don't pride themselves on their marketing skills—perhaps because these are for the people who worry about the details, not the grand design. Although they don't need recognition, they do need to have a sense of achievement and often want to change the world for the better.

Visionaries invariably want to build a big business, often vertically integrated. In other words, they don't just set themselves a cold business target, they strive for a whole set of situations, or a lifestyle, or prestige, or a role in the community. They can be niche players, supermanagers or conglomerateurs, but their ambition and determination put them into a class by themselves. Their attitude toward risk is dominated by a powerful combination. They face their risks squarely, resolutely accept whatever risks they have to take to achieve their goals, and still take risks aggressively. They are not unduly conscious of the need to control their risks, and have a tendency toward putting no controls at all on their risks.

They grow their companies faster than the average and measure their success in terms of annual sales. They tend not to be interested in profit except insofar as it helps them grow to achieve their goals. They are very conscious of putting together all the necessary elements of a super-business—the people, the money and the markets. They have structured organizations and delegate with tight controls. They prefer team players as employees and are more likely than most to give them profit-sharing plans. They don't try and dream up all the good ideas themselves; they draw ideas from everywhere and invite the participation of their employees in their planning process. They are more likely than the average entrepreneurs to have a board of directors, and if they do, their boards are much more likely to be active. Very few have no board at all.

# PART II

LEADERSHIP

# CHAPTER 9

# LEADERSHIP SKILLS

*"Everything seems to have been put on this earth for me to be connected with it.... Everything's been invested by me — the concept, the character. We didn't buy the rights to someone else's idea. I did it my way."*
— Johnny Lombardi of CHIN Radio

*"I'll whip a lawyer's ass, because I'll work eight hours to his two. I often work till 11 in the evening and then I'll be in the office at 5 the next morning. I took night courses to help me understand the business."*
— Klaus Deering of Glenayre Electronics

**W**hen people talk of leaders, they are apt to imagine charismatic personalities who inspire followers to efforts beyond their normal capacities, who set bold and imaginative directions, and who act with decisive forcefulness to keep everyone on track. It's an appealing image, and there are even some people who really do all these things, but they are few and far between. The popular image is actually a composite of these three major leadership skills.

Charismatics lead through sheer force of their personalities, embodying the aspirations of their followers; dynamic leaders are decisive or persistent, pushing change through their organizations by asserting their own priorities; and cerebral leaders communicate organizational visions and objectives that unify the efforts of all their followers. Almost all the entrepreneurs in this book consider themselves to have strong leadership qualities, but very few are strong in all three skills. Many of them, however, are strong in two of the skills.

Another leadership skill, which is rarer than the others, is leadership by virtue of ownership. Pulling rank is not generally a technique that lasts long in an entrepreneurial setting, unless it is backed up by other leadership skills, but some people use it.

And finally, there is one leadership skill that is vital for most entrepreneurship—the ability to make a partnership work. About half of the entrepreneurs I interviewed have a significant partner, who has a major influence on their actions and with whom they must co-operate if they want to succeed. Few people are so competent that they can run a business without some form of partnership; however, the cure is sometimes worse than the disease. Many who go it alone fail. And just as many who enter a partnership agreement fail, usually because they go into it with unrealistic expectations.

## CHARISMATIC LEADERSHIP

Johnny Lombardi is a living legend in Toronto's huge Italian community. It's a rare year when his beaming face doesn't appear at least a couple of times in the Toronto newspapers, his smile hung hugely between his ears, his baldness barely concealed by a thinning thatch of white hair drawn lovingly across his head. The list of his community involvements goes on for pages, and he has been honoured by most of them. He is Toronto's Mr. Multicultural, and even in his seventies, his energy is undimmed, his enthusiasm palpable.

Lombardi's principal business is CHIN Radio, which broadcasts in 32 different languages. Although he doesn't own a TV station, he produces 15 hours of programming in ten languages every week, and runs them on the weekend on the Global Television Network and CITY TV. He can't speak many of the languages himself (even his Italian is rudimentary), but he can relate to anyone. When he was in the Canadian army during World War II, he was the unofficial translator for unilingual officers, because he has such strong empathy he could figure out what they were trying to say. In addition to CHIN, he owns a record company, the restaurant downstairs from his offices, and some real estate, which he has redeveloped, on College Street, just across the road from his radio studios. He is also an impresario when the mood catches him, his biggest event being the free picnic he stages for 250,000 people every Labour Day.

Lombardi projects the image of a man born to lead and comfortable in his role. "I plan what we should be doing," he says. "I bring in all my staff and ask them to check the costs. I ask them for the revenues, the return over five years. When all this is in front of me, I make the decision. I'm the bottom-line man."

He started his radio station in 1966 at the age of 50, the same year his youngest daughter, Donina, was born. He was no neophyte in radio, having been a freelance broadcaster for 20 years, but his principal business at the time was his chain of three supermarkets. He had grown that business from a single grocery store, which he purchased as a young veteran right after World War II. He had found an ideal spot and asked its owner, Imperial Oil, to rent it to him. The man from Esso who was in charge of real estate had lost a son in the war and took a shine to young Lombardi. He gave him a piece of paper and told him to write down what he thought was a reasonable rent. He did the same thing on another piece of paper and put the two in a hat, promising the rent would be whatever was written on the paper drawn from the hat. Lombardi had thought he might as well shoot for a steal, so he wrote down $150 a month, less than half its market value, but the Esso man's piece was drawn. It said $50 a month.

While he was running the grocery business, Lombardi kept his hand in with his first love, show business. He's a born performer. He formed his own band as a teenager when the adult bands wouldn't hire such a young trumpeter. After the war, he rented time from local radio stations and produced his own show. He sold ads to help pay for the production, but he also used the show to promote his grocery store and his band. He continued in this pattern for almost 20 years, associated with many of the big names who later built fortunes for themselves in broadcasting, until he finally won a daytime-only licence for his own station in 1966. The economics weren't promising, but he survived and built his niche until, 18 years later, he started making some serious profits when he received rights to broadcast (and sell ads) 24 hours a day.

Two years later, at 71, he started to think about passing his businesses down to his three children. He put his shares in a trust, which will pass ownership to them in equal shares when he dies. The trust agreement cannot stop them from selling some of their father's businesses (he knows they are most partial to the broadcasting operation), but it forbids any separation in the children's holdings. Lombardi would never countenance any suggestion that his three children might not be able to operate as an effective unit forever. In the meantime, he has to share some responsibilities with them. The trust agreement requires two signatures for every cheque. "I have to get their permission to do things now," he says, almost proudly, if a little uncertainly.

Lombardi is not getting ready to slack off, however. "I've got a bad back and the doctor says I have to get off my feet," he says. "But I can't relax at home. I just can't afford to die, there's too much to do." He's the quintessential stereotype of the entrepreneur. He's adventurous; he flies by the seat of his pants. And he succeeds. Lombardi may not have the polish of a corporate hotshot, but he knows he was born to lead. "Everything seems to have been put on this earth for me to be connected with it. The only thing I've ever wanted to do in life is to be doing what I'm doing. Everything's been invested by me—the concept, the character. We didn't buy the rights to someone else's idea. I did it my way."

There are many charismatic leaders like Lombardi, who have strong personalities and a clear sense of where they're going. They brook no interference with their leadership and are supportive and loyal to their followers, who must, in turn, accept the owner's leadership if they want to keep their jobs. Independent and secure, these leaders often have a sense of destiny. But not all charismatic leaders are like this. Some hold a powerful personal sway over their followers without having to make all the decisions and without being colourful personalities who instinctively hog the limelight.

Jean Pouliot would reject the label of charismatic leader. Small, almost birdlike, with grey hair and thick spectacles, few would recognize him as a stereotypical leader. Yet the owner of Montreal's English-language CFCF TV station and Quebec's newest French-language network, Quatre Saisons, is a charismatic leader. He doesn't have the brash conviction of people like Lombardi. He leads by setting an example of integrity for his employees. He embodies and projects the values he wants to see in his companies.

"People trust me," he says. "When I say something, they know I mean it. When I say yes or no, they may not agree with me, but they know I'm fair. There's nothing under the table. They all know I won't stand any crap of people running other people down. We won't play games. I don't want any special privileges (well, a parking space maybe)."

Pouliot fell into entrepreneurship entirely by accident. As a young man, he never even thought of becoming an entrepreneur. When he graduated in electronics from Laval University in 1945, he went into the army where, at the age of 23, he was made a lieutenant colonel to give him the necessary clout when he went to Germany to check out their radio and TV technology. Three years later, the navy grabbed him to be superintendent of its electronic laboratories. In 1952, he finally joined the private sector with Famous Players, where he found the mentor most people only dream about. "He was," says Pouliot, "the most marvellous guy I ever met."

He continued to rise rapidly through the ranks and by 1957, at the age of 34, he was appointed general manager of Télé-Capitale, the Famous Players subsidiary which owned the TV station in Quebec City. He didn't know what a balance sheet was, but he soon found out. To Pouliot's amazement, when Famous Players was required by the federal government to divest its controlling interest, no one in the management wanted to buy. They thought it was too expensive. Famous Players wanted to sell to management, however, so it said it would change the company's capital structure to reduce the equity to $50,000 and ask the managers to put in $25,000 for 50% of the company. Famous Players promised to put up the rest of the stock and guaranteed all the borrowed capital.

Pouliot bought 5% of the company for $2,500 and subsequently built up his shareholding to 33%. In 1972, he started selling off his holding, and the first batch, representing 6% of the company, fetched him $880,000. "Famous Players was like God," he says, with a passion undimmed by the passing of the years. "They said, 'Pay us the interest if you can and the principal whenever you feel like it. Just don't worry about it.'"

Unfortunately, Pouliot didn't always see eye to eye with the two men who were his partners in the control block. "I was tired of my partners," he says. "They liked the results, but they didn't like the way I did it. They wanted more controls." The antithesis of an authoritarian, Pouliot believes that giving his employees their head so that they can shoot for the moon will bring him rewards that far outweigh the risks of less control and more mistakes (see page 189). "Too many boards of directors are like the Kremlin. I run it like a free enterprise system." He offered to buy out his partners, but they refused, so he quit.

"I was 55 and out of a job. It was the best thing that ever happened to me." Toronto's John Bassett had just bought the CTV affiliate in Montreal, CFCF, from Charles Bronfman, who didn't want the high profile that goes with being the owner of a TV station. But the Canadian Radio & Television Commission, as it was then called, refused to approve the purchase. The timing was perfect. Pouliot was ready, willing and available. He worked out an offer within a week. It cost him $26.8 million for the company, with a little help from a loan of $17 million. Finally, he had his own company. He was soon busy covering all his flanks, starting with the purchase of a cable TV company, then some radio stations (resold in 1988) and 49% of Alexander Pearson and Dawsons, an advertising agency in Toronto.

He catapulted into prominence in Quebec—and created a lot of controversy—when he started Quatre Saisons in 1986. He was unfazed by the technical glitches made by his inexperienced staff, convinced that it was only human nature to criticize anything new and different. He knew it would be a tough job to change people's habits of TV viewing.

Pouliot may not be brash, but he has in spades the courage of his convictions and an understanding of charismatic leadership. "A leader doesn't mean going around giving orders. When I was young, we knew what a leader was. He says, 'I'm going this way, anyone want to follow?'" Pouliot's a bit older and wiser now, but he is still prepared to stick his neck out, and he doesn't mind waiting while the employees make up their minds whether he's worth following. "I get close to employees. The employees have to trust you. You have to go out of your way. You walk around, enquire, listen, try to be friendly. They still think you're trying to screw them, but they don't know how. After three or four years, they realize, 'My God, they're not trying to screw us.' What they want is recognition, especially in a creative business like ours."

### Inner power

Most charismatic leaders have an inner power that gives a sense of invulnerability to their personal style of leadership. It's an unshakeable conviction that they can achieve whatever they set out to do. Inner power also helps them believe they can, by sheer willpower, create whatever external conditions are necessary for them to succeed. It is the antithesis of believing in luck. It's a two-edged quality, however. On the one hand, it empowers leaders to bulldoze their way through situations that would defeat most people, while striving for goals that no one else would consider to be within their reach. On the other hand, it can be dangerous if they become too wrapped up in their messianic drive to achieve their goals and lose touch with reality.

There are two quite distinct versions of this awesome self-confidence. One is almost spiritual in its extreme manifestation of inner power, the other is a more canny audacity. The former develop a missionary zeal, directed by their sense of destiny and built on faith in their ability to carry off anything they put their minds to. These entrepreneurs don't feel the isolation that afflicts most entrepreneurs, because the world is their oyster. They create their own reality. The latter have a profound sense of their isolation, along with a full understanding of their own strengths, weaknesses and vulnerability, but they have no accompanying sense of anxiety. They have acquired an intrepid strength of character that allows them to deal with any setbacks and any triumphs with equanimity (though not passivity).

The missionaries are emotive and invulnerable, the intrepid pragmatists dispassionate, resilient and quietly persistent. The missionaries are team-oriented and visionary, the intrepid pragmatists individualists and realists. The missionaries tend to be enthusiastic, convinced of the infinite potential of all people. The intrepid pragmatists, comfortable with their acknowledged weaknesses, view their fellow humans as vulnerable, prone to error and therefore to be managed with care.

Both, however, believe their willpower can sweep all before them. They know that if they focus their energies with sufficient conviction, they will attract what they need for whatever they want.

The intrepid pragmatists are the tougher of the two. There's an edge to them, a reserve that strangers rarely penetrate. Their dispassionate way of dealing with people doesn't mean they are entirely unemotional themselves (although some of them are), but they do judge everything on its merits. The missionaries will sometimes fail ignominiously, humiliated by the yawning chasm between their visions and their realities, but they will also succeed in ventures no one else would even attempt.

Restaurant owner Peter Oliver acquired the inner power of a missionary when he was a schoolboy. His father was an Englishman who emigrated to South Africa, where he lived in grand style, in a huge house with 11 servants. But he had no job, and when he had a stroke a few years later, he left his family, including six-year-old Peter, with very little money. Oliver's mother nevertheless managed to send him to good private schools, mainly through her husband's connections and bursaries. "At school, I was acutely aware that I was the poorest guy there," Oliver says. "It kindled a desire in me never to be like that again. I used to make my mother stop the car a few blocks away from the school when she came to pick me up, so my friends wouldn't see the car we drove."

Later, at a high school 1,000 kilometres away from home, he rebelled against the discipline, and his mother had to fight to keep him in the school. Peter would rather have been partying with his girlfriends at home. He was, in every way, no better than an average student. Then he found out the rugby team for 15-year-old boys was going on a tour to Cape Town, his home town. "I decided I wanted to get into the rugby team," he says. Practising with the determination that was later to become his hallmark, he was selected for the team and went on to become its captain. "That was a turning point in my life. I realized I could do anything if I tried hard enough."

He still believes that the secret of his success is stick-to-it-iveness. "There's a positive side to every adversity you face," he says. "The key to success is to know yourself. One of my sayings is, 'There's no problem that can't be solved.'" He sets high standards for himself. "The worst kind of thing is a guy who doesn't get the results, even if he's a noble person. It's no good just being good. If you don't make a difference, you're a failure or a waste of time."

Diana Ferguson of Berwick Ferguson Payroll doesn't have Oliver's forcefulness and punch, but she shares his inner power. She is an intrepid pragmatist, who built a string of part-time clerical jobs into a million-dollar business helping companies keep track of payroll deductions. A professional actress and singer, like most of her colleagues, she earned her money in part-time jobs. "I met a lot of brilliant people," she says, "but I nearly starved to death." It so happened that many of her part-time jobs were in payroll departments, which were generally regarded as low-grade jobs at the time. She was always frustrated that the information she received from the various governments was less than informative. "I never knew whether I had the latest information. I thought to myself, someone should do a reference manual for payroll."

That was in 1975. She did her homework, building up files of information, preparing a business plan and testing the market. When she rolled out her direct-mail campaign two years later, she hoped for a response rate of 2.5% to her 8,000 letters. Almost 500 companies signed up. "I realized within five weeks that I had something on my hands that was bigger than my wildest dreams. We sold 1,000 manuals that year."

Ferguson is down-to-earth, with a great sense of fun. She has long brown hair and large facial features, with a big toothy grin. She's a colourful dresser and has decorated her office, which looks like a living room, with expensive art and furniture. She is at ease with herself. "I'm unique and I know it," she says, without a hint of pretension. "I know my own strengths and weaknesses. I enjoy the former and have come to terms with the latter." She wasn't always like this, however. "I had a terrible self-image when I was young. I had to be aggressive, because I didn't think I was as good as I was pretending to be."

By 1984, she had built a thriving business in Canada and decided to replicate it in the U.S. Like so many people, she fell flat on her face, losing a great deal of money in the process. "It was," she says, "the star syndrome at work. I went there on an ego trip. It could be done, but I wasn't the person to do it." She says it with calm acceptance, saying she learned a lot about herself, "which is always useful." She wrote off the investment and went on to build her business further in Canada, reaching sales of $1.2 million in 1987 to a clientele that includes 495 of *the Financial Post 500*. Then she sold her business to the International Thomson Organization for a cool $2 million.

"Other people have said, 'I could have done that,'" she says, "but they didn't. I've accomplished something. I've made a difference. I've made a lot of people in payroll departments richer because their bosses appreciate them more." Now she's going to use her capital to invest in other entrepreneurs in businesses where she can bring some expertise to the table. She thinks she knows why some entrepreneurs succeed and others don't: "Skills are nice, knowledge is better, but the right personality is the difference."

## DYNAMIC LEADERSHIP

Dynamic leaders are hands-on managers. The appeal of personality and values is not for them. They prefer to deal in hard objectives and results. They are adept at clearing away the obstacles to action so that they or their employees can do their jobs and get things done. They are either decisive or persistent. Very few are both. The decisive entrepreneurs are, in a way, the opposite of the persistent ones. They don't wait too long to abandon a failing project while their counterparts will make their projects work if it's the last thing they do in their lives.

Nowhere is the need for decisiveness greater than in smaller firms competing with giant companies. Against the power of immense resources, flexible responses to changing markets is the only viable strategy for entrepreneurs. Jack Donald of Parkland Industries has seen it from both sides of the fence, because he has worked in small and big companies (see page 165). He has grown the company he started from scratch into a mid-sized company which competes with multinational giants in the oil business. He has seen the paralysis of analysis in large companies, and he's not going to be caught in the same trap. "Too often in big companies," he says, "there are too many maybes. You've got to let people get on with their jobs, so you have to give them an answer or persuade them to find the answer themselves." He delegates extensively to his employees, to the point of watching them make mistakes, always provided, of course, the damage is not too serious. "It makes them grow, because every right decision improves their self-confidence. If you dump on someone for making a mistake, it impairs their decisiveness."

### Perseverance

The dynamic leaders who are persistent would rarely adopt Jack Donald's approach. That doesn't mean they're inflexible, just that they are single-minded in their pursuit of their goals. Their perseverance is an extremely powerful leadership attribute. It is important not only because it is an antidote to the extraordinary number and height of obstacles to success, but also because it is the most effective way to develop the feel for emerging patterns that gives entrepreneurs their ability to recognize opportunities before anyone else.

Klaus Deering lived off his dogged perseverance for more than 40 years, through highs and lows that would have demoralized most people. He finally walked away from it at age 63, a successful and wealthy entrepreneur, but his lived-in face maps the anguish of starting from scratch four times in his life and losing it all twice. A great big, weather-beaten bear of a man, Deering looks more like the lumberjack he once was than the president of Glenayre Electronics, a manufacturer of radio telephone systems, mobile and rural cellular telephones, and telephone answering and paging systems.

When he bought control of Glenayre in 1969, he was "44 years old, with no job, no education and no money." The company then had annual sales of about $100,000. He scraped together $2,500 to buy the company, after persuading friends to contribute another $15,000, which was enough to buy 80% of the company. He later built his interest to 23%, before he started diluting it to finance the firm's growth. In his 18 years at the helm, he took Glenayre to sales of $34 million in 1987, not bad for a man in a high-tech industry who never made it to university.

Deering comes from humble stock. His mother and father left Germany to farm in the southern Ukraine, but moved again in 1896 to northern Manitoba, where the government had set land prices unimaginably low to European ears. Although neither of his parents had any formal education, their entrepreneurial instinct rubbed off on Deering, who is uncomfortable in structured settings to this day. Despite his obvious unease at his lack of formal education, he hasn't succumbed to any sense of inadequacy. Quite the contrary. "We did very well until we became intellectual," he said a year or so before he sold out. He had hired, in quick succession, two super-qualified hotshot general managers when Glenayre's sales passed $12 million. He figured he needed more structure, but the PhDs and the MBAs didn't help. One of them changed the systems and made impossible promises on the delivery of software. "He really [devastated] the company," Deering says, with considerable force. "One project was delivered 18 months late. They got into organization charts and so on. Politics. I've got nothing against MBAs and other intellectuals; it's just that they're usually unsuccessful."

These views do not exactly endear Deering to his fellow entrepreneurs in the high-tech sector, but it doesn't bother him. He understands with great clarity where his real strength lies. "I'll whip a lawyer's ass, because I'll work eight hours to his two. I've never been able to delegate and take three-month holidays. Until we reached $12 million a year, I handled every receivable. I used to personally check work in progress at each month-end—that's two-and-a-half hours' work. Long hours, persistence, learn, learn, learn. I often work till 11 in the evening, and then I'll be in the office at 5 the next morning. I took night courses to help me understand the business."

The learning paid off for running the business, but he never did master the technology of his product: "Electronics to me is a black art," he says. Yet, through sheer dogged persistence, he developed an intuition for technological decisions. "I can read a 20-page R&D proposal, and I can always rationalize it to a simple problem. I can get them to agree on a solution." It drives his technical people up the wall. His engineers used to come into his office and tell him they were sick of his being right for the wrong reasons.

In fact, Deering consistently plunged into industries he knew very little about. When he first came into Glenayre, he had just gone broke in a mining venture. "I thought I could learn to be a miner, but I was being mined by them." Although he's been broke twice, he has never had to declare bankruptcy, because he's always paid off all his bills. He had businesses in logging and sawmills, the advertising industry, manufacturing TV sets and mining before he found Glenayre. His failures were generally caused by lack of sophistication, but his perseverance proved more powerful in the end.

Deering nevertheless acknowledges the difficulties of relying so heavily on perseverance. After he had stepped down from the chairmanship of Glenayre, he said, "I'm a great guy to get something going and drive it to a certain point. But now we need another guy who's more attuned to the market and who can do a better job of choosing products and so on. I don't want to take it any further now." Two years after he ceded the helm, Glenayre's sales had doubled to more than $50 million. In 1989, it was taken over by Trans Canada Glass, which has become a key link in Cantel's national network of cellular telephones.

## CEREBRAL LEADERSHIP

Cerebral leaders articulate ideals for their businesses, giving their employees a framework in which to exercise their initiative. Sometimes cerebral leaders select as their ideal the quality of their product. They commit themselves totally to quality, allowing the ideal of a perfect product to embody the values of the company. Others choose more abstract ideals that define the purpose of their business.

Many cerebral leaders are intuitive lateral thinkers, able to come up with all or most of the ideas themselves, but that is not a prerequisite. The critical skill in cerebral leaders is not coming up with the ideas; it is communicating their concepts with such a clear sense of purpose that their followers can identify with them and work together in pursuing them. The best ideas in the world will not work if the people implementing them do not understand them.

John Seltzer of GBB Associates has the unusual distinction of leading a firm of professionals although he does not himself have the professional qualifications of his colleagues. His firm of consulting actuaries has become one of the top firms in

Canada, and Seltzer's leadership skills so impressed his colleagues at George B. Buck, the giant U.S. firm that bought control of GBB, that they asked him to be their chairman too.

Now retired, Seltzer's irrepressible energy, which will keep him going at full speed until he drops, is still apparent. He just loves to build businesses. Having taken GBB and Buck as far as he could, he jumped into new ventures as soon as he withdrew from actuarial consulting. In the four years he was chairman of Buck, he added 16 new branches to the ten it had when he started. He transformed it from a U.S. firm to an international one, travelling almost constantly as he built alliances and contacts throughout Europe and the U.S. He's calm and friendly, almost jolly, with a ready smile never far away, but he's also a stickler for detail, meticulous and demanding. A very private man, he keeps his feelings under lock and key, yet he has a strong empathy that makes it easy for clients and employees to confide in him.

He started his career in an insurance firm, then bounced between actuarial consultants and trust companies, before realizing that the only way he was going to find a firm that suited his ideals was to start his own. When he was laying the groundwork for his own firm, he and Barry Sutton, his actuary partner, decided to add a third partner who could bring to GBB money, good software for actuarial consulting, or solid leads to clients. They found candidates for all three roles, but the best offer came from George B. Buck, one of the leading firms of consulting actuaries in the U.S., which bought a third of the firm from Seltzer and Sutton. "Buck had a superlative professional reputation," he says, "although I later realized they had enormous deficiencies in business development." Buck's software (which GBB bought in an arm's-length deal), however, proved successful for GBB and the partnership prospered.

Buck bought control of GBB Associates four years later, in 1976. GBB was by then doing extremely well, growing much faster than Buck, and the people at Buck drew the appropriate conclusion. They asked Seltzer to take over as chief executive in New York. Seltzer declined, preferring the environment of Toronto to that of New York. The next time there was a changing of the guard at Buck, however, in 1984, the board asked Seltzer to be its non-executive chairman and he accepted.

When Seltzer took the chair at Buck, he presided over a firm employing 1,000 people and grossing $120 million a year, including an impressive $10 million from GBB after only 14 years in business. "But they had no idea how to run their business," he says. "People used to leave board meetings because a client was on the phone. I stopped all that. The meetings start on time now and no one leaves until it's over—although we do allow people to go to the washroom." An even bigger problem was getting the directors to focus on their business rather than their professions. "Board meetings were an occasion to chat about coffee and tea and professional questions. They could talk all day without arriving at a decision."

When his appointment was made, he compiled a list of 250 items that Buck's board, its chairman and its president should be doing. Each was classified as to whether it involved information only, a discussion or a decision (although some involved more than one category). At his first board meeting, he presented the list to his colleagues and asked for deletions and changes. They made three changes and agreed to operate on that basis. "It still works now. Every time a new member of the board is appointed, he receives a copy of the list. I was able to put in rational terms what they should be doing. I can apply the pros and cons and make sense of it. I led them out of their collegial system."

## LEADERSHIP BY OWNERSHIP

Only a tenth of the people in this book ran their companies with the attitude that they derive their authority from their ownership rather than their power to influence or lead people. That's an attitude far more common in large bureaucracies and tends not to last long in entrepreneurial firms, because the unstable environments in which they operate usually make it difficult to maintain ownership without an enthusiastic staff.

These leaders tend to deal with their followers in a contractual way, relying on their employees' self-interest to motivate them rather than trying to find their hot buttons themselves. Few of them are warm people, and if they do get enthusiastic over anything, it's more likely to be over something technical connected with their businesses than over people. They pay a price for this attitude, however. Few of them grow rapidly.

## PARTNERSHIPS

Ramona Beauchamp built her fashion agency, Ramona Beauchamp International, on raw willpower and talent. She succeeded because she could anticipate the needs of her market. At a time when fashion models were still viewed as expensive clothes pegs, she foresaw that designers would soon start looking for models who were alive and could relate to their audiences. She trained her models to act and dance, so that she was ready with her vivacious "talents" when the designers needed them. She then used her understanding of how people can best present themselves to start a management consulting business for executives who want to create the right impression. Against the advice of everyone she talked to, she also started a school for children, teaching them how to act for television. It wasn't the pictures on the screen that sold the parents, it was the incredible self-confidence it built in the children when they saw what they could do in a medium they all understood.

Unfortunately, Beauchamp was not a good businesswoman. She started her business in 1969. As soon as she started generating some revenues, she realized she needed some help with the business side and hired someone to do her books. In 1975, that person embezzled every penny she possessed. Ashamed of her incompetence, she told almost no one, but she did learn her lesson. She nurtured some close friends, whom she knew she could trust implicitly, and built them up to the point where she could give them significant responsibility. One of them had worked in her agency for years, the other she hired away from Eaton's.

"I'm good at packaging and marketing," she said then. "I have to hire someone who's good at business. I'm not a good negotiator. I'm terrible. I give in. If someone says they are having a hard time, I give them a course free. So my partners handle that side." Ever generous, Beauchamp gave them each a third of her business. "I thought," she said much later, "if I gave them as much as I could, it would give them an incentive. I wouldn't be taking the whole pie." It was a move she lived to regret.

In early 1987, well before the stock-market crash, Beauchamp completed all the paperwork to go public on the Vancouver Stock Exchange. She could see the promise in her corporate consulting, and her marketing would be helped by being a public company. But she reckoned without her partners, who didn't want to expand the corporate business. They wanted to stick with fashion shows. Not only that, they felt Beauchamp ran too expensive a shop. They figured they could make a lot more money by being more careful with their expenses. They hired a new person to run the agency, outvoting Beauchamp when she protested.

The new manager and Beauchamp's two partners cut staff by half, doubling the student/teacher ratio, and started using cheaper materials. They cut back on service. "We've always had a reputation of being classy," Beauchamp said soon after her partnership collapsed. "Our structure was superior to anything I'd seen. I slept at night. They didn't pay attention to how people are treated when they come in the door."

It was too much for Beauchamp. She quit and sold her share of the business. Although her partners later came round to seeing her point of view and switched back to her way of running the company, it was too late to save the partnership. They are now on good terms, and Beauchamp has smelled the flowers for the first time in many, many years, but she is deeply disappointed. "If I had to do it over again, I would have kept control."

Beauchamp's story is not an isolated one. An extraordinary percentage of partnerships end up in messy divorces. Half the people in this book have partners—two-thirds of them are individual partners who are active in the business, and the rest are evenly divided between corporate partners and individual silent partners. There are unmistakable patterns in the success ratios of these businesses.

The silent partner usually doesn't want to be involved in the day-to-day operations, so the operating entrepreneur can get on with running the business. The problems that do arise tend to be operating difficulties rather than personality clashes or strategic differences.

Corporate partnerships are often fraught with difficulties. The objectives of the large company are seldom in tune with those of the small company. The big business may be seeking an entrée into a new market, or keeping a hand in an emerging technology, or even dabbling because an executive wants to try something new. Many large companies are trying to find a way of structuring partnerships with small companies, but it will work only if they accommodate the objectives of the entrepreneurs.

Individual partnerships, like Ramona Beauchamp's, can succeed, but they work best if the leader retains voting control. The best partnerships among the entrepreneurs in this book all had minority partners who accepted the role of the leader and who were happy to play second fiddle. The leaders responded accordingly, seldom going ahead with a plan that did not win the agreement of the minority partner. Equal partnerships also work well, particularly if they have a shot-gun clause. The problems posed by these partnerships can be enormous, but they are dwarfed by the eruptions that can destroy family partnerships. Benoit Métivier, former President of IPL in St. Damien, a small town in the Beauce region of Quebec, can attest to that. IPL had annual sales of $55 million in 1988 and net income of $3.1 million. It produces 500 different products, mostly in auto parts, containers and packaging materials, which are exported to the U.S., Europe, Australia and Japan. Its factory is equipped with the most modern machinery, and the quality of its products is given high ratings by the auto companies. Much of that success can be attributed to Benoit, the second son in a family of seven children.

Métivier's father, Emile, started IPL in 1939 to manufacture toothbrushes and built it slowly to annual sales of $6 million in 1971 before he died of cancer. He left his four sons with equal shares in the business and they elected, naturally enough, the eldest son, Rémi, to be president. Rémi took personal charge of sales and threw himself into the task with vigour. He increased sales significantly to about $20 million, before the company started stagnating. By the time the recession came in 1981, the family knew that something had to be done. The administration was chaotic, Rémi's focus on sales was getting him into fights with production, and morale was plummeting.

In 1982, the family appointed Benoit president. He immediately restored co-operation between departments and started building team spirit. Four years later, he had doubled sales, started a major modernization program and rationalized IPL's product line. Profits, however, had not moved up in line with sales. In early 1987, he decided he had to quit because he couldn't work with his brothers any longer.

Benoit is a conservative man. He grew up with a father who took enormous risks, and he swore he'd never be the same. "My father's time was tough," he says now. "He was always buying companies, and we were always over our head in debt. He made all his children live the same way. We all worked 70 to 80 hours a week." Benoit is a good family man who believes in a balance between work and family, so he was in constant fear of becoming a slave to his business. When he ran the family firm, he made sure the risk-taking subsided. He slashed the debt/equity ratio and took the company public in 1985. "I put it on a solid base," he says.

Gentle, warm and sensitive, Benoit is immediately likeable, with his crumpled clothes and with his bashed-in face around his crooked nose. He's open and interested, always seeking understanding. He's also tenacious and loves working with people, but he could never start a business from scratch. Most of all, he has a horror of repeating the experience of one family in which a messy transfer of the family business between generations so embittered some members of the family that they would cross the street in tiny St. Damien to avoid having to acknowledge one another.

Benoit believes in consensus. He would work at persuading his brothers that he had the right approach, but he was slow to assert himself with Rémi, who was still smarting from his loss of the presidency. Rémi would order the vice president of marketing to do things which directly contravened Benoit's directions, and Benoit would not explode. He would work it through, gradually chipping away at the dissent. He went to great lengths to compliment his brothers on their good ideas, all the time proclaiming that he didn't have many good ideas, he just knew how to implement them. Benoit had worked for years in administration and on the shop floor. He knew about production. His brothers all liked sales. He built a top-class team of managers, radically improving quality control.

Although he got most of what he wanted, the battles with his brothers began to tire him. "You have got to have the respect of the family," he said a year after he quit. "I can't keep banging the table and saying I'm the boss." His collegial approach left a lot of grey areas and his brothers took advantage of them. "I like business, even when it's hard, but if you can't have a climate of unanimity in the firm, it's not worth it. Power for the sake of power is not for me. Money for the sake of money isn't either." He quit and the Métivier brothers appointed the youngest brother, Julien, as chief executive.

Benoit is resigned to his departure now, having severed all ties with the management, although he remains on the board. He talks of the achievement of having worked together successfully for 30 years. But he can't hide his disappointment. He hopes his brothers will succeed; however, he is too sensitive to decisions he feels may turn out to be wrong. If he could do it all again, he would have bought voting control when he had the chance during the 1981-82 recession.

# CHAPTER 10

# LEADERS
# DO IT THEIR WAY

*"I do most of my managing by wandering about. I go on the shop floor every day—not for the sake of checking up, I just like to talk to them. I know 80% of my 200 employees by name. I can identify every part on the shop floor."*
— John Buhler of Farm King Allied

*"Everyone knows what they have to do, so it requires very little supervision. The managers here have the easiest management jobs in the world. There's not a lot of room for initiative— you set up a system and they follow it."*
— Karl Magid of Lulu's

**W**hen Francine Brulé wanted to say thank you to her staff of five women a few years back, she took them all to New York for the weekend. She arranged for stretched limousines to ferry them around, she took them to a Broadway play, she lunched them at the Rockefeller Plaza, she fêted them at a fancy discotheque. From Friday morning to Sunday evening, her sales staff lived the life of the rich and famous.

She doesn't take them to New York every year, but her Christmas parties never fail to leave their mark on the young women whose extraordinary energy and enthusiasm helped her firm, Les Agences Francine Brulé, grow to annual sales of $10 million in its first eight years. It's Brulé's way of maintaining morale in the wholesale fashion business that is so pressurized that few employees can take the pace for long.

With 18 lines of clothing, Les Agences Francine Brulé has become a pressure cooker, squeezed by late deliveries and fickle fashions. It's a feast-or-famine business. "It's eight or nine months of madness now," she says. "Burn-out is a big problem. The pressure's so strong, you cannot relax." A prodigious worker herself, Brulé draws out every ounce of youthful energy in her employees, all of whom are saleswomen or potential saleswomen, even the receptionist. There is no time for "management," she just wants her employees to sell, sell, sell. She doesn't motivate them by tempting them with promotions and supervisory responsibilities. She pays them good commissions, demands top performance and makes sure they have fun. She gives them a lot of short vacations during slow spells. And when they let off steam, she wants the benefits to last.

She leads this manic charge by sheer force of character. She's immersed in every detail of her business. When a new line comes in, she and her husband, Pierre Brosseau, are in the shop over the weekend ticketing the clothes. She's fully in control of herself and her destiny. When she walks into a room, everyone else can feel her palpable energy. At 34, her face shows no sign of the pressure, lit up by an infectious smile.

Typically, she didn't blanch at the crucial choice faced by all young women who go into business—she had three children in less than five years. She says she always made time for them, aiming to play with them for two hours a day and taking care never to be away from them two nights in a row. But with many meetings starting at 8 a.m. and days that often ended well into the evening, that wasn't always possible. Something had to give. The parallel full-time jobs of building a business and raising three infants were too much for her and she began to lose control. She couldn't find the time to groom herself to be the image of a fashion queen. The 50 surplus pounds she acquired having her second and third babies clung to her despite valiant efforts to shed them. In desperation, she appointed her best saleswoman, Natalie Audet, general manager. It never really worked, although it did give her time to recover her svelte figure and restore her vital good looks. Two years later, she was back in the thick of the action, and the General Manager went back to selling.

Brulé is completely unpretentious and direct, uninterested in her lawyer husband's prestigious contacts in the world of politics. She also sees her business with clear eyes, unfazed by the glamour that blinds so many of her competitors. Her uncompromising business view extends to her employees. She doesn't spend much time worrying about their state of mind. She wants them to be ambitious and good saleswomen. They don't even need to have dress sense, just as long as they can move the merchandise.

Brulé is a stereotypical entrepreneur. She has the vision, she has the drive and she makes all the decisions. Her leadership of her admiring employees is based on her inner power and her sound business judgement. She is a one-person show and it can be no other way. If she is to persuade a fashion manufacturer to distribute its products through her firm, she cannot easily delegate the supplier contact to an employee. "Why," she asks, "would anyone give their collection to Francine Brulé if they can't even speak to Francine Brulé? And if the salespeople speak direct to the manufacturer, why should they work for me?"

Brulé may be stereotypical, but she is not typical. She is a solo leader. Other entrepreneurs are osmosis leaders, managerial leaders, system leaders and figureheads.

## SOLO LEADERS

Solo leaders are the one-person shows. They include a remarkable number who lead through inner power; they also tend to be enthusiastic and committed to the quality of their products (see Appendix C, Table 10.1). They are seldom adept at articulating concepts to their employees, whom they often feel don't need to know where the firm is going. Solo leaders seldom seek consensus, seeing their employees more as implementors than as decision-makers.

Francine Brulé says she has great respect for her employees and says they can all make decisions, "but they never make a decision without telling me," she says. "I'm the one with judgement. I'm not too tactful. I've been doing it a long time." She does, however, bounce ideas off them. "It's a family. If I have an idea, I ask them their opinion. It motivates them." In a sales organization, everyone has to know what's going on, but Brulé's leadership style means that only she knows enough to be the hub.

The computer offers the potential for her to do even more business without losing her place at the hub. That, and her faith in herself, dissolve the limits on Brulé's ambition. She looks at the eclectic collections of companies owned by many of the leading modern entrepreneurs and muses she can do the same thing. She already has extensive interests outside her firm, including sizeable investments in real estate and the stock market (she's on the phone two or three times a day with her broker), and she owns a small publishing company which has produced a coffee-table art book. Even if she grows to sales of $50 million, however, she will never stop being a solo leader.

She has unlimited confidence in her ability to achieve whatever she sets out to do. She grew up in a poor family and decided she was going to break the cycle. As a teenager, she went to Toronto to make her fortune, armed with only $300. She worked for four years in a clothing manufacturer, then took off to travel before returning to become a salesperson with a distributor. When she was ready, she quit to start her own firm. "The only person who blocks you is yourself," she says. "If the world could understand that you don't have to have talent, you just have to want it. It's a gift of life. I'm very religious. I'm made like that. I have so much energy. I've got a natural charisma." She has indeed achieved everything she visualized, including a Mercedes Benz and a magnificent mansion in the heart of anglo Montreal. "Life sends me what I need when I need it. Everything happens on its own."

## OSMOSIS LEADERS

John Buhler of Farm King Allied won't allow any of his employees to send inter-office memos to him or to one another. "They're only to cover your ass," he says with his ever-ready chuckle. But he's not joking. When he bought the Winnipeg subsidiary of Allied Farm Equipment Ltd. in 1981, he fired all the executive assistants at Allied. Most especially, he says, he fired all the people who typed inter-office memos and all the people who filed them. He felt bad about it, but knew he would have felt worse if he hadn't done it.

Buhler is a turnaround artist, who buys companies cheap and makes them fly. When he acquires a new company, he asks everyone what their job is and if they don't know, he lets them go. Like many entrepreneurs, he has declared war on bureaucracy and goes to great lengths to avoid any suggestion of formal structures or rules and regulations in his business. He has been known to allow an inter-office memo, such as instructions to his staff when he was installing his computer system, but then he has to be able to break his own regulations, or he would start to feel like a bureaucrat.

His view of inter-office memos is only the tip of his leadership iceberg. When he bought Allied, he also fired the personnel manager, the parts manager and all the quality control people. The departure of the quality control unit created chaos for a while, but most of the production workers loved it. Buhler's philosophy is simple. The good workers don't need quality control, so, rather than hire quality inspectors to control the bad workers, why not simply get rid of the bad workers?

Buhler is an osmosis leader. (The *Collins English Dictionary* defines *osmosis* as "diffusion through any membrane or porous barrier.") These entrepreneurs seek out extensive contact with employees throughout their enterprises but, unlike the solo leaders, they develop managers rather than run everything themselves. While they respect the role of their managers, however, they do not hesitate to exert active and aggressive leadership at any level in their organization. These are the quintessential entrepreneurial leaders, hands-on and involved.They often pride themselves on their decisiveness (a good thing, since they make so many decisions) and rarely lead through their inner power (see Appendix C, Table 10.1).

Buhler has a powerful personal bond with his workers, as do all osmosis leaders. He respects his managers' authority, but his affection is reserved for the people on the shop floor. He values them as much as he values his managers. He spends a lot of time walking around his plants talking to his production workers and salespeople—not to check up on them, but just because he likes talking to them. He says he knows 80% of his 200 workers by their first names. When he strolls up to a lathe and chats with the operator, he knows every inch of the machine, and he knows that worker's history with the firm, down to his most recent productivity performance. They talk like fellow workers, delving into the technicalities. There's a respect and, on the part of Buhler, a transparent joy at being on the floor, where the action is.

When he started quality circles at his factories, Buhler insisted that they report to him through a leader whom they elected themselves. He has adopted every recommendation they have made. In this quest to develop leadership among his workers, he also hired a management consultant to teach them how to go about it, and is delighted that employees are beginning to understand they can get through to management. And he still doesn't have a personnel manager.

To keep the barrier between his workers and himself as thin and porous as possible, Buhler has the simplest of management structures. Everyone reports to him. They all spend time working with one another, of course, but there is no reporting structure, except for a weekly meeting of all the managers. He even negotiates the union contract himself. It takes him 45 minutes a year. He has even managed to persuade the union to accept wage scales that incorporate wage premiums for things like attitude and productivity, as well as training and seniority.

The big advantage of Buhler's extensive contact with employees throughout the organization is that it gives him a remarkable degree of control over the company's operations. He knows every salesman's collection record and the productivity record of everyone on the shop floor. He signs every cheque that goes out of Farm King Allied, not because he doesn't trust anyone, but because it helps him know what's going on. Osmosis managers know all the skeletons in their enterprises' cupboards.

That makes it tough to be a manager in Buhler's firm. His knowledge of how everything works in his business is the wellspring of his leadership. But if the owner is into everything, what's left for the managers? Buhler is not a solo leader, however. He delegates to his managers and appreciates the importance of persuading them that his ideas are right if he wants them to implement them properly. "I'll spend weeks and months trying to get management to see my logic, but sometimes I just have to say, 'This is the way it has to be done'—and 18 months later they see it."

Buhler is a little unusual for osmosis leaders because he

possesses remarkable inner power. He is totally secure in himself. He has no pretensions; he is self-deprecating and projects the image of a jolly, easy-going man. But he is emotionally very strong, able to withstand almost any setback, able to lie in wait indefinitely for the perfect opportunity, without any trepidation or self-doubt. He is also not afraid of failure, convinced that he can always provide for his family, because no person and no setback can take away his energy and his talents.

## MANAGERIAL LEADERS

Jack Donald has been pumping gas since he was a schoolboy. In 1987, at the age of 53, the company he started ten years earlier and in which he is still the biggest shareholder, became Canada's newest integrated oil company. By buying a refinery that Shell Canada no longer needed, Donald's Parkland Industries put the last piece of the puzzle into place, rounding out the oil- and gas-producing properties, the drilling rigs and the Fas Gas service stations that blanket Alberta and spill into Saskatchewan. A licenced mechanic, who still loves to get his hands dirty, Donald has left his love of machinery far behind, to become one of the stellar oil-patch entrepreneurs in Alberta.

A large man, with hands like frying pans and a teddy-bear face often creased in a smile, Donald is not what he seems. He dresses casually in jeans and a plaid shirt with no tie, like most of his employees, most of whom he knows by their first names. With his powerful physique and his obvious affinity for the nuts and bolts of his business, he looks rough-hewn and tough, just like someone in the oil patch should look. But he has a sensitive side. He is happiest when he's dealing with people. He is also an art lover. Pioneer sculptures and paintings, painstakingly assembled in countless visits to art galleries and auctions all over western Canada and the U.S., are prominent in and around his office, along with numerous magazines and collectors' guides devoted to western art.

He doesn't talk much about his artistic interests, however. He may be understated and unpretentious, but his plans are on a grand scale. He wants to employ a lot of people, and he wants to weld them into a superb organization that works like clockwork. He has the people skills and he is a canny strategist, so it's no surprise that annual sales at Parkland Industries have risen from $4 million in 1978 to $110 million in the year ending June, 1988, a compound growth rate of almost 40% a year.

Along the way, Donald has learned to be a highly effective manager. Managerial leaders show much greater respect for the lines of authority than do osmosis leaders. They are open to ideas and initiatives from employees at lower levels, but what contact they do have with these people tends to be social or casual. Any actions they might take as a result of these contacts would be through the managers, not direct. They are good delegators and generally monitor their subordinates closely. They make very few decisions without reference to their managers, and frequently rely on their projection of personal integrity as their most important leadership skill (see Appendix C, Table 10.1).

It takes some discipline for Donald to fit this mould as well as he does. His hands-on experience means he could do all of their jobs as well as or better than they could. He has paid his dues in every aspect of his business, having worked in gas stations, refineries and in sales. He started out doing the same thing he did in his summers at school, pumping gas. He quickly rose to become manager, before moving to a Texaco refinery where he worked as a senior lab technician for two years. At age 23, he left the world of big business to start his own firm, an auto service centre in Edmonton. That lasted only three years before he went back to being an employee. For the next four years, he was a salesman for two oil companies in Edmonton and Calgary, before BA Oil bought out his employer and he went back to being an entrepreneur, at 30 years old this time.

Over the next seven years, he built a chain of gas stations, taking business courses by night while his wife Joan ran the gas bars for him (she's now assistant corporate secretary of Parkland). He eventually sold his chain to Turbo Resources, the high-flying integrated oil company that was the darling of the stock markets during the 1970s. At Turbo, he became the marketing vice president, responsible, as he describes it, for putting the people together, while the secretary treasurer Jack Killick crunched the numbers and president Bob Brawn struck the deals in the orgy of acquisitions that went into building up Turbo.

The early years at Turbo were thrilling. The trio at the top developed into a tight-knit team that wowed the oil patch. Donald built the company from 50 to 215 stations in only five years, but the company as a whole couldn't adjust to the rapid growth. The hiring went out of control and cash was wasted to the point where the company slipped into trouble and lost its credibility. After Donald and Killick both left in 1976, Turbo's decline started in earnest. At age 42, Donald was on his own again, although this time he made no mistakes. He built his Fas Gas stations more steadily than he had at Turbo. It took him 12 years to build the chain to 87 stations in 1987, before he made his first big jump,when he added 46 properties by buying a small chain called Armenco in 1989. Parkland is solid. It has survived the severe downturns in the oil industry in the 1980s with barely a flicker, sales dropping in only one year (1987) and profits increasing every year from 1982 to 1988.

Even with sales of more than $100 million, he still has only 15 senior and junior managers. Not surprisingly, there's no formality in his management style. He calls management meetings only when there is a problem big enough to make him feel like calling a meeting. He goes round the table asking all of them in turn to report on their problems and opportunities. Yet, although he knows the answers to most of the problems, he lets them figure it out for themselves: "You have to work damn hard at refusing to make decisions for people."

He acknowledges the trickiness of changing into a manager after so many years of running small, hands-on businesses. The biggest change for him was that he had to learn to watch his own behaviour carefully. When Parkland became big, Donald couldn't spend enough time with all his employees for them to be able to comfortably "read" him. "You find your every word has greater repercussions," he says. "People take different meanings out of your words. So you can't shoot from the hip anymore."

Most importantly, he doesn't try to force this style onto his managers. One of his most trusted advisors is Andy Goruk, who has run his drilling rigs from the beginning. "Andy is the best rig man in Alberta," says Donald, "because he has the technical and people skills." Goruk, who likes to run a hands-on operation, could never learn to delegate like his boss, so Donald doesn't try to force him. He won't expand the drilling operation beyond a size that Goruk can handle with his style. If he has to expand, he will put together a parallel operation, leaving Goruk free to run his show without vice presidents. Donald builds his business around his people.

Few entrepreneurs can build really big companies unless they grow out of being solo or osmosis leaders. Rod Bryden of Kinburn (annual sales of $900 million in 1988) and Marcel Dutil of Canam Manac (annual sales of $644 million in 1988) are both managerial leaders. The span of control in companies this size makes it close to impossible to be an osmosis leader who can maintain contact with employees at every level. Close to impossible, that is, but not impossible. Jimmy Pattison of the Jim Pattison Group is still an osmosis leader even after his annual sales topped $1.5 billion. Mere size hasn't stopped him from keeping an iron grip on every corner of his sprawling empire.

## SYSTEM LEADERS

Just outside Kitchener, in prosperous southwest Ontario, there is a gigantic nightclub called Lulu's. It's the third largest nightclub in North America, and the *Guinness Book of World Records* credits it with having both the longest and the second-longest bars in the world. Lulu's is owned by Karl Magid, a quintessential entrepreneur who has experimented with just about every technique known to capitalism to make money. Yet his leadership style defies the stereotype of the entrepreneur. He is a system leader.

System leaders run their organizations through systems, which they create to make their employees' decisions a matter of following guidelines. Once the system is in place, they can sit back and watch it work. There is little need to have any contact at all with employees at lower levels. The entrepreneurs run their businesses through elaborate reporting systems, contributing little in the way of leadership through ideas or personal values (see Appendix C, Table 10.1). It is also the only style in which it is not uncommon to find leadership by ownership. They tend to make plans on their own, after consulting their employees. Their day-to-day decisions, however, tend to be based on a high degree of consensus, if only because the system ensures that both entrepreneurs and their managers fit their decisions into the context of the system. Unlike the first three leadership styles, they often let their managers learn through their mistakes.

Magid fits this mould, except that his system is so watertight that there's no room for managers to make mistakes. Six and a half feet tall, Magid is languid and soft-spoken, not at all like the hustler he says he has been since he was 16. Yet he has sold everything from balloons through magazine subscriptions to vacuum cleaners. In the 1940s, he was the youngest licensed street vendor in Toronto, hawking ribbons when the Argonauts were at home. He used to ply the crowds at parades, selling them balloons or souvenirs. At age 18, he put down $800 to start his own Arthur Murray School of Dancing. He's even operated a weight-guessing booth at carnivals. At age 23, he went into the real estate business, which landed him in the restaurant business when he couldn't find a tenant for one of his developments.

"It's all the same thing," he says. "Now I'm hustling drinks instead of balloons." Actually, he still hustles balloons—1,500 of them a night at Lulu's, each one colour-coded to signify the intentions of the person who bought it. Yellow means a shy, coy person, white is a virgin (a woman with two white balloons is a born-again virgin), red and blue signify women or men respectively who want to have some fun, and silver means the holder of the helium balloon "wants to get lucky." Purple takes care of the next step. Magid opened Lulu's right next to Highway 401 in 1984. He bought a washed-up, 75,000-square-foot K-Mart store and turned it into one huge singles bar, which can accommodate 3,000 people officially (although there are more than that on a good night). The whole area is furnished with oak furniture, all the same height, so it looks like a giant maze when it's empty. He has installed a magnificent sound system, which is the envy of the many bands who play there, including Chubby Checker, the Platters and more modern groups. The huge sunken dance floor in the centre is surrounded by numerous fast-food stalls and specialty bars. Although it is only open on Thursdays, Fridays and Saturdays, Lulu's draws people from all over southern Ontario, often by the busload, and has 20 acres for them to park in. It is quite simply amazing.

Magid runs his nightclub with an iron hand. He watches every ratio daily and works to an elaborate plan that maps out every detail of the operation in advance. He leaves nothing to chance. He monitors the activity from a wood-panelled control room high above the floor, where he spends most of his time when he's in the nightclub. Furnished with a deep shag rug and plush furniture, and equipped with a fridge and bar, the real reason for the control room is the $60,000 TV system that monitors every inch of Lulu's. Nine closed-circuit cameras, placed at strategic points around the floor, can be controlled from Magid's aerie. They can zoom in on a transaction at any one of the cash registers, with a sharp enough image to see the change on the waitresses' trays and the writing on the order slips. There's also a machine that can plug into any of the cash registers and print out exact copies of the slips being produced on the floor.

The cash registers are all connected to the main computer, which prints out daily summaries of cash receipts, inventories and gross profit margins. Magid makes sure the proper percentage of his $6 million in sales falls down to the bottom line. The employees all know about the system, but its Big Brother aspect doesn't seem to bother them. For Magid, it's the only way to control such a big operation. "I designed it all myself, so I know every nook and cranny. I can walk through the place and tell you in ten minutes if anything's wrong."

He didn't hit on Lulu's overnight, of course. He had worked his way up from a 100-seat restaurant, to a 120-seater and finally to a 200-seat restaurant, before he finally decided he had so many ideas he couldn't fit in that he had to go for a big one. "It could have been 125,000 square feet or 50,000," he says, "but this one was available at a good price in a good location." He does all his own design and acts as his own general contractor. That way he controls costs and keeps his breakeven down to a reasonable level. He says many restaurants fail because the owners can't wait to get going, so they pay $15 a square foot and wind up working for the landlord. Not Magid. He put up $1 million for Lulu's the first year and $½ million the second and got his money back by the end of the third. "Lulu's doesn't owe me any money," he said in early 1987. "I hate owing money. I pay it back then get on a free ride. A business should pay back the investment in a year."

He has analyzed the techniques he has developed over the years and distilled it into a formula that prevents most mishaps and makes him a lot of money. "The managers here have the easiest management jobs in the world," he says phlegmatically. He has broken down every function to make it so simple that "any fool" could do it. Everyone knows what they have to do, so it requires very little supervision, leaving Magid to dabble in his real estate business and cut back on the prodigious hours he has put in for most of his entrepreneurial career. He leaves the management now to his general manager (who used to be his bank manager) and seven assistant managers. The only things he still does himself are booking the entertainers and negotiating their contracts.

## FIGUREHEAD LEADERS

Michael Potter bought Cognos in 1977, when its annual sales were $5 million, and turned it into one of the great high-tech success stories, with annual sales that almost reached $108 million in 1988. He's still chairman and chief executive officer, he still holds the largest block of shares in the company (30%), but he doesn't pretend for one minute that he can, or should, run the company's day-to-day operations. He gave that job to a top-notch executive whom he hired to impart the disciplined structure to Cognos that he could not provide and without which a company that size cannot survive. He is a figurehead leader.

Figurehead leaders defy the popular image of entrepreneurs. With their hands-off style, they don't try to run their businesses, leaving that task to their hired experts, whom they monitor only lightly. They concentrate instead on setting an example, establishing a tone for the business or acting as a resource for their employees (see Appendix C, Table 10.1). They rarely lead by inner power or decisiveness. It is perhaps the purest form of leadership, and works only if they hire the best talent available. In their planning, they almost all ask their employees to participate in the process, acknowledging that their own views may have to take a back seat. And they tend to limit themselves to active management of the firm only in areas where they have special expertise or interest.

When Potter first suggested to his colleagues that they should hire "a real pro with structured experience" to run the day-to-day operations at Cognos, some of the inside directors felt it wasn't necessary. The company had, under Potter's leadership, built up an extraordinary head of steam with its software package, Powerhouse, which enables programmers to use powerful application software to enhance the programs they write for specialized customers. But Potter knew he needed help and with the support of the majority of the board, he and two outside directors began looking at management development in the fall of 1986. The result was the hiring of Tom Csathy as president and chief operating officer.

Csathy has impressive credentials. He worked for IBM for 20 years, then spent three years as the CEO of Burroughs Canada. He inspires something akin to awe in Potter. "We've gone from not-so-good to much better. We succeeded [previously] because we were smaller and playing in the minor leagues." In the Cognos that Potter had developed, the process of making decisions and developing strategy reflected his own character—sensitive to the individual needs of the employees and oriented toward consensus. Potter knew how to maximize his employees' creativity, but he was less adept at imposing the rigorous discipline to translate that creativity into profits. Csathy brought a different feel to the company. "He's not autocratic," Potter said at the time, "but he accelerates the process of consensus-building. With Tom, the process of decision-making will have much more structure. There's no cure for a decision not made."

Potter feels no loss in giving over so much responsibility to Csathy. Despite his big-business background, Csathy has slipped easily into the culture at Cognos. "He's a pace setter," says Potter. And Potter still has a critical role to play in the company. Only three of the top ten executives report to him now, but they are all concerned with the long term—corporate development, research and marketing. His leadership is now more tightly focussed on setting a corporate tone or culture, keeping Cognos opportunistic, creative and entrepreneurial.

As such, he has a significant impact on events in his firm, but he does it through building a consensus rather than through the autocratic exercise of power. He motivates people by giving them a piece of the action. As soon as he bought 100% of Quasar, the predecessor company of Cognos, he distributed 25% of the shares to 86 employees. This progressed to an annual event that gives all employees share purchase opportunities and key employees stock options. He also gives people enormous autonomy, secure in his belief that the culture and sense of ownership in Cognos employees guarantee they'll do their best. "I let people make mistakes to a very high degree," he says, adding that he doesn't "allow a person with good intentions to feel that a mistake damages his career."

Potter has an acute sense of what's important to people. He spends a great deal of time with a broad cross-section of employees at all levels of the company, finding out about their problems, helping them understand their strengths and weaknesses, telling them when they're off track. However, he doesn't do this the way an osmosis leader would. He operates at a more subliminal level, imparting his values and getting a feel for the mood in all areas of the company.

This gives him a good feel for projects or ideas that offer potential for rapid growth. He wants to remove all constraints from creative people by promoting opportunism. This is what gave Cognos its first and best breakthrough. One of the programmers, Bob Minns, decided he needed a master program to help him write the programs he was developing for Quasar's clients. So he went ahead and developed it without telling anyone until it was finished. When Potter found out about it, he immediately recognized its potential and it became the report-writer component of Powerhouse. He believes that formalized management throws too many resources at small ideas that are working, rather than creating "an environment where individuals feel they can try something on their own."

He sees himself as more of a coach than a leader. "I have none of the attributes of a strong leader," he says. "I am not a persuasive speaker and I'm not particularly decisive." Like many people, he equates leadership with inner power and decisiveness. Nevertheless, he does have strong leadership qualities. He transmits his personal values to the people at Cognos, giving the company a strong culture that nurtures creativity. "There's a subtle way one's personality can be imprinted on a company," he says quietly, "and that includes the good as well as the bad. I'm not punctual, for example. But respect for the individual in Cognos is high. It's important everyone be given a chance to grow. We're egalitarian."

He is also extraordinarily persistent, prepared to work relentlessly for a goal on occasions. In a company where people are encouraged to go their own way, it takes enormous perseverance to forge a consensus. That strength was instrumental in turning a single brilliant program into a brilliant software package and marketing it throughout the world.

## CAN ENTREPRENEURS CHANGE?

Two and a half years after first being interviewed for this book, John Buhler was no longer an osmosis leader. When his annual sales reached $20 million, the lack of structure in his leadership style became a problem, so he hired Leonard Harapiak, a former minister of agriculture in the NDP government of Manitoba, to be general manager and chief operating officer. Harapiak has taken over much of the day-to-day supervision of Buhler's factories in Winnipeg and Morden, leaving Buhler time to work on his next acquisition and do what he does best—turnarounds. "I realized," he said a few weeks after hiring Harapiak, "that if I am going to achieve my objective of having 1,000 employees by 1993 [he had 200 then], I can't go on running the company the same way. I just can't stretch myself that far."

He doesn't attend the weekly management meetings anymore; he just reads the minutes. He finds, to his great surprise, that it is a pleasureable experience to step back from a problem and leave it to his general manager. He's hoping Harapiak will be an osmosis leader. As for himself, he has started to enjoy the role of managerial leader and is thinking about becoming a figurehead. He's considering moving his office completely out of the factory and into the downtown core of Winnipeg.

Buhler expects he'll turn back into an osmosis leader as soon as he makes his next acquisition, but for the time being he has changed. Karl Magid and Jack Donald also learned to adjust their leadership styles. They ran small firms for years, operating as hands-on solo or osmosis leaders, then changed their styles when they could no longer cope using their original leadership styles. Mike Potter, on the other hand, says he hasn't changed his style. By hiring Tom Csathy, he added a critical skill to the Cognos mix without changing his own contribution.

Many people believe that entrepreneurs cannot change their style. This is almost certainly untrue. The ones who don't have to change probably don't, like Potter, but the ones that have to adapt often do so. The usual pattern is for entrepreneurs to make rapid progress, then rest for a while so that they can absorb the changes, before they resume their progress. Venture capitalists, particularly, find this frustrating. When they say entrepreneurs don't change, they usually mean they don't change fast enough for their liking. It's nonetheless true that many entrepreneurs fail, often because they lack one of the seven elements of entrepreneurship, and often because they lose control when they grow too quickly. However, it's not clear how many of them reform and go on to succeed in other ventures.

Oscar Grubert of Champs Food Systems best expresses the transition from an entrepreneurial approach to a management style more appropriate for a large organization: "In the early stages, it's your ability to get the loyalty of people who will work above and beyond the call of duty to help you satisfy your objectives. These kinds of people need emotional satisfaction or stroking and almost a paternal image leading them. When you make the transition, you require specialists in an organizational structure. They need less paternalism, they need goal-setting leadership, with clearly defined job descriptions. People who can act in a boardroom environment—decision-making, goal-setting and accountability. They also need stroking and so on, but achievement of goals and appropriate remuneration give them their emotional satisfaction."

It took Grubert five years to make his transition. His firm had 3,500 employees in 60 restaurants, with sales of about $85 million in 1989. He's had his share of failures on the way—G. Willaker's and Gabby's Texas Steakhouse, for example, have not become household names, despite the Grubert touch. But he's had some big successes, too—24 Mother Tucker's in Canada and the U.S. and his chain of 22 Kentucky Fried Chicken franchises in Manitoba. Tall and slightly stooped, the soft-spoken Grubert is widely admired by other Winnipeg entrepreneurs. He is in full control of everything around him, and talks in sentences so well structured that interviewing him is like taking dictation.

"When you're in transition, you learn that your business has value, so you set some minimum investment standards. You look at growth potential. We don't knowingly take a negative cash flow for more than three to six months. One of the disciplines of the transition is to listen to those you surround yourself with. True entrepreneurs don't like to listen. You have to learn that criticism of an idea is not a personal attack. You have to start making decisions based on reason, not emotion. It's never easy. It takes some adjustment. If you can't make the transition, you should sell."

Half the entrepreneurs in this book said they had changed their style and half said they hadn't. For some of those who changed, the change was not so much a change in style as the accumulation of wisdom from their greater experience. Rod Bryden of Kinburn articulates the feelings of many when he says, "If you look back ten years, lack of experience in business would have made my leadership more tentative on the one hand and more aggressive on the other. I was compensating with firmness for the absence of experience that earns respect." Many others comment that they become less governed by their own feelings. They have learned not to tolerate bad management from people they like, and they have learned to tolerate irritating habits from top-notch performers.

Jean-Luc Giroux has been, at various stages in his career, an osmosis, a managerial and a figurehead leader. Much like Jack Donald, he's a managerial leader now, who encourages his managers to be independent thinkers and to show leadership within his company, Gentec. A burly man, Giroux is irrepressibly likeable, bursting with enthusiasm and curiosity. He describes himself as a bulldozer, but his lively step and mercurial personality suggest a more agile and flexible character. A highly committed Canadian and Quebecker, he has decided to build a network of contacts and associates throughout the country as his personal contribution to nation-building. That attitude got him into a lot of trouble once, so he has to control it, but he hasn't abandoned it.

Giroux and his silent partner, Marcel Lacroix, (who own one-third and two-thirds respectively) bought Gentec in 1978, when it was on the verge of bankruptcy. A few years earlier, the federal government had selected Gentec and Lumonics as the two companies it would back in an effort to develop commercial capability in laser technology, and licenced to them the technology it had developed. Lumonics went from strength to strength, winding up in the fold of Sumitomo Heavy Industries in 1989 when it felt it could no longer survive without more clout to compete internationally. At Gentec, however, the laser division never got off the ground. When Giroux took over, sales were $1.2 million, and he quickly realized that he would have to pare the unprofitable divisions if he was to turn the company around. The top candidate for the axe was the laser division, which was what had given the company its appeal. He knew that he could not afford more than $300,000 for R&D on the lasers—and his research manager had told him it would take a couple of million dollars to develop the technology for commercial applications. He could, however, salvage the technology of using lasers for measurement instruments. He decided to concentrate on the mechanical and laser measurement instruments that Gentec was producing profitably and abandon all the other product lines. The strategy worked and Gentec soon moved comfortably out of the red. Giroux became a local hero. Asked repeatedly to address seminars and conferences and to advise the provincial government on its technology policies, Giroux responded with his natural enthusiasm. "I was always on the go, participating in all kinds of associations," he said later. "Everyone came here, saw it worked and copied my products." He quickly found he didn't have much time to spend on Gentec's affairs and freely acknowledges he abdicated his day-to-day responsibilities. He had become a figurehead leader, but without a substitute leader to take care of business while he assumed a high public profile.

In 1984, the rapid growth vanished, as sales fell to $2.8 million from $4 million in 1983. He realized what he had done. He cut his outside engagements to the bone and assumed a profile so low he became invisible. "Now I'm taking care of three things," he said shortly afterwards. "Number one is my business, number two is my business and number three is my business." His office reflects his priorities—it's plain and unadorned except for pictures of all Gentec's products to remind him why he's there.

The figurehead style went out the window as he burrowed into every nook and cranny of Gentec. It was not a pretty sight. "Everyone thought they were great because Gentec had turned around," he says. "One of my vice presidents had a drinking problem, another wasn't performing because he had marital problems, and the engineers were lazy." Worse still, when he had started delegating to his vice presidents because he was too busy telling everyone else how to succeed, they didn't delegate in turn to the junior managers. His middle management was accordingly weak, and he had to rebuild his team, giving it a whole new spirit of management.

He became, once again, an osmosis leader. He started a junior management committee, which reported directly to him. Made up of the foremen, accountants and administrative people, the committee met every two weeks. "It was very hard," he says. "There was a lot of bickering between them. Everyone had his little kingdom. We had to destroy that. We've got to communicate. If we're not doing it with 60 people, how will we do it with 200?" The meetings continued for six months, by the end of which he had parted company with three key managers, including a foreman. Senior management was concerned at being by-passed, but the bulldozer knew what he wanted and was not going to be diverted. He had rejuvenated junior management and restored his acquaintance with Gentec at every level.

By 1988, when his sales had reached $10 million, he felt able to loosen his day-to-day control. He doesn't deal directly with the junior managers anymore, and he's no longer wearing his second hat as marketing manager. He has become a managerial leader who sees his leadership skills as being his business judgement and co-ordinating ability. Although he spends a lot of time visiting every department in Gentec, it's mainly social now. He doesn't break the line of reporting. He's also upgraded the quality of the people who work with him. "I don't have the technical expertise to make decisions on new product lines," he says. "So I surround myself with good guys and ask them for their opinion. And I accept their views. You have got to have teamwork."

CHAPTER 11

# POWER AND PERSUASION

*"You get involved with the employee's whole family. You play the clergyman, the family advisor, the psychologist. That's how you get their loyalty. If 90% of your people aren't loyal, you might as well quit."*
— Oscar Grubert of Champs Food Systems

*"We don't fire people who disagree. We have go-for-the-throat kind of people working here. The culture is so well formed now that if someone doesn't fit, the machine just spits them out."*
— Basil Peters, Peter van der Gracht of Nexus Engineering

**T**he true measure of leadership is whether a leader can consistently persuade a group of followers to do what he or she thinks is best, even if the followers have to submerge or modify some of their own wishes or needs in accepting that lead. Sustained, successful leadership entails striking a satisfying balance between organizational and individual needs.

These simple, perhaps obvious, observations are sometimes lost in discussions about leadership techniques, perhaps because so many "leaders" prefer to focus on the achievement and retention of their status, ignoring the dynamic process of leadership itself. People in a position to exercise leadership often do not lead. Some of them don't have an agenda, others prefer to avoid the risks of leading. Either way, it is easier to retain the status of leader by abdicating to the followers or becoming an autocrat. Whether they defer to their followers or ignore them, these "leaders" do not try to strike a balance between organizational and individual needs, which is the crux of leadership. Many leaders hold their positions because they know more about their organizations than anyone else. They can prescribe, with precision, what is best for the organization and reasonably expect their followers to appreciate, sooner or later, that they are worth following, because they are usually right. This is a restrictive strategy, however, because these leaders cannot expand their organizations beyond the limits of their own expertise without losing their ability to lead.

It is more common for leaders not to know exactly what is best for their organizations. The strongest leaders may have clear views on the desired result or process, but they borrow ideas and information anywhere they can find them. Most often, they rely on their own followers to devise many of the specific courses of action necessary for the organization's success. The critical act is for the leaders to lend their weight to the concepts of what is right for their organizations and consistently to persuade independent followers that it is to their own advantage to act on that premise. And when all the camouflage is removed, they can do this in one or both of only two ways— with a carrot or with a stick.

The tradition of business leadership is profoundly authoritarian. The models of the army, of feudal social structures and of automation on the assembly line still offer the best insights into the workings of modern corporations. Many have tried to change this reality by exploring motivational techniques to capitalize on individual self-fulfillment on the job, but not much has changed. The discipline of the bottom line in an increasingly competitive world has reduced both the margin of error and the time available to align individual and corporate goals. The cult of productivity standardizes jobs and categorizes people.

This is, however, true more often in big businesses than in entrepreneurial firms. Leaders in big firms risk losing all control if they cannot install systems and rationalize operations so that they can grasp the intricacies of their span of control. This is more important than eliciting superb performances from their staff. Because of the momentum of big firms, secured by their enormous financial resources and marketing clout, a large firm can show respectable growth with barely adequate management of its resources. Moreover, there's insufficient in-

centive for people in the organization to excel, because credit
for successes is seldom fairly apportioned. Inevitably, the focus
of managers' efforts in big companies shifts to career advance-
ment, as opposed to job performance. The traditional power of
authoritarian business leaders resides in their ability to allo-
cate resources or veto the actions of their subordinates. The
power of their subordinates lies in their ability to act, and that
includes sabotage.

It's an entirely different matter in entrepreneurial firms.
Short-term survival is by no means assured, so performance on
the job assumes far greater importance. There can be no fudging. The performance of entrepreneurs is measured objectively,
not only because mistakes have a direct impact on their own
income and wealth, as owners, but also because the source of
the mistakes is so much more obvious in small firms than in big
ones. And even if they perform well, entrepreneurs can still be
swamped by sudden changes in the environment, which may
seem like ripples to big firms, but which can sink smaller firms.

Offsetting this necessity for superior performance, entrepreneurs have much more flexibility than leaders in big businesses, because they wield absolute power within their firms.
As owners, they have the right to be wrong. However, this
power is absolute only in the short term. Whether they like it or
not, entrepreneurs constantly bet their ownership as they
grow and change, so retention of their ownership is contingent
on continuing good performance. Entrepreneurs who do not
control more than half the voting shares in their companies
generally survive only if they see themselves as employees.
Minority shareholders who lead their firms as if they controlled them often run into trouble when things go wrong,
because the dynamics of absolute power invariably breed
latent resentments that flare out of control as soon as there is a
prospect of a change in leadership.

As long as entrepreneurs wield absolute power within their
organizations, they are not driven by a need for power. Entrepreneurial leadership is oriented toward performance, which
alone can maintain their hold on their short-term power. It is a
precarious situation, but it is also exciting and stretches their
leadership qualities to the limit. It affords a unique backdrop
for both the carrot and the stick—they have enormous power to

monitor and control their businesses and unlimited opportunity to create an environment in which they can encourage
their employees to perform beyond what they perceive to be
their own limits. This chapter looks at three elements in this
mix—their techniques of control, which are the stick, and their
reliance on loyalty and their efforts to create a culture that will
support their objectives, which are the carrot.

## CONTROL

The Jim Pattison Group includes 40 or so companies, depending on what he's sold or bought recently, with annual sales of
about $2 billion in 1989. Its owner, Jimmy Pattison, controls it
as well as or better than most companies one hundredth the
size. He first sets clear objectives for his subsidiaries and their
managers. Then, through assiduous monitoring of their performance, regularly and in person, he makes sure the objectives
are met.

When one of his subsidiaries wanders from his chosen path,
he's a pocket tornado. He fully trusts his management teams to
implement his direction and philosophies, but if they cannot
solve a problem despite all the assistance he gives them, the
management has to go. If the new management can't solve it
either, he will re-examine his philosophy in that particular
business—why he's in the business and what he brings to it that
can differentiate his company from the competition. If he
cannot find the flaw in his philosophy in a troubled company
with good managers, he sells the company or liquidates it. No
hard feelings: "If you don't understand a business, you shouldn't
be in it."

Pattison is a tiny man, at five feet six inches and 100 pounds,
with delicate hands that hint at the artistic inclination that
makes him a virtuoso performer on the piano and trumpet. He
looks almost frail, but his personality is robust, aggressive and
domineering. He is brutally intolerant of people who don't earn
his respect quickly and has a mercurial temperament. He can
be engaged, relaxed and positive one minute and belligerent,
irritable and detached the next. Like many entrepreneurs, he
likes to push people to see how much they'll yield, testing their
resilience. He has few illusions about his own strengths and

weaknesses, expressing, in a candid moment, a quiet annoy-
ance at the number of mistakes he's made along the way.
Acutely conscious of what he can achieve, he is driven by his
obsession to reach his full potential. He is not an easy man to
work for. He is intensely loyal to his employees, but his
dramatic and unpredictable changes in direction sometimes
leave them floundering between admiration and frustration.
He follows his own unerring instincts and doesn't always share
with his key executives the thinking behind them. He so totally
dominates his group that it's not easy for the people who work
for him to make decisions when he's not there, no matter how
much leeway he gives them to manage their businesses. He is
scrupulous in letting his managers manage, but he won't hesitate to change a decision (his or anyone else's) if he feels it is
endangering the health of a company or the group. Most of his
key employees, not surprisingly, prefer to make decisions with
his blessing.

No detail is too small for him. He'll spend hours wandering
around warehouses, inspecting washrooms, talking to truckers
or switchboard operators in his companies. He figures each one
of his 7,000 employees is a priceless source of information on
how his companies are doing. He likes to see for himself. He
spends countless hours in his corporate jet visiting every
corner of his empire. He hasn't written a letter to anyone in his
businesses for 20 years.

His quarterly meetings with each individual company in his
group are legendary for the extraordinary attention Pattison
pays to detail. He combs through their financial and operating
reports with meticulous care, aided by his seven corporate experts. He probes the morale of staff in each company, examining the performance of the key personnel.

Osmosis leaders like Jimmy Pattison aren't the only ones
who control their businesses tightly. About half the managerial
leaders in this book follow the example of osmosis leaders and
spend time walking about their operations to sniff out what's
going on. This technique is less popular among the system and
figurehead leaders, who prefer to keep track of what's going on
in their companies through the grapevine. Of course, all successful entrepreneurs monitor their progress with the help of
detailed financial and operating statistics.

Many entrepreneurs go beyond the conventional means of control to use idiosyncratic methods, some of which may appear bizarre to outsiders, but which work for them. The most comprehensive of these is Karl Magid's elaborate control system in Lulu's. He is unusual, though. A lot of entrepreneurs sign every cheque that their firm issues, not to check up on everyone's spending, but to help them keep a handle on where their money is going. Whatever the motive, it is an effective control mechanism.

John Gillespie, formerly of Pizza Pizza, had a control tool that few people even recognized as such—his telephone number. Every order for a pizza goes through a central telephone number that is advertised everywhere (967-1111 in Toronto, 737-1111 in Ottawa and so on), so the company can monitor the business being done by every franchisee. Because every complaint also goes to that number, he knew exactly where the quality problems were. Another of Gillespie's control techniques was to send inspectors disguised as customers to his Pizza Pizza stores. After they'd bought their pizza, these people filled in a confidential report commenting on the food and the service. Just in case the inspectors became too friendly with the franchisees, Gillespie also had a few people who kept an eye on the inspectors. It is not uncommon for restaurants to use variations of this technique.

At least a few entrepreneurs use inter-office memos to keep track. One entrepreneur has copies of every inter-office memo deposited in a central file, which he and his partner sit down and read from time to time. Serge Racine of Shermag has every inter-office memo carbon copied to his attention. A former economics professor, who got his Ph.D. from Georgetown University in Washington, he is acutely conscious of the need to know what's going on in his rapidly growing company, but he's not secretive with the mounds of information he collects. He never closes his office door and encourages all his employees to take anything they need from there, even when he's out.

With sales of almost $50 million in 1989, Shermag is one of Quebec's success stories of the past few years. Its solid-wood furniture has belied the dark reputation of furniture firms as one of the four "soft" industries in Quebec's declining manufacturing base during the 1980s. Racine bought his first furniture factory in 1978, when he was city manager of Sherbrooke in the Eastern Townships. He had been teaching regional economic development at the University of Sherbrooke, but quit in 1972, when he decided to study his subject in the trenches. Five years into his job as city manager, a Montreal firm that made rocking chairs was on the brink of bankruptcy and decided its only hope was to transfer its operations to Sherbrooke. Its investors dropped out at the last minute, however, and Racine decided to put in $50,000 of his own money to resurrect the company.

He could afford it, because he was independently wealthy from his dabbling in real estate, but the firm quickly spun out of control. He invested again and again, until he had poured in his entire wealth of $400,000, and it was still going bust. He decided to quit his $65,000-a-year job and run the factory himself, at a salary of $21,000. The big loss in the first year was more than cancelled by the second year's profit, and Racine bought two more small companies. By the end of 1981, although he had a stable operation employing 35 people, he was restless. In 1981-82, he bought three large factories and the expansion started in earnest. Sales in 1982 were $2.5 million. In the next four years, he multiplied that by ten, then doubled it again in the following three. He now sells all across Canada and in the U.S.

Small and rounded, Racine has a friendly bustle about him. He's neat and tidy to a fault, not a greying hair out of place and immaculately dressed. His intellectual background has given him a fondness for theorizing, and he's happiest discussing the role of entrepreneurs as the new priests in Quebec. Every six weeks, he takes off ten days to read all the latest books, which he discusses with his key executives at their next regular meeting.

He controls costs on the factory floor by inviting the employees to participate in the savings from superior productivity. He negotiates with them a unit cost for each of the factory's products. If they make 5% more than expected, they receive half the savings in unit costs, which is paid to them in any way they want. The workers receive 75% of the savings for the next 5% of extra productivity, then 100% of anything over that. Productivity increased 27% when he introduced the first plan.

Racine sees his role in Shermag as the synthesizer of all information. He gets daily reports on production and marketing. "I'm at the cross roads. I'm informed on the economy, on sociology, the region and our industry. I receive the raw information and take decisions on my responsibilities and give suggestions in other areas. I am the judge for competing opinions." His spirit is democratic, his controls are watertight.

Perhaps the most unusual control technique was devised by Joe Shannon. Based in Port Hawkesbury, on Cape Breton Island, he runs a mini-conglomerate of firms in ten different industries. Each of his companies keeps a telephone message book where carbon copies of every message are filed. Shannon reads them from time to time when he drops in and says it gives him a good indication of who the bad managers are and which accounts are problems. His controls extend far beyond the telephone books, however.

Shannon runs his businesses with an iron grip on costs. His offices are spartan, shorn of decoration, characterless. He doesn't even have a full-time secretary. His only obvious concession to his success is his large Mercedes-Benz. He employs more than 100 people in his diverse businesses, which included, at the time of writing, a concrete firm, trucking companies, real estate management, cable TV, a nursing home, a high-tech business in point-of-sale machines, a retail tire outlet, highway construction and offshore supply to the oil industry. He keeps thoroughly informed on every one of them, and then some. He also tracks the numerous businesses he would like to be in, but isn't, as well as the businesses he was in until he sold out, but would like to be in again.

Lean and restless, Shannon is a legend among entrepreneurs in the Atlantic provinces. His father was a barber who had ten children, all of whom left Cape Breton to make their way in life—except Joe, a born entrepreneur. He always seemed to manage well, no matter how tight conditions were in one of the most depressed regions in Canada. He set the pattern early. When he was a child, a plane crashed behind his home one day. Everyone in the area wanted to see the wreckage, but couldn't, because the hill leading up to the crash was too icy. Shannon paid all the children in the neighbourhood to borrow their sleds for the day, then charged the adults a fee to be pulled up the icy hill to see the wreck.

He didn't leave the island as a young man because he landed a job as a truck driver. It wasn't long, however, before his entrepreneurial spirit took over and he quit to start his own trucking firm. In the next five years, he built up a fleet of five or six trucks, one of which he still drove himself. It was all too much. "I was doing the office work, the maintenance, everything and doing it all poorly," he says. "I had to decide to be a businessman." He stopped driving trucks and never looked back.

A typical osmosis leader, Shannon is constantly on the move, visiting each of his businesses regularly, always probing for clues of potential problems and opportunities: "I talk to so many people," he says, "that I know enough about everything to be dangerous. They never know when I'm checking on an operation." He's another entrepreneur who signs every cheque that leaves his companies. And he talks to all the general managers of his subsidiaries every day. Almost nothing is written down, except for the financial reporting. Every day at 8 a.m., the general manager of each division receives a print-out that tells him where he stands against budget.

Not many entrepreneurs watch their businesses as closely as Shannon. Jean Pouliot of CFCF and Quatre Saisons is at the opposite end of the spectrum. He runs his $100-million-a-year business just as effectively, but is relaxed about controlling events or people. He believes in letting his employees do whatever they think is best and showing lots of appreciation for their efforts.

Pouliot refuses to impose his views on his managers, because he's convinced they succeed only when they do their job in their own way. "Then they *have* to make it work," he says. "If they do it my way, I limit myself to my own talent, and that's not much." His approach does not leave much room for tight controls. He receives the normal flow of financial and operating statistics that the head of any company that size would receive, but he doesn't pore over them. "So often people are so busy getting information for someone else, they don't have time to do anything." He does not even lose sleep worrying about cost control, a subject that might have exercised most entrepreneurs who were engaged in spending tens of millions of dollars starting a new television station. "We're cost-conscious, but we're not in business to keep expenses to a minimum." That attitude extends to people, too. He doesn't try to pass a new regulation every time a person makes a mistake, to ensure that it won't happen again. He reasons that people listen to their own experience more than regulations.

## THE JOYS OF POWERLESSNESS

Jean Pouliot's approach is not widespread among the entrepreneurs interviewed for this book; nevertheless, he is at the cutting edge of a new approach to leadership. Modern economies, dominated by the knowledge and service industries, place a premium on employee initiative rather than obedience, and demand a different kind of leadership. Strict controls inhibit initiative, which can exist only when people feel free to act in contravention of the rules. There must still be controls on projects once they're being implemented, of course, but these controls work best when they are almost self-administered and applied only after the initiative has been taken.

There are many entrepreneurs like Jimmy Pattison and Joe Shannon. Their style works and will continue to work for strong, competent people who can cope with the flood of detail generated by hands-on control. There is even a handful of extraordinarily talented entrepreneurs who are capable of powering the rapid growth of their firms entirely through their own drive and initiative. But they are now rare in an increasingly complex world.

Entrepreneurs who want to develop initiative in their employees are finding another way. They are achieving better results by creating an environment in which employees can set their own goals and standards within the parameters of the objectives of their businesses. Sometimes that takes the leaders to destinations where they don't necessarily want to go, but they don't mind paying that price if it means they can draw on their employees' initiative.

Leadership under these circumstances poses vastly different and difficult challenges. It amounts to moving simultaneously on two conflicting fronts: persuading followers to submerge or modify their own needs and wishes; and encouraging them to develop their own strategies for their jobs. That amounts to integrating the leader's priorities into the priorities of each individual follower. It requires not only that the employees recognize the legitimate role of their leader, but that they also listen to the leader's views and absorb them into their own behaviour patterns. This enables them to exercise judgement compatible with their leader's, which is quite different from what normally passes for motivation. When goals can be achieved only through employee initiative, the entrepreneurs in this book are most effective when they let their key employees set their own courses in their own bailiwicks. The entrepreneurs reserve only a few areas where they can bring special expertise or leadership skills to bear. By defining their own turf and ensuring that their views in those areas are respected, the leaders can then defer to the views of their employees without having their authority threatened. By empowering their most talented managers, entrepreneurial leaders acquire influence in an environment where they are powerless to command.

The trouble is that people with initiative simply don't listen. It's not an isolated phenomenon. They hear the words when people speak to them. They understand them perfectly well, often indicating agreement. Then they go off and do exactly the opposite. It's not deliberate or even willful, but everyone does it. It's the principal reason why people find it so hard to change their behaviour, whether it be dieting or managing. People operate on automatic pilot for most of their lives. When they drive a car, for example, people make almost all decisions automatically—to the point where they sometimes arrive at their destination without having even noticed how they got there. The same is true of work. Decisions, even those bearing on a completely strange situation, are invariably made without any real consideration of the underlying assumptions or of fresh alternatives. They are habitual reflexes, formed over the years by constant repetition of thought processes that often comprise extraordinarily complex and extensive reasoning.

The automatic pilot is the subconscious mind, which runs people's lives whether they like it or not. The conscious mind can instantly absorb ideas, analyze them, and accept or reject them. The subconscious has no analytic capacity. It operates mechanically, incessantly, a deeply embedded program planted over time by the conscious mind. It changes only when it is bombarded with a new idea or habit that is sufficiently powerful to erase an old idea. Changing the subconscious program is easy for young children, because they have so few old ideas to displace. It's a different matter for adults, who often are not even aware of the programs governing their behaviour.

Traditional leadership avoids these obstacles to change by training followers to obey the letter of their instructions, which keeps the whole process in the conscious mind. People who are trained to show initiative, however, act on the basis of their own subconscious when they are asked to do something. If entrepreneurial leaders want to change their followers' behaviour, they have to change their subconscious programs.

The subconscious program can be changed, but it requires persistence and focus. There are two main techniques: repeating the message so often that it finally "sinks in" or giving recalcitrant followers such a shock when they deliver their disapproval that the followers never forget that moment, or that message.

The most common shock treatment is to let people make their own mistakes. This is only useful, however, if they understand the nature of their mistakes and accept responsibility for them. And this, in turn, is only useful if they are not punished for making a mistake. Punishing them only creates undue conservatism through the fear of making mistakes in future. The shock treatment is a risky approach to leadership, because it's so easy for the message to be blurred. Constant repetition is usually the most effective way of getting employees to listen, but it's a slow process. A message may have to be repeated up to 30 or 40 times before it penetrates the subconscious. This is frustrating, of course, and may also be expensive if a business can't afford to wait that long for results.

The solution to the dilemma—the secret, perhaps, of entrepreneurial leadership—is to create an environment that makes the slower process of constant repetition work much, much faster. This environment centres on loyalty and the conscious creation of a corporate culture. If employees are loyal to one another, to the entrepreneur and to the business, they will instinctively absorb messages that they need to change their behaviour more quickly, because they are more sensitive to the objects of their loyalty. By the same token, an appropriate corporate culture multiplies the examples of desired behaviour and imbues employees with a bias toward actions that are consistent with the leader's and the organization's objectives.

## LOYALTY

Oscar Grubert of Champs Food Systems rates loyalty highly. "If 90% of your people aren't loyal," he says, "you might as well quit." Grubert attributes his business success primarily to his ability to get the most out of the people who work for him, and he goes to enormous lengths to earn their loyalty. "You get involved with the employee's whole family. You play the clergyman, the family advisor, the psychologist. That's how you get their loyalty."

All but a handful of the entrepreneurs in this book rate loyalty as important to their success. That's sharply at odds with the conventional wisdom in many other parts of the business community, where it's become a cliché to dismiss loyalty as an old-fashioned concept whose time has passed. There is some powerful evidence to support that view. Staff turnover is high; valued employees flee to the competition carrying all their trade secrets with them; and it is now commonplace for people to work for half a dozen or more different employers during their varied careers. Even the employees who do stay with the same employer for extended periods are too often not conscientious, preferring to pour their energies into hobbies rather than their work.

Like all clichés, this is only half true, however. The complaint over the fickleness of employees is as old as recorded history, a reflection, as always, of employers who have failed to catch the interest and enthusiasm of their paid help. The entrepreneurs in this book do not believe this needs to happen. They observe overwhelmingly that most of their employees are ready, willing and able to be loyal. They also believe they cannot run their businesses without loyal employees who really care about their organization.

Not every entrepreneur agrees. "No one owes me their life," says Steve Chepa of Dicon Systems. "But if you make a deal, you stick with it. It's no more than a normal part of ethical behaviour." He sees his job as rewarding his employees for the services they render him in such a way that they want to stay with him. "If they do run off because they found a better deal, I can't ask them to sacrifice their interests for mine."

Most have greater expectations of their employees than Chepa. Indeed, loyalty thrives on expectations. People are unlikely to be loyal if they believe there is no long-term benefit for them in being so. Most of the entrepreneurs in this book acknowledge that they cannot expect loyalty until they have earned it. That means they have to be loyal to their employees before their employees will be loyal to them.

They earn their employees' loyalty through two principles. The first is mutual respect. "Loyalty," says Michael Cowpland of Corel Systems, "must be based on mutual respect and mutual co-operative rewards." He knows what he's talking about. When he and Terry Matthews were running Mitel, he filled his rapidly growing needs for senior people by promoting from within the company. That was a fine demonstration of loyalty, but it was flawed. It's a fine idea to give people challenges that stretch their potential, but in a firm growing very fast, not everyone can double their capabilities every year. A person learning on the job makes more mistakes and that inhibits other people in the company from fulfilling themselves. Since he left Mitel and started Corel, Cowpland pays more attention to earning the mutual respect of his employees by giving them bosses who are worthy of their respect.

Respect is a function of attitude, not skills. Everyone, without exception, is worthy of respect for something. People who deserve respect for something that is not important to the business should be encouraged to go somewhere else, where their skills will be respected. Entrepreneurs who put people in jobs they can't handle are not showing any respect for them either. Good attitudes cannot be built with employees who don't fit in.

The second rock on which employee loyalty is built is their feeling that the organization has a useful purpose and philosophy, that they are making a worthy contribution to it, and that someone is listening to them. "When people have a say in how an organization works, it's easier to be loyal to that organization," says Claude Lessard of Cossette Communication-Marketing (see page 264). "People become disconnected from their organization when there's no one left to listen to them."

When employees are encouraged consistently, over a long period, to air their grievances or suggestions, and are listened to by their bosses, they develop the attitude that their company is a good place to work, even if only because they helped fashion the environment themselves. Once that sentiment prevails, people stop worrying about what's wrong with the business and start chasing what's best for it. A major benefit of this process is that people who don't agree with the entrepreneur's values soon emerge from the woodwork and drift away when the entrepreneur doesn't accept their suggestions. Those who are left can then develop a more cohesive view of the firm's objectives.

The distinction between loyalty to an entrepreneur and to the organization he or she controls is often blurred. Many of them see their firm and themselves as one, so loyalty to one is indistinguishable from loyalty to the other. The entrepreneurs in this book prefer loyalty to their businesses, but those who believe their employees should be loyal to themselves personally are not just being vain. The employees cannot be loyal to the firm if they don't believe in the person who's controlling it.

Most entrepreneurs also try to avoid situations where employee loyalty is dispersed. Oscar Grubert, for example, tries to ensure that his employees don't develop loyalty to any one manager. "If he leaves, you lose the whole staff," he says. "You have to create an atmosphere that shows the employees it's a good *company* to work for." He holds regular meetings with all his middle managers to give them a sense of community, and he hosts a number of social events every year. The company newsletter tries to develop a sense of pride in working for the company. He knows that he has to make his company successful to give his employees confidence that Champs Food Systems is a stable company worthy of their long-term commitment and loyalty.

The larger and faster growing firms are less concerned with employee loyalty to managers. Marcel Dutil of Canam Manac sees the best focus for his employees' loyalty as the top person in their particular team. If that person's employees are loyal to their team, the loyalty will spread to the company. This is consistent with Dutil's approach to leadership—he encourages rivalry among the various divisions of his group. "Not too much," he says, "not if it means hurting each other." The friendly rivalry helps his bottom line, and he's lost few enough people in key jobs that he doesn't fret about the downside of dispersed loyalties.

Less than 10% of the entrepreneurs in this book make loyalty to their clients a priority. This goes against the grain of the conventional wisdom created by *In Search Of Excellence* (Thomas J. Peters and Robert Waterman, Jr.), which raised devotion to the customer to a new level of worship. The entrepreneurs may be more realistic, however. Customers inevitably change their tastes, as the troubled companies showcased in *In Search of Excellence* demonstrated only too clearly. This forces a business to choose between changing its customers or its product. Both are vital to a business, of course, but excessive loyalty to the customer eliminates the second option. A business is more likely to succeed if the employees can focus on the business itself, or the entrepreneur, as well as the customer.

Personal and organizational loyalty are not incompatible, because loyalty to an organization is transmitted through personal loyalties. Everyone, from an entrepreneur to a janitor, can earn the loyalty of fellow employees by themselves being loyal to their organization and its members. Loyalty is the magic catalyst that turns highly motivated, individualistic people into team players. It's loyalty that convinces people to consult with and listen to their co-workers, so that they can orient their actions to the greater good of the organization rather than their own selfish interests.

## DEVELOPING A CULTURE

The first meeting with Basil Peters and Peter van der Gracht, chairman and president respectively of Nexus Engineering, can be disturbing for the uninitiated. Both in their mid-thirties, they talk at breakneck speed, mostly in verbal shorthand, nodding their heads vigorously in agreement, until van der Gracht decides his partner is wrong (no euphemisms here) about something. He turns on him, intellectually, almost physically, to attack his ideas in a trenchant stream of bald criticism. Peters listens calmly and dismisses his partner's attack with a deft counterattack. The battle is on, for anything from a minute to half an hour. Not long afterwards, another battle erupts, this time with Peters as the aggressor. The two trade arguments with an energy and intensity that only later becomes recognizable as a pattern with which both are comfortable.

Their competitiveness is not exactly friendly, because both need to win in the worst way, but it is not antagonistic. It is more like a ritual, developed to challenge each other's sacred cows, obliterate sloppy thinking and relentlessly squeeze out intuition. Peters is tall and strapping, with light blond hair and eyes that drink in everything around him but demand attention. Van der Gracht is smaller, olive-skinned and dark-haired, with brown eyes that bore into his listeners. Both emanate high-voltage energy, although Peters seems to be holding his in check, while van der Gracht pumps his out aggressively. "We're basically competitors—it started at school," says one of them. Despite the striking difference in their looks and characters, it is often impossible to remember who said what, because they speak interchangeably for and against each other. "But it's not disruptive, it's creative conflict or constructive confrontation. Competition is good, internally and externally."

There are no signs of the two partners mellowing. The main change in the past few years is that they are more confrontational with other people. "We have go-for-the-throat kind of people working here," says one of them. "We don't fire people who disagree." They have obviously thrashed out a lot of their differences to arrive at consensus on many issues, but they gain no satisfaction from what they have resolved. They are constantly looking out for more areas about which to start an argument.

Like the uninitiated visitor, their employees were initially amazed at these antics, but they soon discovered the utility of the arguments. They test ideas before they go into production, subjecting them to a rigorous examination to make sure that they will work in production. "We keep our mistakes in the R&D room," says Peters. "Once an error gets into production, you're in trouble."

It works for Nexus. Since they started in 1982, the two partners have force-fed annual sales to $24 million in 1988. They brought in Tom Holgate and Marc Phillips as partners to finance the growth, ultimately merging Nexus with Holgate's and Phillips's company, Channel One Video, a distributor of satellite equipment. The combined company now has 100 products in electronic equipment for handling TV and audio signals. Peters and van der Gracht see "no impediment" to increasing sales to $100 million, but concede they're not quite sure how they'll progress from there to a quarter of a billion dollars. There is, however, no doubt in their minds they will get there. "We couldn't say what products we'll have in ten years," says van der Gracht, "but we can say how we'll be managing people, what markets we'll be in and what our revenues are likely to be."

The two planned their venture while still at university, where Peters got his Ph.D. and van der Gracht his Master's degree (he's two years younger than Peters and took two years off to work for Northern Telecom between his undergraduate and his Master's degrees). They started Nexus the day after they graduated and proceeded to spend $1 million developing their first product—modulators for TV signals from satellites. The modulators decode the satellite signal for small, rural cable systems or for apartment blocks where there are few subscribers. In case anyone might have thought they lacked chutzpah, the intrepid two chose a product for which there were already several well-established manufacturers, in the expectation that they could deliver a product 90% as good at half the price. They succeeded.

The business grew rapidly, reaching $3 million in sales in their third year, and they moved to an old warehouse. They tore down all the interior walls to improve the communications. The only walls left make up the common meeting rooms along the exterior wall looking onto the street. The barn-like interior is decorated with big, colourful banners hanging haphazardly from the ceiling. The open architecture reflects their management style. Peters and van der Gracht are almost obsessive about open communications. Their bi-weekly company news-letter, *Nexus Snooze*, is a hilarious eye-popper, jammed with racy commentary and doubles entendres on the social and work activities of Nexus employees, including a few judicious jabs at Peters and van der Gracht. In the middle of a meeting, someone might bounce into the room and want to know who the guests are and what they're discussing. It's not disruptive, just consistent with the fission reactions that energize every-one at Nexus, keeping them alert and interested.

There are more serious sides to the communication blizzard at Nexus. Once a quarter, all Nexus employees are invited to complete an anonymous survey intended to gauge their mo-rale. They are asked to articulate how they feel about their jobs and how their feelings have changed in the past three months. They are asked specifically to comment on their managers, by name. A summary of these comments is circulated to the 26 senior and middle managers who meet every Friday for two hours to discuss the management philosophy and reinforce the culture. There's no hiding in these meetings. Peters and van der Gracht also hold a meeting of all employees to read out the most significant comments, positive and negative. "It is," says Pe-ters, "very important to fix problems." After the information has been distributed, all the survey returns are shredded.

It's not all intensity and confrontation at Nexus, however. There's a Friday beer meeting (with free beer to encourage attendance). There are monthly events like sports days or barbecues. Any excuse will do for a party. "We have a funda-mental respect for people," says van der Gracht. "The company that sweats together stays together." He's only half in jest. There are no status symbols, not even reserved parking spots, and free pop, coffee and juice for all.

Peters and van der Gracht spend a quarter of their time polishing and maintaining the corporate identity. "The culture is so well formed now that if someone doesn't fit, the machine just spits them out." But employees must be more than open-minded and alert. They must perform. Peters expects top managers to receive about half their total remuneration in bonuses.

The other side of this coin is training. Peters and van der Gracht say they spend half their time on training. "Twenty percent of our people are enrolled in a course," says van der Gracht. They design self-development programs to stretch people. They give classroom instruction if there are enough people interested. They pay for the tuition and the books in outside courses. At one stage, the entire accounting department was attending night school. Altogether, they spend almost 3% of their revenues on training.

The culture developed by Peters and van der Gracht would not suit every business, but it works like a charm in their environment, where young people are grappling with fast-paced technological innovation. Two-thirds of the entrepreneurs in this book work hard at developing a culture to suit their particular environment. Their cultures are often a reflection of their own personalities and can involve everything from detailed instructions on how to behave with customers, to persistent reinforcement of preferred ways of dealing with fellow employees, to an insistence on the importance of individual initiative. The key is that these leaders know what they want and they propagate, at every opportunity, their concept of what their business should feel like.

Probably the most detailed and structured corporate culture in Canada, in big or small companies, was developed by Frank Stronach of Magna International. He has built a concept of the ideal corporation that is immensely powerful, although many people find it a bit rich for their blood. When Stronach stepped down as chief executive officer in the spring of 1988, the stock-market analysts agreed the company would benefit from having a less "erratic" leader than its founder. However, the spirit of Stronach will live for a long time in the company he built from nothing to a giant company with annual sales of $1.5 billion in 1988. With his strong personality, curiosity and open-mindedness, he has created a structure that breaks new ground in the way it apportions responsibilities and obligations among the major players in his business—the investors, the management and the employees. Notwithstanding the skepticism of the business community, the Magna culture is a sensitive and intriguing concept which may yet prove to be a model for other firms.

His system is based on a unique satellite structure. By the end of the 1980s, the company had more than 120 subsidiary companies, arranged in a series of groups attached loosely to the corporate head office. No unit is allowed to grow larger than 200 employees, although there are a few closely watched exceptions. When one reaches that size, it is split into two units. That way, bureaucracy is kept at bay and the company can sustain its extraordinary growth rate.

Stronach has created a Magna charter of rights, which defines how the company should be run. It provides the basis for controlling management excess by giving the board of directors the right to remove managers who contravene its terms. Management, on the other hand, are given the power to operate effectively by allocating to them Class B shares with 500 votes each, while employees and investors hold Class A shares with one vote each.

The plant managers run their autonomous units as entrepreneurs, secure in their power to run things as they like, provided they meet the criteria laid down in the charter of rights, which includes making a reasonable profit and creating a co-operative, fair labour climate. It's a ground-breaking document, which has created a lot of interest among other entrepreneurs. It divides the company profit, in fixed percentages, among shareholders (20%), employees (10%), R & D (7%), top management (6%) and charity (2%). The rest is reinvested in the company. There are also some stringent limitations on the powers of management if they take undue risks or if they fail to perform.

Just to make sure everyone keeps their attention focussed on the long-term prospects of Magna, Stronach has also built in a system of remuneration that rewards long-term employees. Senior managers all have 15- or 20-year contracts, and the company contributions invested in the DPSP vest fully in the employees only after 15 years' service.

He also believes labour should receive its just reward. "I feel strongly that labour has a moral right to some of the profits they help generate," he says. "It always baffles my mind when you hear all the motherhood statements about how we have to work hard. If I was an employee, I'd say, 'what for?' You have to have a reason. There's only one legitimate reason—and that's to say, 'I'll share with you.'

"Business cannot be dictatorial anymore," he says. "Great

strides have been made, especially in the last 20 to 30 years, to create better environments for the working people. The days when you could pound the desk with your fist and demand things are gone, and it's a good thing." As a determined pounder of desks himself, this represents a bit of a turnaround for Stronach, but it is a genuine enough sentiment. He thinks business and labour have failed dismally to adapt to the new environment and considers it management's responsibility to adapt first.

Since he stepped down as CEO, Stronach has made labour relations a priority. He has developed a concept for a labour charter of rights, which will give Magna's employees some power to influence their working conditions. The heart of the charter of rights for labour will be an advisory board made up of five people who have earned a high profile through their work in social and humanitarian endeavours. The board will have staff and enough money to investigate complaints by Magna employees and advise the company on practices which it feels are unfair to the employees. The staff will speak a number of languages, to guarantee good communication with all employees. The charter also sets wages by a formula based on wages in comparable firms, so that wage increases cannot be a strike issue. Health issues will be settled by binding arbitration.

Stronach sees Magna as a bank that will invest in businesses with a corporate charter of rights. "It is a bank that focuses on human capital." He has also defined a regeneration process that allows for the splitting of cells in his universe to create new cells. In his eyes, there's no reason why Magna shouldn't keep increasing at 30% a year indefinitely.

# CHAPTER 12

# MANAGING GROWTH

*"We've got a system like the army. Five levels of management. It's my engineer's mind."*
— Vern Simpson of Swift Sure Courier

*"We are who we are because we have made it. No individuals have done it, we've all done it. The group has made me look good, and each one of them too."*
— Lawrence Bloomberg of First Marathon Securities

**W**hen he hires his managers, Steve Chepa of Dicon Systems doesn't try very hard to tell them what their jobs are supposed to be. And once they're working, he doesn't spend much time holding their hands. At Dicon, managers succeed when they grab the initiative and decide for themselves what their job is and how to do it. Chepa wants people to pick holes in his organization. If people come to him with a proposal, even one that trespasses on someone else's turf, he is delighted to give it the go-ahead, as long as they have thought it through properly. In this Darwinian environment, weak people get short shrift. "I won't defend anyone who can't protect his own turf," he says. "I believe in letting natural forces find their own level."

That extends to Chepa's own turf. He enjoys making his managers fight to prove they are better than he is. He challenges them, to see if they challenge him back. A perceptive student of human nature, he talks of the competitive jungle inside Dicon with a detached calmness, almost like a persistent academic, scientifically testing people's limits. He is acutely conscious of his own strengths and weaknesses and seems fascinated by the game of seeing how close he can nudge his managers to their full potential. Secure in his understanding of the contribution he can make to Dicon, he tells all his managers he expects them to be better informed than he is, or to find another job.

"As people grow," he says, "you won't get the best out of them by defining their jobs tightly. Some are more than what you thought, others can't handle it. Job descriptions have to change depending on the people in them and the people around them."

It makes for a mercurial organization chart. When he holds a meeting, he doesn't worry about who *should* be there, he assembles the people who can contribute to the subject at hand. A meeting about a new product may involve the product manager and a clerk who is handling some aspect of it, but it won't include the vice president of finance until they have to decide on pricing. Until recently, he barely called any meetings at all, other than those required to deal with a crisis. The basic strategy of the firm was discussed by the four or five key managers only when they were all in town and could have lunch together.

As he began, in 1988, to move his company from annual sales of about $15 million to more than $20 million, however, he had to change his own style. He instituted regular monthly meetings for his senior managers, scheduled on the same day every month for the whole year. "The communication gap has grown," he says. "We need structure now." But he isn't going to let the need for structure turn Dicon into a hierarchical bureaucracy as it heads for sales of $50 million or more. He's pushing his employees to become even more individualistic, asking them all to do a mission statement for themselves. If he can make it work, he'll have a company that brings new meaning to the teachings of Adam Smith. The sum total of the individual aspirations of all his 250-plus employees will be an invisible hand that guides Dicon toward a set of goals that Chepa defines, but enforces only lightly.

None of this causes him any anxiety. He knows the productivity will be impressive. He has complete confidence that he can apply leadership to align the aspirations of any people who stray too far. "Dicon is a whole that's made up of parts of different perfection," he says. "The aesthetic value is to put together all these different talents and skills and end up with a machine that beats everyone else."

It's an exciting approach, if not a safe one. His approach is similar to that of many entrepreneurs in this book. He delegates significant authority, but keeps a close watch on the results. He generally avoids a structured organization, ruthlessly stamping out incipient hierarchy and holding meetings only when he has a specific reason for them. He likes to hire people who get things done without any fuss and preferably without his involvement. He encourages them to seek personal fulfillment and growth in their jobs. He loves the art of doing business, he loves to make his business machine hum, but he's not a rah-rah team leader who wants to make his firm a family. He's more interested in individuals than in groups. It's dynamic, it's stimulating, and it's not for entrepreneurs like François Vachon, whose approach is at the opposite end of the spectrum from Chepa's.

Vachon is a part-owner and president of Cartem, which makes cardboard packaging for the food and beverage industry. Cartem is a fast-growing, dynamic firm in a mature, slow-growing industry. Its main plant is in Ste. Marie, south of Quebec City in the Beauce region of Quebec and far from most of its customers in Montreal and New England. Yet Cartem made a name for itself in its first 11 years, growing quickly to sales of $12 million in 1988, and winning several Mercuriades awards (the most prestigious business awards in Quebec and the example that inspired the Canada Awards for Business Excellence).

When Vachon hires employees—and he hires them all himself, because he is personnel manager as well as president—he is the opposite of Chepa. He defines the jobs of his employees with precision and looks for people with the specific skills to perform those specific jobs. He looks for people who will fit in with the Cartem culture. Although he is not exactly looking for yes-men, he does want people who will follow directions. Very much the team leader, Vachon takes candidates for a job opening on a tour to meet the workers with whom they'll be working, to see if the existing employees feel the prospective employees will be compatible. If they pass this test, the new employees go on probation for ten weeks, then, after three to six weeks, if their colleagues still like them, they are hired permanently. The most important criterion for Vachon is that they like working with people. "Not paper, or tables. They must be able to manage people."

This preoccupation with fitting in comes from Vachon's profound sense of community. He is an active member of associations for the Beauce region, he belongs to the three industry associations that affect Cartem's product and he belongs to the leading association of entrepreneurs, the Groupement Québecoise d'entreprise. He doesn't collect these associations casually. He cares about every community of which he feels a part, and he's passionate about improving economic conditions in the Ste. Marie region. He feels acutely his responsibility for building something great and wonderful for the present and future enjoyment of his employees, his shareholders and his community. "We don't build enterprises for our children," he says. "We build it for ourselves and our community. If the kids can build on it, that's great, but if they can't, that's too bad."

He was the Development Officer of the Ste. Marie municipality, when he first found out about the predecessor company of Cartem. The 38-year-old packaging firm in Ste. Marie had just declared bankruptcy. Vachon and five of his local friends decided it was worth saving, so they bought the assets of the failed firm, renamed it Cartem and set out to build a business that would set an example and be an inspiration to the region.

Two of the six equal shareholders decided to work in their new company, and Vachon, with his neatly trimmed Edwardian beard, quit his job with the municipality and became president. He has a perpetually surprised look that comes from his openness and eyes that are magnified by thick glasses. However, that impression evaporates as soon as he begins to talk, invariably at breakneck speed. He is absorbed by his business. Intense and determined, he knows exactly where he's going, what he wants and how long he expects it to take him to get it. It was the challenge he'd been waiting for. He threw himself into the task with abandon, researching the market, the technology and the distribution systems. In his second year, he delivered a comprehensive five-year plan, which opted to shoot for the most advanced technology in the world so that Cartem would be able to offer the best quality in the area.

In his office, decorated elegantly in mahogany and lush cream-coloured carpeting, there's a large wooden carving of a beaver with a stick in its mouth. Vachon says it represents Cartem, because the raw material is the same and the beaver's main characteristic is, like Cartem's, perseverance. Also like a beaver colony, although Vachon doesn't say so, Cartem is built on teamwork. He never fails to give credit to his team, and one of his top priorities is to inform every employee what's going on at their company before they read about it in the media. Twice a year, he holds a meeting of his 100-plus employees, giving them a detailed report on the company's affairs and inviting them to ask questions. Once a month, he meets with the union representatives.

He is as convinced of the importance of developing employees as Chepa is, but he chooses the direction in which they develop, not the employees themselves. It takes four years to train an operator of a printing press, and Cartem trains its own, making sure they fit in with the culture. Vachon seeks team players with skills that fit the openings, Chepa seeks people who feel right for the job, in the expectation they will wind up doing something completely different anyway. Vachon is as structured as Chepa is unstructured. His meetings are as regular as Chepa's are erratic. Vachon pays close attention to the seniority of his employees, Chepa is concerned only with what they know. Both men delegate to their managers, whom they then monitor, but Vachon gives them far less rope. A mistake would hurt the others in the team.

Despite these enormous differences, both men run highly successful manufacturing firms of a comparable size. Each uses the style that works best for him. Their different approaches to making their leadership stick illustrate the three elements of management that bear most directly on effective entrepreneurial leadership—the selection of employees, organizational structure and the art of delegating and making decisions.

## HIRING

In surveys of small business every year, there is always one item at or near the top of every list of major problems: the difficulty of finding good employees. That's probably not a reflection of the available talent, since so many successful small firms are inordinately proud of their employees. It's more likely a reflection of the employers' frustrated expectations. A strong leader in a small firm knows how things should be done and no one can do it as well as he or she can, so there's bound to be dissatisfaction with employees who don't have the same enthusiasm, commitment and skills.

Most successful entrepreneurs look at it a little differently. The people in this book said again and again that when their employees perform poorly, they blame themselves for picking the wrong person or failing to train them adequately. They can afford to take the blame, because they know they have a significant edge over leaders in bigger organizations and in fields other than business. Most of these leaders do not choose their followers themselves. Either their followers choose them or they inherit their followers with their jobs. And almost all of them are content to live with that disadvantage, at least partly because most of them believe they will move on to new challenges sooner or later, so there's little incentive to invest too much energy in developing the right kind of people for the organization. Successful entrepreneurs, however, are in their businesses for the long haul. They know they will pay dearly later on for bad hiring decisions or failure to train employees properly. And they're in a position to do something about it, because they have the power to choose their employees themselves or set the rules by which they are hired.

The entrepreneurs in this book were asked what they look for in the people they hire. The seven most popular characteristics are:

| Characteristic | Percent responding |
|---|---|
| 1. Appropriate experience | 44% |
| 2. A good attitude | 42% |
| 3. Compatibility with existing employees | 42% |
| 4. Ambition | 30% |
| 5. Good character | 29% |
| 6. Initiative | 27% |
| 7. Good judgement | 21% |

Note: For a full listing, see Appendix C, Table 12.1.

This is not a comprehensive list of all the factors those entrepreneurs consider when they hire, because the responses were unprompted and therefore include only the factors at the top of their minds when they were interviewed. There would be other considerations for any specific job that are important but not highly visible to the entrepreneur. This list does, however, indicate clearly where these entrepreneurs place their emphasis when they hire.

Further analysis of these responses uncovers another interesting fact. The entrepreneurs appear to fall mainly at opposite ends of a spectrum. At one end are those who seek in their employees one or more of three characteristics—experience, compatibility and ambition. At the other end are those who seek one or more of good attitude, initiative and good judgement. A few entrepreneurs cited as many of one group as the other, but almost 80% showed a strong tendency to favour one group of traits over the other.

The ones who seek good attitudes, initiative and good judgement are individualistic, seeking to challenge their employees to greater individual efforts (see Appendix C, Table 12.2). They might be called, in a new phrase coined especially for them, Theory K leaders. They measure their success by their results and are less concerned with team playing. Many are not concerned with an employee's track record, which they consider often to be the source of too many bad habits. They like to see personal growth in their employees and are quite happy to adjust their plans to accommodate changes in the direction of their employees' careers. Chepa shares many of these characteristics.

The ones who seek experience, compatibility and ambition, are more group oriented. They might be called Theory Q leaders. They concentrate on building effective teams and give a high priority to the interests of the team in their day-to-day decisions. They tend not to be interested in the personal growth of their employees, preferring instead competence in their field and compatibility with the group. Vachon is typical of this group.

The latter are a little more complicated, however, because they, in turn, fall into two camps. For some of them, their team is an extension of themselves, designed to implement the leaders' wishes just as the leaders might have done so themselves. The others see their teams as groups of people who share responsibility and authority. They lead the team, but they allow themselves to become part of the group's dynamics, accepting that they will sometimes cede leadership, temporarily, to others in their team or to the team as a whole.

The first kind of Theory Q leader is almost a stereotype of entrepreneurial leadership. One good example is Johnny Lombardi of CHIN Radio/TV International. He likes to talk about his team and about how much he listens to their advice, but there's no confusion about who makes the decisions and sets the tone at CHIN. The entire operation is a reflection of Lombardi's character. His managers, including two of his three children, understand very well the importance of respecting that, as much for the integrity of the management as for their own futures. Lombardi is a devoted team player, but he's the designated leader.

Lawrence Bloomberg of First Marathon Inc., the holding company for stockbrokers' First Marathon Securities, is a different kind of team player. He runs marathons, as do several other executives in his firm. They often run them together. You don't have to run marathons to be hired by First Marathon, but Bloomberg makes sure all new employees fit the culture he and his colleagues have created. He feels they are good at selecting employees. And when they make a mistake and a person doesn't fit in, they don't hesitate to fire them. "If you don't, you weaken the whole structure," he says. "This culture is our culture, so we're sensitive to people who don't fit. People we don't like don't last. That's very important to us."

The First Marathon culture is "aggressively opportunistic," as hungry for the challenge of mastering the cut and thrust of financial markets as for the rewards that top performance brings in this industry. First Marathon wants people who have the killer instinct, who want to make money. And the entrepreneurial environment ensures that those kinds of people make a lot of money for themselves and their employer. That's a reflection of the company's hard-driving president and biggest single shareholder.

Bloomberg was a vice president and director at Pitfield, Mackay, Ross before he started First Marathon in 1979. He specialized in selling equities to institutional investors and felt the credit he received in position, responsibility and earnings didn't reflect the quality of his contribution. He wanted the challenge of being the president of an investment house. By 1979, he'd waited long enough. The impending deregulation of the stock broker industry persuaded him there were opportunities aplenty. He persuaded three other institutional equity specialists to join him in a new firm. Their main focus initially was naturally institutional equities, but they soon broadened out into the raising of funds for corporate Canada. Five years later, First Marathon added a discount brokerage operation (Marathon, Brown) which soon grabbed about half the growing market share of discount houses. Bloomberg later invited in, as a 50% partner in Marathon, Brown, the people-in-a-hurry at Central Capital Corp., which is growing faster than any other major financial institution in Canada.

Bloomberg's company grew at a rate that surprised even the investment industry, which is used to huge multiples and mind-boggling incomes. From a standing start in 1979, revenues were $7.5 million in 1980, the company's first full year. Three years later, revenues were more than double, and the same again three years after that. Most impressive of all for a fast-growing company, which is always at risk when markets slump suddenly, it made a profit in 1988. That was the year the entire industry was devastated by the fallout from the crash of October, 1987, and First Marathon's revenues were down 21%.

Bloomberg is a small, slender man, unselfconsciously handsome and approaching the age when he can start looking distinguished with his smattering of greying hair. The burning intensity of his desire to succeed, and succeed big, makes him ruthless with anything that wastes even one minute in his consuming drive to achieve his ambitious goals. He sometimes seems to be about to erupt like a volcano. A man of few words, he does away with pleasantries, getting to the point with almost brutal directness. That decisiveness has enabled him to provide almost flawless leadership to his company, focussing on the right issues at the right times, to steer it at full throttle through the treacherous waters of a highly competitive industry.

There's another side to him, however. The compulsive perfectionist is also a powerful team builder. "At any time in an organization, somebody goes down for a period," he says. "They need to be supported then. You provide the role of friend, confidant and motivator, then they come back stronger." He also understands the contribution other people make to his company's success and recognizes it (perhaps remembering his own experiences before he started First Marathon). "We are who we are because we have made it. No individuals have done it, we've all done it. The group has made me look good, and each one of them too." Bloomberg places a high priority on the two-way loyalty that has kept him working with some of his colleagues for 20 years and more.

He sees as a critical part of his job the creation of an environment that attracts the kind of employees he wants, and he's fiercely proud of the people who work with him. Each stage in First Marathon's expansion has been tied to the hiring of a person with significant expertise in that area. The result is a team of people who are more expert in their own areas than their president. Bloomberg shares his leadership. In a core group of six people who run the firm on a daily basis, there are three who have major responsibilities, including setting priorities. "The fact I've survived with the guys who work here is terrific."

## ORGANIZATIONAL STRUCTURE

Entrepreneurs abhor red tape and bureaucracies, but that doesn't mean they don't build some elaborate organizational structures themselves. Structured organizations are not necessarily bureaucracies; they only become bureaucracies when their structures start having a life of their own. Bureaucratic structures are designed and operated strictly for internal purposes. They treat the customer as no more than an intellectual discipline that provides a framework for the design of internal processes. This narcissistic focus of bureaucracies inevitably breeds an obsession with process, to the point where fast decisions become impossible and inflexibility the norm.

Successful entrepreneurs sometimes need elaborate structures, but they go to a lot of trouble to make their structures transparent, so they can reflect, without distortion, their business objectives. And they monitor each department's effectiveness with the customer, feeding the results back into the system.

Vern Simpson of Swift Sure Courier has a fair-sized firm with annual sales of $22 million in 1988, but that's small in the $800-million-a-year courier industry. He specializes in the personalized service that the big companies can't do well, and figures he could expand up to $80 million without stepping on any toes. Even at his current size, however, Swift Sure handles more than 10,000 jobs a month, and Simpson has to be organized.

He started in the courier business in 1976, when he had a heavy construction firm and needed to send time sheets and parts back and forth all across Ontario. He couldn't get the service he needed, so he started his own system, which he gradually expanded into Winnipeg, then Montreal and Vancouver. It was still only a hobby really, a distraction that amused him as his enthusiasm for the construction business started to wane. By 1979, however, he wasn't making any money at construction, so he sold all his equipment and turned his full attention to his courier sideline.

Since then, he has built a far-flung empire, with offices in Toronto, New York and London. A huge map in his office has an impressive covering of coloured pins for his offices (white), his agents (blue) and the places where Swift Sure has delivered (red). But all was not well when he started to grow rapidly. His troubles started when his business reached $10 million in

1985. His worst problem was the turnover among his drivers, who are the key link in providing personalized service. The kinds of people who use Swift Sure all have quirks, so it can take several weeks for a new driver to figure them out. That became impossible when Simpson was losing a third of his drivers every month. His unstructured organization couldn't deliver equal opportunities to the drivers to make good commissions, so they quit or transferred into other jobs.

Simpson brought in a consultant who helped him devise a whole new structure. He graded everyone's jobs from 1 to 7, starting with vice presidents at 1. He calls it his group of seven. Then he formalized descriptions for each job and tied salary ranges to them, right up to the level of vice president. "We've got a system like the army," he says. "Five levels of management. It's my engineer's mind." Salary ranges for the bottom three grades are public knowledge. "People were changing jobs like Cokes in a Coke machine," says Simpson. "Now we have rules. We're much more professional. They don't have to depend on drinking with their boss."

The new system has worked for Simpson. It's not uncommon now for there to be no turnover at all among his drivers in the course of a month. Nevertheless, he is conscious of the need to avoid the trap of becoming "sterilized" by the system, so he makes a big effort to keep Swift Sure entrepreneurial. A big man, with big-boned engineer's hands and a mane of greying hair, Simpson is self-deprecating and unpretentious, still an engineer at heart. He's not a naturally compassionate man, but he works hard at creating the right attitude among his staff. He sends a note to his employees in every paycheque saying what they're doing really well, and he never misses an opportunity to pepper them with information. He also sends out a newsletter, which he writes himself, to all his employees and customers every two months. "You gotta keep telling people they're the best," he says. "After a while they start thinking they are the best and acting like it."

Simpson will keep Swift Sure entrepreneurial despite its army hierarchy, without which it probably couldn't survive. But most entrepreneurs prefer to eliminate organizational structures. That's how John Bragg of Oxford Frozen Foods has built his mini-conglomerate in rural Nova Scotia. Bragg feels he does not yet have a professional organization, but that hasn't stopped him taking his business from annual sales of about $10 million in 1983 to more than $100 million in 1988, an annual compound growth rate of 55%.

Bragg says he's the biggest blueberry farmer in the world. He has a huge 8,000-acre farm in Nova Scotia and two more in B.C. and Maine. Yet the output from these farms is still not enough to feed his plant in Oxford, N.S., which has cornered 25% of the Canadian market for frozen blueberries and which is where he makes his real money. He ships his product all over the world, including Japan, the most demanding customers of all (the quality standards of the Japanese are 30 times as stringent as those of North American customers).

This is only one element of Bragg's empire, even if it is the one closest to his heart. He also owns the biggest cable TV operation in Atlantic Canada, with a string of small local systems all around his home province and a share of the major systems in Halifax and Dartmouth. He's a half-owner of three hotels, a major real estate development in Halifax and half a lobster packing plant.

There's no corporate head office for this string of businesses. Bragg sits alone at the centre of the web. The cable operation is run by a former schoolmate. "I know him well," says Bragg. "I have complete trust in him. He knows which things I want to have a say in." His cable TV business in Maine is also run by a man (a "mentor") who had worked with Bragg for years before joining his company. He will invest in a venture only if he has total trust in the person running it day-to-day.

Quiet and understated, Bragg loves to talk about how people succeed, but he doesn't get carried away with his own success. He is laid back and seems determined to remain essentially the local boy made good. His family has lived in the area for five generations. His father, grandfather and great-grandfather were all local entrepreneurs, and he takes his responsibilities to his community seriously. When he hires people, the most important criterion is that they should fit in with the local area. And whenever he finds promising people in the Oxford area, he will hire them regardless of whether he has a job for them.

Bragg has two basic approaches in running his businesses. The frozen food operation is his golden goose, and he is deeply involved in its day-to-day operations. All the rest are run by his associates. Although he is not involved closely with these firms and can go for weeks without seeing the managers of some of them, he makes it clear what information he needs and has confidence he'll be called in when he needs to be.

Altogether, more than 15 people report directly to John Bragg. His relationships with all of them are one-on-one, and he almost never holds meetings with all of them. About a third of them are in Oxford Frozen Foods. "We control 25% of the blueberry market here," he says, "so our decisions don't affect just Oxford, they affect the whole industry. I have to be right on top of everything." He used to interview and check the references of every manager hired at Oxford, but he's too busy to do that any more. He is still deeply involved, however, and continues to make all the key decisions. A measure of his involvement is his difficulty in motivating people to take charge.

Bragg is more typical of entrepreneurs than someone like Simpson. His organizational structure is simple. Everyone has a job to do and they do it. If they are not clear on what they are supposed to be doing, they have "a long talk" with Bragg. There's little need for meetings with large groups of other managers. Bragg sorts out their priorities with them, they do their job, and Bragg makes decisions in predetermined areas where he feels he should retain authority. Then he lets them get on with it and monitors them as closely as he feels is necessary. It's that simple.

Between the two extremes of Simpson's formal structure and Bragg's decentralized collection of independent profit centres, there is a third approach used by many of the entrepreneurs in this book. These people have an ad hoc structure that is not respected religiously. It serves more as a guide for dealing with situations than as a genuine channel for the flow of information and decisions. Steve Chepa has always had a formal structure for his Dicon Systems manufacturing plant, because the logistics of manufacturing demand it. For product development, administration and sales, however, his ad hoc structure has worked well for him. That way, when he needs some fast action, he can cut through the lines of authority without disturbing relationships and hurting people's feelings.

It takes a strong leader to work with this kind of structure, and few entrepreneurs can continue this approach when their firms grow bigger, as Chepa himself has found out. Two-thirds of the entrepreneurs in this book with ad hoc structures have sales of less than $10 million a year, compared to a quarter of those with sales of more than $10 million (see Appendix C, Table 12.3). The larger companies with ad hoc structures are generally those where employee creativity is critical to the success of the company.

## DELEGATING AND MAKING DECISIONS

The final element in entrepreneurial management is the delegation of authority. The critical measure of delegation is the degree to which leaders are prepared to live with decisions by employees which the employees consider to be important and with which they do not agree. The entrepreneurs in this book delegated at six different levels:

1. The solo artists make all the decisions themselves, without reference to their employees.

2. The next level is made up of entrepreneurs who seek and accept input from their employees on important issues, then make all the decision themselves, alone.

3. In the first level of genuine delegation, leaders give their employees significant authority and allow them to make decisions in areas for which they are responsible, but they monitor those decisions and their results closely and regularly. When an employee makes a decision the leader considers to be bad, the leader may reverse it, or let it stand after reprimanding the employee. Regardless of the action taken, the leader's judgement is always assumed to be best.

4. Once leaders decide their employees' judgement can be as good as their own, they can allow decisions to be

made through consensus. These leaders allow the cumulative judgement of their key managers to match their own, and rarely go against a consensus even if they disagree. The leaders are still closely involved in all the major decisions, and their opinions carry more weight than anyone else's, but they don't always insist on having the last word. They do, however, still monitor the results of the decisions with great care.

5. At the next level, leaders don't apply the discipline of group consensus, but allow individual employees to make their own decisions. Although they fully expect them to make mistakes, often significant ones, they are content to let them learn their lessons through experience. They trust their employees' ability to find their way out of the holes they dig for themselves. These entrepreneurs continue to provide the overall direction themselves, but they don't monitor their employees' decisions as closely as the third and fourth levels do.

6. Finally, there are the entrepreneurs who make very little attempt to influence or even monitor most of the decisions their employees make. They reserve some decisions for themselves, but they abdicate their authority for the rest. Often, they do this after hiring the best people they can find and giving them full rein. These kinds of employees would quit if they were offered anything less. The leaders are then free to target their own skills to the limited number of areas where their businesses face long-term challenges and opportunities, or where a severe crisis demands their immediate intervention. They can also act as a resource to their employees if they should need a second opinion.

Among the 100 entrepreneurs I interviewed, there are successful examples of all six approaches to delegation and decision-making. Some of them are heavily concentrated in one or two leadership styles. The first two levels of delegation, for example, are used by none of the system and figurehead leaders in this book. The fourth, fifth and sixth levels are similarly not used at all by solo leaders and are very rare among osmosis leaders (see Appendix C, Table 12.4).

Vern Simpson is a good example of a targeted decision-maker. He can afford to give his managers a lot of rope, because he has designed a system that creates its own checks and balances. "I sometimes bounce ideas off the core group of managers," he says, "but they accuse me of telling them what to do. So I usually make up my own mind." Simpson doesn't try to control his managers very closely. He has an executive meeting once a week, but he never chairs the meeting. The chair is always the person in charge of the area being discussed at the meeting. Once a month, he holds a "blue flag" meeting at which the agenda is made up of the most important issues raised by his key executives in response to a memo Simpson sends to them. Simpson almost never interferes with decisions his managers make, which occasionally leads him to wonder if they don't have too much freedom. "Very occasionally, I abort a decision because it's too big a disaster. They don't forget that."

A good example of an entrepreneur who delegates at level five, allowing his employees to learn by their mistakes, is Jean Pouliot of CFCF and Quatre Saisons. He sees himself as a catalyst, who creates an environment in which people can reach for the stars. "I encourage young people to make mistakes. We will never be first by copying what's there now. Young kids are afraid of mistakes, so our message is, 'For God's sake, try things.' Other people's experience is worth nothing."

Rod Bryden of Kinburn decides by consensus. He says there are only three reasons for any disagreement: different objectives, different facts, or people applying different qualitative factors to the facts. "Generally, it's the facts that don't agree," he says. "The second most common is the objectives are different." He won't approve a decision until this process is complete and everyone agrees. Especially himself. He would never knowingly agree to a course of action he didn't believe in, if only because every time he's done so, he's regretted it. "The individuals in the company are determined to do the best thing for the company," he says, "so they are as unwilling as I am to act in a way that doesn't win my approval. As long as people have confidence in me, I am a lightning rod for decisions."

More than a third of the entrepreneurs in this book delegate at the fourth to sixth levels. This does not fit well with the stereotype of white-knuckle entrepreneurs who can never let go, but that still leaves three out of five entrepreneurs who control their operations with a grip of iron. Half of these people are genuine delegators who keep tight control of their managers, and the other half make all the decisions themselves, mostly with some input from their staff but sometimes without any input. François Vachon and Steve Chepa are both tight delegators. Peter Oliver and Johnny Lombardi are solo decision-makers.

Don Watt of The Watt Group makes decisions with input from his managers, but he also typifies the kind of direct and forceful decisiveness that lies behind so many entrepreneurial success stories. Watt is a devout iconoclast. His ingenuity has fathered many innovations, including the square screw-on lid. He also invented the photo-symbolic packaging images that now decorate many packaged foods and most supermarkets. If his mouth-watering images of fresh produce covered with cool beads of water are a commonplace sight today, they were revolutionary when they first appeared. "The industry thought it should not be done," he sniffs now. "The professions teach wonderful self-imposed prisons."

He first decided to go into retail design in the early 1970s, when it was a badly fragmented area. The architects, industrial designers and graphic designers coming out of the school system were all specialists who sneered at each other's expertise. It was a golden opportunity for Watt. "I wanted to take over the design of space. My ignorance didn't seem a barrier. I didn't have the myopia of experience."

The customers weren't all ready for his ideas, however. When he got the job of redesigning the packaging in the bakery department at Dominion Stores, they refused to let him redesign the bakery. "They told me to stick to packaging, which was what I was hired for." So Watt went to an executive vice president at Loblaws and told him he could help him overtake Dominion. By 1972, he had the Loblaws' account, which was not then as prestigious an account as it was when Watt had finished with it. At the time, Loblaws was in such bad shape that its owners, The Weston Group, were thinking of selling it. Dominion Stores was then tramping all over the competition and was the undisputed market leader in Ontario's big market. Ten years later, Dominion Stores was discouraged, soon to be virtually disbanded, and Loblaws, already dominant in the Ontario market, was moving powerfully into other provinces.

Watt is short and soft-spoken, with regular features that make him look solid and dependable. He has the skin of a serene man who sleeps well at nights (not that he needs much—he sleeps only five hours a day). A graphic designer, he started his own firm in 1966 and quickly established a reputation for himself, winning such prestigious assignments as the design of the CP logo. When he began to find the scope too limiting, he added management consulting and strategic planning to his design practice. His custom-built office is stuck away in an obscure and dusty corner of Toronto, jammed against the railway lines alongside the Don Valley Parkway. It's all open plan, exposed ducts and bright colours. A sculpture of a woman sits incongruously on top of the divider that cordons off the boardroom.

Secure in his reputation, Watt sets himself high standards. "If I can't be as good as anyone in the company, I shouldn't be here," he says. "So many designers lose their ability when they stop doing it." He has created a structure that lets him do what he does best—solving design problems. He has divided the office into two parts, administration and design, and he spends very little time on the former. He hired an accountant with a degree in business administration, who administers the firm, while Watt and his top designers spend their time designing, largely divorced from the detail of scheduling and administration. "I draw, think or write six hours a day," he says. "I'm not going to let my experience be wasted. As a manager, I'm lower second quartile. Management of people is what I do when I have time."

That sentiment may be intended for shock value rather than insight; he doesn't mince words when there's a job to be done. "It's not a democracy." He writes a lot of short memos to his key people, which tersely outline a situation, describe the direction he'd like to take with it, list a few options and ask for their comments. Although he always seeks their opinions, and sometimes uses them, he makes the decisions alone. Like all osmosis leaders, he works through his managers, but never hesitates to cut across the organizational structure to work on an important project with people at a lower level.

He's not an easy man, but he gets results. "I'm constantly pushing people to do things they might not like doing. I'm used to being disliked and feared. I always deal with issues on their merits. People hate my memos."

# PART III

## STRATEGY

# CHAPTER 13

# PLANNING FOR CHANGE

*"We have no corporate plans, very little manage-
ment, no paper. I seldom write a memo a week."*
— Ken Rowe of The IMP Group

The president and sole owner of The IMP Group in Halifax is
not a fan of strategic planning. At least, he says he isn't. His
group consists of nine separate businesses with 1,800 employees and annual sales reputed to be about $200 million in 1989.
His companies are in three main groups—aerospace, marine
supplies, and hotels and real estate—and, to hear him talk, the
whole thing just fell into place by pure happenstance.

Ken Rowe is certainly flexible, prepared to change direction
the instant circumstances change, yet that doesn't mean he
really refuses to make plans. They may not be elaborate strategic plans at the corporate head office, and he may not write
them down, but he thinks strategically and has an intricate appreciation of the strategic problems and the most promising
options for each part of IMP. His subsidiaries all prepare formal
plans in varying detail according to their needs. In his aerospace division, for example, he has a comprehensive ten-year
plan, which is prepared with his active involvement. The hotel
and real estate arm of IMP, on the other hand, doesn't look
much beyond three years at a time.

Rowe prefers to describe his strategy as making money.
"This company's not interested in what's going to happen in 15
years," he says. "Unless it has a return in a short period, we're
not interested." He does admit, however, when pressed, to
having a long-term vision on which he bases some of his
decisions about expansions and acquisitions. His basic strat-

egy for his subsidiaries is to pick a niche, become the top firm in that niche and then add new products. The pattern has been to expand into areas related to his existing businesses, so that he can build some synergy into each part of his conglomerate.

Rowe is a chartered corporate secretary, so it's only natural that he runs his companies according to the book, with thorough and detailed operating statistics. His tight-fistedness is legendary in the Maritimes, where he has a reputation as a tough taskmaster whose attention to the bottom line brooks no incompetence in his managers. But he's also widely admired for his acumen in restoring troubled companies to good health, which he could never have done without being such a tough manager.

His enormous self-confidence is softened by a quiet sense of humour that lurks under the cool effectiveness he projects. He's a handsome man with a lean, square face and hooded eyes that hide his feelings, if not his sharp mind. He speaks with the clipped language of a man who knows exactly where he's going and doesn't want to waste any time getting there. He appears to be plagued by few doubts about anything that touches his business, as he articulates a stream of fully formed ideas without hesitation in his brisk English accent.

He started out on his own in 1967, at age 33, when he bought two failing companies in the foundry and steel fabrication business. He had been working for Great Grimsby Coal, Salt & Tanning Co., which he had joined in Britain when he was 25, fresh from an apprenticeship in the merchant navy. At Grimsby Coal, which manufactures fishing gear, he started at the bottom and rose quickly through the ranks until he was number two in the company, "telling them what to do." When he was 30, Grimsby Coal transferred him to its Canadian subsidiary, where he could run his own show as managing director. The company couldn't move fast enough for young Rowe, though, so he quit three years later to go on his own.

He soon expanded into the business he knew best, fishing equipment. Over the next ten years, he built up IMP's marine division, through internal expansions and acquisitions, into what is now the largest supplier in North America of every conceivable kind of fishing equipment, from nets to inflatable boats. He has also expanded into Europe where he has a significant operation, based, of course, in Grimsby.

He then entered a new field, although still in the transportation business: aerospace maintenance. Ten years later, in 1980, he took that business into the major leagues when he won the contract to service the Aurora Long Range Patrol Aircraft. Meanwhile he had expanded, logically, into commercial aviation and offshore supply to the oil rigs in the Atlantic. Since he was repairing aircraft, it was natural to expand into parts, so IMP started manufacturing electrical harnesses for military aircraft, which in turn led the group into plastics injection moulding. The final leg of his group is real estate and hotels, which he entered three years after he started IMP by buying a company that owned the Halifax Holiday Inn and some real estate.

By the time IMP reached its twentieth birthday, he had assembled a sizeable mini-conglomerate, with sales of $100 million a year. But Rowe was still hungry for growth. He had been searching hard for complementary businesses to round out his aerospace division. He came close to buying Canadair, the Montreal-based manufacturer of executive and commuter airplanes, but couldn't compete in the political game that eventually awarded Canadair to Bombardier. Then he made a bid for Leigh Instruments in Ottawa, which specializes in avionics, but was defeated by a British giant, Plessey, which was favoured by Leigh's management.

Rowe handled the setbacks with aplomb, secure in the knowledge he would find a good fit sooner or later. Sure enough, less than a year later, in the first quarter of 1989, he finally found an avenue for expansion in his aerospace division, when he successfully bid for control of Innotech Aviation Enterprises. Based in Montreal, Innotech earns revenues of $60 million a year selling and servicing business aircraft and building custom interiors for aircraft like the Canadair Challenger. At about the same time he bought Innotech, he concluded a deal with the Soviet airline, Aeroflot, to build a series of hotels, commercial buildings and aircraft hangars in the U.S.S.R. Their first project, worth $70 million, is to build a 420-room hotel and office complex in Moscow.

He won't stop there, of course. He has found three niches, become a major player in each and will continue to add products. Now that he has built his company into such a large conglomerate, however, he might have to rework his image to accommodate his new status as a corporate patriarch, solidly installed on the board of the Royal Bank. He is not pretentious and has a lifestyle far below what his wealth could afford. He will remain an entrepreneur, because he loves the game and he loves to win. He is successful because he can recognize opportunities and capitalize on them. And he may just admit one day that he does strategic planning for his group.

## ENTREPRENEURIAL PLANNING

The idea of strategic planning has fallen on hard times in the 1970s and 1980s. It was all the rage in the 1960s and early 1970s, when scientific management, in its exuberant adolescence, created expectations in managers all over the world that they had the power to manage the future. All they had to do was think it, and it would come to pass. The shock troops for this new ideology were the young graduates of the North American business schools, who swarmed all over the continent, armed with the jargon of futurism and dazzling their bosses with their sophisticated models. There was even concern in Europe that their management technology would crush all other economic systems, putting in their place a sterile meritocracy.

It was always doomed, of course. The expectations for strategic planning were unsustainable even in normal times, but the credibility of the whole idea was destroyed by the severe economic dislocations following the first OPEC crisis in 1973. The glorious strategies of the 1960s never did connect with the real problems and opportunities in the trenches. The ensuing collapse in support for strategic planning obscured its real value, and it acquired the reputation of a bureaucratic boondoggle. Strategic planning became associated in too many people's minds with elaborate prescriptions for action that were bound to fail, because they were based on pedantic assumptions created in isolation by programmed robots. Rob Peters of Peters & Co. captures the feelings of many when he says, "The guys I've had trouble with are Harvard MBAs who have five-year plans they stick to" (see page 240).

Many entrepreneurs believe, like Ken Rowe, that planning precludes flexibility. But when these people protest that they do not plan, they are talking about the pejorative stereotype of strategic planning. Careful analysis of what they do, rather than what they say, reveals them to be conscientious planners. Planning has evolved; it hasn't gone away. All large businesses plan today, as do almost all successful entrepreneurs. They just don't like the word.

Among the 100 entrepreneurs in this book, only four honestly do not plan. Yet 25 flatly denied they planned when asked the question directly. It's astonishing how many successful entrepreneurs insist, with a straight face, that they never plan, that they operate from day to day by crisis management, only to pull out of their bottom drawers shortly afterwards detailed plans for up to five years into the future. Of the 21 planners who said they didn't plan, almost half had substantial documents containing some degree of planning. Five (including Rowe) had one or more full-scale, written plans. Another five had less developed plans, although they were documented. The remaining eleven all had specific plans, which were not elaborate and were not documented, but the entrepreneurs had gone through the process of strategic thinking and had developed their tactics accordingly.

A strategy does not have to be written down to qualify as a plan. It's true that written plans are usually more realistic and better thought out than unwritten plans, if only because they have been exposed to the glare of critical assessment without the protection of verbal fudging. However, unwritten plans can still contain all the key elements of a sound strategy.

Phil O'Brien of Devencore, a firm of commercial real estate developers in Montreal, will never write down a plan. "I'm allergic to paper. I don't own a briefcase. I believe in discussions. I'd rather our office space were a bunch of tents in a park." He's only half in jest. A boyish and light-hearted man, O'Brien thinks it's important to enjoy working. He has arranged his business so that he can do what he does best, which is put deals together, and delegate what he dislikes, which is administration. He has built an impressive network of Montreal's business elite through many years of working on volunteer committees and is an inveterate booster of his city. And he does have a plan—unwritten, of course, but carefully shaped in annual regular sessions away from the office, sometimes in tents.

Two to four times a year he takes his 12 key employees into the wilderness far north of Montreal, where they spend four days exploring where they think the company should be going. He's had occasions when two of his people weren't talking to each other and a canoe trip solved the problem. "I put them in a situation where they are not controlling the environment," he says. "It helps them get rid of their baggage." He never plans an agenda. He finds people don't want to raise subjects off the agenda for fear they'll offend the boss, and sometimes these are the things that need to be discussed most. "I use the meetings to keep a sense of humility in the organization."

About two-thirds of the entrepreneurs in this book write down their strategic plans (see Appendix C., Table 13.1). Some do it for their bankers; most do it to clarify their ideas in their own minds. Almost none of them prepare strategic plans to inform their employees where they are leading them. To many entrepreneurs, written plans sound a little too much like procedure manuals, and they're afraid that if they circulate them, their employees might treat them like a bible and actually try to follow them. If the plan has to be shared with employees, most entrepreneurs prefer to spread the word themselves, orally and in bits and pieces.

It's understandable why people with unwritten plans should say they don't plan; it's a lot more curious when people with carefully written plans deny they plan. This is probably because they almost never consult the piece of paper on which their plan is written, so they forget it exists. The value that entrepreneurs derive from strategic planning lies in the process of working through a plan, not in the piece of paper at the end of the exercise. Accordingly, entrepreneurs often view their planning documents as notes for the goals and strategies which they have formulated in their own minds. They don't make decisions on the basis of their strategic plans. Their decisions are based on the strategic thinking that emerged from the process of developing a plan.

However they do it, entrepreneurs who do plan perform better than those who don't. Among the entrepreneurs in this study, the average growth rate of the four businesses that do not plan is significantly lower than the growth rate in the businesses that do plan. The non-planners are successful—so far—but they are exceptional. The hundreds of thousands of Canadian entrepreneurs who don't plan fail more often than those who do plan. Moreover, the non-planners are not even as flexible as most of the planners, because they don't go through the process of identifying all their strategic options until it's too late. Many of these non-planners switch to strategic plans in their second or subsequent businesses, when they graduate to become successful entrepreneurs. The point has not been lost on investors and bankers, who now generally insist on a thorough strategic plan when smaller firms seek financing for new businesses or even for refinancing existing businesses.

Entrepreneurial planning, however, has none of the logic and elegance of the forward planning performed by bureaucracies, which deploy their weighty resources in well-ordered manoeuvres. Entrepreneurs are scramblers, constantly leveraging their limited resources to expand their capability in order to make some progress toward their objectives. They often have to go sideways, sometimes even in the opposite direction, on the path toward their objectives. Every step they take, though, either advances their strategy or builds a key resource.

The key difference between entrepreneurial planning and the strategic planning practised by large organizations today is flexibility. Planning, entrepreneur-style, is rooted in the creation and recognition of opportunities. Without adequate resources, however, the plans based on these opportunities are seldom reliable, because the opportunities can fade or vanish as competitors react to their initiatives. But there must still be plans. Plans significantly improve entrepreneurs' performances as long as they can recognize changes in their circumstances, and are prepared to throw their plans out the window and prepare new ones immediately. Entrepreneurial plans are not written in stone.

A plan allows a firm to let go of the past. It gives a forward context to present decisions, improving the selection of tactics to exploit opportunities. Each plan is the base for the next revision of strategy, when subsequent experience proves its assumptions wrong. Entrepreneurial planning is a dynamic process, more like constant replanning. It does not decide anything, it is a parallel activity, influencing as well as reacting to day-to-day decisions.

Most of the entrepreneurs in this book say that their plans work out more or less as expected. This doesn't mean they are brilliant forecasters. It means their plans adjust as quickly as they do to changing circumstances. The parallel functioning of strategic planning and day-to-day decisions blurs the distinction between the plan and strategic thinking. If the strategy is expressed in sufficiently broad terms, and the tactics are changed as frequently as the situation demands, and the details of implementation are left to the ingenuity of the entrepreneur and his team, then it is indeed possible for events to turn out much as a plan envisages.

If strategic thinking is the prize of planning, then the assumptions that go into them are the booby prizes, because they almost invariably turn out to be wrong. However, they are still necessary for a plan. They provide a context for strategic thinking through the analysis of present and future situations and through the development of options for future initiatives.

The disenchantment over the repeated errors in these supporting struts of strategic thinking has led to some bizarre prescriptions for effective planning. One of the better, though still dangerous, suggestions came from Tom Peters and Bob Waterman, Jr. in *In Search of Excellence*. They advanced the seductive idea that no strategy can anticipate the surprises and discontinuities that lie in wait for the people who are chosen to implement it, so the best solution is to sever the link between implementation and strategy. This way, the implementors can react quickly to changed perceptions of the marketplace as they implement the strategy. They might even try several different approaches to implementing the same strategy and choose, with the benefit of hindsight, whichever one was best.

That's fine as far as it goes, but it's a very short step to the realization by the strategic planners that it's a waste of their time putting too much effort into their strategies, because the implementors aren't going to pay much attention to them. This is true even when the implementors are also the planners, as is the case with entrepreneurs. They become careless. The plans become cursory. Their businesses become reactive and start misinterpreting trends when something unexpected happens. They lose their way.

Successful planners make their strategies central to their implementation. The flexibility comes when the strategy doesn't work. The planners analyze the hiccoughs they encounter and then reformulate the strategic plan. Flexibility lies in communication between setting and implementing strategy, not in severing the link between them. Since most entrepreneurs combine the roles of planner and implementor, they have the advantage of perfect communication between the two functions.

## THE COMPONENTS OF PLANNING

Good planning seeks to answer three fundamental questions: the needs of the customer, the future direction of the competition and how to gain competitive advantage. The essence of strategic thinking is creating a competitive advantage. There are numerous techniques to achieve competitive advantage, including a low price, a differentiated product or service, superior service and personal influence on customers or suppliers, to name just a few. A competitive advantage, once established, must then be maintained, so that the business can stay ahead of the inevitable reactions of competitors and customers.

There are six major steps in planning:

1. *Analysis of the firm's competitive situation.* This covers, among other things, market analyses, probable technical, social or other changes in the industry, studies of changing customer needs, SWOT (Strengths, Weaknesses, Opportunities and Threats) analyses, the sources of competitive advantage, and information on existing and potential competitors and their strategies.

2. *Identification of opportunities.* This is the special expertise of entrepreneurs, the ability to recognize patterns, turn them into opportunities and make a commitment to seize them.

3. *Establishing overall objectives.* This breaks opportunities down into specific and manageable bites so that they can be

pursued in concrete steps. The process includes determining the firm's overall direction, identifying target market segments along with the appropriate products or services, and setting specific goals.

4. *Establishing a time frame.* A time frame is important in a plan, because it is the catalyst for setting priorities. However, it is possible to plan without a time frame if the plan depends on external circumstances which cannot be predicted, or if the plan is not specific about some of its elements.

5. *Action plans and allocation of resources.* This includes the logistics of projects to get the business there from here. Part of this involves the skill of committing resources only as they are needed, in order to conserve what resources the entrepreneur has. And part involves the skill of being decisive and flexible, which together enable entrepreneurs to implement plans effectively and at a minimum cost.

6. *Control and feedback.* This is part of implementation rather than the actual plan, but it's crucial if the plan is ever going to mean anything. It means monitoring events as they unfold to see if the assumptions on which the plan is based are reliable and, if necessary, going back to the first step when it becomes apparent the plan is not working.

Entrepreneurs use all of these concepts, but they generally prefer not to express them in these rather theoretical terms.

The first two are the basis of the first element of entrepreneurship, an orientation toward opportunity in an environment of scarce resources (see Chapter 4). The last two are part of competence, the third element of entrepreneurship (see Chapter 6). The middle two—setting objectives and putting a time frame on them—are examined in the next two chapters.

# CHAPTER 14

# THE FOUR TYPES OF PLANNING

*"I don't believe in visions. I don't have a vision. I'm more concerned with a sense of direction. Vision implies you can see the light at the end of the tunnel. A sense of direction means you know where the tunnel is. The purpose of strategic thinking is to synthesize what we're good at and what direction technology's moving."*
— Ian Sharp of I.P. Sharp Associates

The entrepreneurs in this book plan in one of four ways: project-planning, goal-setting, direction-setting, and full-scale planning. The first three types of planning are components of full-scale planning. Some entrepreneurs select whichever component of full-scale planning most suits their needs or personality; others evolve from one type to another, winding up as full-scale planners. All of them use their type of planning to give a forward context to their current decisions.

## PROJECT-PLANNING

John Seltzer built his firm of consulting actuaries, GBB Associates, by giving his consultants a free rein to find their own market niches and develop them. He rejects the usefulness of managing people, preferring to hire self-starters who feel they have their own businesses within GBB and who neither need nor want direction from him. "I'm not one for long-term strategic planning—or even short-term," he says. "I'm not a believer in the theory of strategy." But he is a believer, of course. He just means he doesn't develop strategies in isolation, without consulting the people who will implement them.

Seltzer is not an overpowering leader. He seldom reveals anything of himself or his feelings and he doesn't expect others to share their feelings with him either, but he has an unerring appreciation of people's strengths. The whole idea of military-style strategies and corporate games repels this gentle and cerebral man. He is nonetheless an expert strategic thinker and has the steely determination to enforce his vision, even though he avoids giving orders and limits himself to gentle persuasion or the carrot of a challenging assignment.

Once a year, Seltzer and his senior consultants write down for their board of directors what they're going to do in the next year. They look at the services they provide and the industry classifications of their clients. "In the last few years, we've tried to look at areas we're not in, but should be," he admits. Inevitably, he develops strategies to correct the omissions. It's worked, even if he won't call it strategy. A few years ago, GBB had almost no clients among the financial institutions, an industry where Seltzer himself had worked for many years. He hired a new consultant and suggested he might like to go after the banks and trust companies. Two years later, GBB had as clients three of the five biggest banks and a Schedule B bank, and had generated some work with the investment houses.

That approach doesn't always work quite so smoothly. He was, at one stage, concerned that GBB was winning almost no government business, so he asked some of his newer consultants to try and break into that market. When they had no luck either, Seltzer hired a consultant to tell his firm what they were doing wrong. His approach is a typical example of project-planning: he selects a critical area for development and then starts a concerted program to develop business in it. Even if the implementation of his plan is flexible and ad hoc, he still identifies a target market and works at finding the right formula to penetrate it.

He applies the same principle to the services GBB provides. A few years ago, his clients began to complain that onerous legislation was making the administration of their pension plans increasingly complex. Seltzer picked up on it immediately and began to lay plans to develop the capability of administering pension plans on behalf of his clients. Seltzer has a clear idea of where his firm's competitive advantage lies, where he wants the firm to go and what kind of firm it should be. He plans new products, but there's no big plan.

Project-planners identify and plan projects that are strategically important, because they represent a significant departure from their existing lines of business. The plan does not cover parts of the business that are not tied in to the project, but it does offer a focus for the short-term and long-term decisions of the leading people in the business. Also, of course, the planned project usually defines, however subconsciously, the planned context of the entire business because of the steps that have to be taken to select the project in the first place. Project- planners are often niche players (see Appendix C, Table 14.1).

## GOAL-SETTING

Goal-setters tend to be the most aggressive entrepreneurs. Their simple goals, like a first-place finish for athletes, focus their minds and give them the energy to persevere through all manner of setbacks, complexities and changes in strategy. The people around them often describe them as dynamic. John Gillespie, formerly of Pizza Delight and Pizza Pizza, now chief executive and part-owner of Goliger's Travel, is a goal setter. "I'm always making goals," he says. "I set a goal for each five-year segment of my life—personal and business. I write it down and put it away. It's surprising how close you get."

This man is driven. There's a bustle about his every movement, an eagerness to get on with his life. He is articulate and incisive, his thoughts spilling out in torrents of words, barely able to keep up with his racing mind. He can listen, too, and can be warm, even charming, but only if he's genuinely interested in the subject. He keeps his ego under tight control, reluctant to share his thoughts or join discussions if he can't see some advantage in airing his views. He is in far too much of a hurry to spend time on peripheral niceties. His office at Pizza Pizza, decked out in green leather on grey carpeting, was cold and spare, symptomatic of a man so absorbed in his work that he is oblivious to his surroundings. It has nothing to do with taste. It's just that his surroundings are not important to him.

He has a youthful face and was a little overweight when first interviewed for this book, but the physical softness hides a capable, tough and uncompromising man in hot pursuit of the results he wants. He ran his pizza franchises as he would have run them had he been the franchisee, with tight cost control and fierce attention to service. He's not ruthless, because he has no interest in winning at other people's expense. He's just dedicated and uncompromising. He won't let other people's sensibilities slow him down or distract him from his chosen course. The only regret he has about his lifestyle is not having spent enough time with his children. He completely missed the first five or six years of his first-born's life, and he still sees his children only on weekends, figuring he'll play catch up with his grandchildren. The only person in his family whom he sees a lot is his wife Linda, who is deeply involved in his job (they met when they started out as partners in Pizza Delight).

Gillespie came from a poor family and money is important to him. By the time he was 37, he had created two huge successes, and suffered twice as both of them crumbled before his eyes. The first time, with Pizza Delight, he started with no money, built a franchise chain of 100 stores and then lost everything in a dispute with the franchisor. He was devastated, but had no time to mope; within weeks he had joined Michael Overs at Pizza Pizza. Overs gave Gillespie, who was already recognized as a hot property in the franchise business, 20% of the company (for no cash) and a clause in the shareholders' agreement that specified he was to have management control.

In the nine years after he joined, Gillespie powered Pizza Pizza from 16 stores to more than 100. Then the partnership shattered. Gillespie exercised his management control a little too firmly for Overs, who fired him. Gillespie eventually collected $4 million for his shares, which he claims was less than half what they were worth, but he wanted to get on with the rest of his life.

During his enforced inactivity, when he was still president of Pizza Pizza but unable to work there by court order, Gillespie tackled his new circumstances with characteristic directness. He knew he would be under stress, so he lost 35 pounds and went on a health kick. He sold his house, cut cash flow and scouted his contacts for a new challenge. Soon after he pocketed his $4 million, he joined forces with the Goliger family and merchant-banker Lincoln Capital Corp., to become a part-owner, president and chief executive officer of Goliger's Travel (International). His goal, just as it was at Pizza Pizza, is simple: he wants to be number one in any market he enters.

He sets goals for his life up to age 50, because he considers his prime years to be between the ages of 40 and 50. He was 38 when he took the helm at Goliger's in 1988. He said then that he intended to increase the number of Goliger's outlets to 200 from 60 in five years. It promises to be an interesting decade for Goliger's.

Goal-setters are often deal-makers or maestros, the former not caring much what kind of business they're in as long as it advances their goals, the latter not prepared to deviate from their craft, which defines their goals. The goals they set for themselves are specific and quantitative. It could be a certain level of annual sales or profit or number of employees. It may be market share or asset base or even, in at least one case, acquiring the wealth to be able to afford a private jet.

The importance of the goals is that they provide a focus and a motivation for the entrepreneurs and their key employees. They also provide clear measures of their progress. These entrepreneurs usually don't know how they're going to reach their goals. Many of them find that when one promising line of endeavour does not live up to their vague expectations, unexpected progress in another counterbalances it.

## DIRECTION-SETTING

This is the opposite of goal-setting. Direction-setters abhor specific goals. They are less concerned with where they'll be in five or ten years' time than with how they will have got there. This is not to say that they don't care what they achieve. On the contrary, many of them are ambitious. It's just that they don't want to limit themselves to specific targets. They may want to mine a particular niche they feel is worthy and interesting. They may want to improve their standing relative to their competitors within their line of business. They may even want to build a business that meets the personal needs of their team of top executives. Sometimes they seek to contribute to the achievement of broader goals within their communities.

The direction they choose for their businesses might encompass several different projects or products, all selected carefully to be consistent with the chosen direction of the firm. Some of the projects will succeed and some will fail, but direction-setters don't need to worry too much about trying to guess which ones will do well. As each project gathers experience in the marketplace, the direction-setters will know which ones should be nourished and which ones starved of funds.

Rob Peters is one man who just loves his business. The firm of stockbrokers he started in 1971, Peters & Co., has clients all over North America and Europe, thanks to its solid expertise in the oil patch. It is one of the few firms based outside Toronto and Montreal to have made a national name for itself. It hasn't been easy. The oil industry has been a roller coaster of highs and lows beyond the imaginations of most people. Although Peters & Co. has survived and thrived through it all, its owner wouldn't claim any credit for having managed its affairs astutely, which is what in fact he's done. He has learned more than a few lessons, to be sure, but he doesn't see himself as a manager. He sees himself primarily as a practitioner. He loves to make big deals.

He intensely dislikes "the professional managerial role." He joined Nesbitt, Thomson, as it then was, when he was 25 and rose to become manager of the Calgary branch by the time he was 28. One year later he quit to start his own firm with a partner, whom he later bought out. He couldn't take being a manager anymore: "You're a baby-sitter more than anything else. You learn about hierarchy and politics."

This resistance toward managing colours the way Peters develops his plans. He gives individual managers a lot of rope and encourages them to develop business for the firm in their own way, within a broad framework set by the limitations of the firm's capital base and location. He holds the power of the ultimate decision-maker, but he rarely uses it. He claims, with a boisterous laugh, that, although his executives pay lip service to his leadership, they really ignore him. In reality, his presence is so commanding within the firm that few people would stray for long from the parameters he communicates so well. He dominates any group he's in. When he talks, he projects his booming voice on the wings of his infectious enthusiasm, often breaking out into boyish laughter. Superbly fit, bursting with energy, he fills a room with his presence. He also knows his business and has an openness to new ideas that encourages people to be imaginative.

The decor of his plush office is given over to horses. The walls are plastered with pictures of show jumping and polo games, leaving gaps only for the numerous trophies he has won. He is an ardent polo fan, having played in Africa, India, Argentina, the U.S. and the Caribbean. (The Calgary Cup, which was first contested in 1892, is the oldest polo competition in North America.) He also owns a 4,000-acre ranch where he keeps a commercial herd of 200 head of cattle and 100 racehorses, mostly other people's but some his own. Peters is involved in ranching up to his neck, as he is in any activity he undertakes. When it's haying time in the late summer, he leaves the office early to help out with the haying. He has no hobbies, only a large collection of vocations.

The pivot for running Peters & Co. is the meeting Peters holds with his key staff every morning at 7 a.m. He goes round the table, reviewing current information and deciding on courses of action. Strategy for the day, the week or the year is a critical part of these discussions, but it is never formalized. It more closely resembles a dynamic consensus that evolves continuously. Peters is the primary source of ideas by sheer force of personality, but he rarely bucks the consensus view of his or anyone else's ideas: "You've got to be righter than wronger!"

These early-morning discussions usually set the firm's direction and define where its competitive advantage lies. Peters then isolates the resulting initiatives, tracks them carefully and feeds the ones that turn out to be more profitable. There is an executive committee, composed of the five most senior people, but it meets irregularly, almost solely when there's a major decision to be made. Peters has not used it to set a direction for the firm.

His zest for life is refreshing. He is open to any new idea. When Calgary was booming in the 1970s, he jumped in with both feet, investing in all manner of businesses with the compelling enthusiasm of those times. It seemed then that everything Albertans touched would turn to gold. He diversified out of Peters & Co., attempting to build a personal conglomerate of promising firms. He bought, among other businesses, a trendy restaurant called Kipling's, a taco restaurant ("the food was awful"), a company making ski-lift chairs, a trust company, major shareholdings in a couple of oil firms (Poco Petroleum and Chancellor), a shopping centre in Saskatoon, an option on some land and a company that designed and manufactured a high-tech, slant drilling rig.

When the bust came, it all turned to dust. He had to let the option to buy the land lapse, losing $100,000 in the process. The slant drilling rig came onto the market just as oil prices collapsed, and the company had to operate it itself, rather than sell or rent it to drilling companies. The share prices of Poco and Chancellor have been bumping along at devastating lows for a couple of years. The restaurants went bankrupt. Peters recognizes now that he was investing with his heart, buying into firms because he liked their products.

The experience has not dimmed his enthusiasm one iota, although it has injected some sober conviction in him that he will never again invest in something he knows nothing about. He learned about direction. His investments are now mostly in or with Peters & Co., and he is trying to move the company into a role more like that of a merchant bank. He wants to stay small, he knows he has to have quality research, and he knows he has to have superb block traders, the people who move around big blocks of stock for institutional investors. He knows he has to build on his intimate knowledge of the oil patch (the energy business accounts for 80% of his revenues), and he knows that his bread and butter will come from the institutional investors who dominate the Canadian market (and provide two-thirds of his revenues). But decisions on what kinds of deals he'll look for, or what kinds of products he'll deliver, or what markets he'll exploit will have to wait until the moment he's ready to move.

Another direction-setter is Ian Sharp of I.P. Sharp Associates. His strategy is driven by his product, which is computer services. He led his company to annual sales of more than $60 million in 1987, before selling to Reuters for $62 million. Sharp's company became a leader in the time-sharing business in the 1970s, when few companies could afford the massive price tags of the biggest computers. However, the falling prices of computers, culminating in the introduction of personal computers, turned the time-sharing industry on its head. The machine that Sharp bought in 1969 for $3 million was one of the largest in the world then, but 20 years later, it is outperformed by a $3,000 personal computer. Many of the customers of the time-sharing firms decided they would be better off buying their own machines and doing their computing in-house.

A number of time-sharing firms soon went out of business, because they thought they were selling time on their big machines. Sharp, however, understood that the technology of time-sharing is the software that links data bases and network technology. The applications of this technology are not in independent links to many end-users, but in linking one company's network of thousands of terminals spread across several continents. The technology of time-sharing has become pervasive, although few may realize it. Hotel and airline reservation systems are based on time-sharing technology, as are credit cards, automatic teller machines and the global financial markets.

Sharp intuitively understood this market pattern in the early 1970s when the time-sharing bureaus were in their prime. His strategy was and is to focus on the technologies for time-sharing, data bases and networks, to keep the three technologies moving forward together and to build application programs that depend on the combination of the three. The bigger the data bases are, the harder it is to gain access to their information at a reasonable price. Data bases now often contain more than a billion bytes of information (equivalent to about 150 million words or about 1,500 fair-sized books), so an error rate of 0.1% would mean a million numbers wrong. The technology for data bases is critical to ensure there are no mistakes in entering the data, storing it, updating it and getting at it.

All this was far beyond the imaginations of everyone, probably including Sharp, in the early 1970s, but he was spared the fate of most of his competitors by his orientation toward his technology rather than his customers. "We're not customer-driven, we're customer-sensitive," he says. "We're technology-driven. We don't try to solve bank problems. We try to find those problems in the bank that are amenable to solutions with our technology. Then Xerox may have the same problem and we can solve that too."

He develops his technology systematically. Each branch of the company is encouraged to develop new applications by persuading their customers to fund the research. However, there are always a number of potential applications that individual programmers cannot sell to clients, so Sharp spends about a quarter of his payroll on "unfunded" applications. Even with this enormous commitment, there is still a long wait before projects are funded. Many programmers get tired of waiting, so they quit to develop their ideas on their own. If an unfunded project reaches the stage where it appears to have commercial potential, it is transferred to an application development department, still within the branch that came up with the idea. There, perceived customer needs are brought into the equation and applications are developed to test the market. Once it has been proved commercially, it is made available to the worldwide organization.

It's a brutal system, internally competitive and creatively chaotic. Sharp himself is idiosyncratic, a small, ascetic man who defies the conventions for a president of a mid-sized company. He rides to work on the subway, dressed in tweedy, slightly rumpled suits. He projects a self-effacing image, with slight hesitations in his speech that camouflage an incisive and bold character. His eyes look like they might be laughing but are more likely mocking - almost disdainful, but not quite so. He spends up to a third of his time travelling to the far-flung outposts of his empire, yet he is never absent. By signing on at the nearest computer, he can plug into the firm's electronic mail system, which is his primary means of communicating with his staff. He has a computer at home, of course, but doesn't have one in his office, preferring to stroll down the corridor, get a print-out of his mail and read it at his leisure.

Sharp's mild and courteous manner hides his reputation for being a difficult boss. He says himself he's not a believer in democracy. "Business has to be a dictatorship—the more benevolent the better." He tried, shortly before he sold his company, to hire a president to handle day-to-day operations, but he didn't last long, because his style was too different from Sharp's. He wanted to deal only with people who reported directly to him. Sharp didn't object to a different style; he just didn't want his president behaving that way.

He is a typical osmosis leader. He believes in keeping in touch with employees who are on the firing line, maintaining a close connection with his firm's major contracts and application developments, so that they can serve as his entrée into the murky future. "I don't believe in visions. I don't have a vision. I'm more concerned with a sense of direction. Vision implies you can see the light at the end of the tunnel. A sense of direction means you know where the tunnel is. The purpose of strategic thinking is to synthesize what we're good at and what direction technology's moving. Price is one edge. A better edge is uniqueness. We have tended to focus on the latter."

## FULL-SCALE PLANNING

Full-scale planners come closest to the popular image of planners, although their version of it is far from the stereotypical straightjacket. Their plans are comprehensive views of the future that pinpoint options for initiatives. They are not decisions about planned courses of action; they give a future context to present decisions and offer guidelines for future decisions. Full-scale planners are more likely to feel they create their own opportunities rather than grab opportunities that come floating by (see Appendix C, Table 14.2).

Full-scale planners go through all six of the planning components mentioned in Chapter 13. It takes a certain amount of patience and discipline to work through a full-scale plan, but the entrepreneurs who do it are unanimous in their view of the purpose of planning. Again and again, entrepreneurs said something like Normand Carpentier, president of Camoplast: "The planning process is essential, the *plans* are useless. The moment it's out, it's obsolete."

Carpentier is perhaps more inclined toward full-scale planning than most entrepreneurs because he used to be the head of the industrial products division of Bombardier. The division supplied its parent with snowmobile component parts as well as snowmobile suits and industrial and protective clothing. In the late 1970s, the division was struggling as demand for snowmobiles sagged. Bombardier was unwilling to invest much money in it, so Carpentier suggested the company sell the business to him and his partner, Michel La Salle. (La Salle later sold his interest to the Société d'Investissement Desjardins.) Six months later, Bombardier agreed, putting a price of $10 million on the division and keeping a small shareholding itself. It was January, 1982. Carpentier and La Salle had put their names to a $2-million personal loan and an $8-million corporate loan from the Royal Bank at unprecedented rates of interest, just in time for the recession.

There was no snow that winter, so demand for snowmobiles fell even further. Although Carpentier had a good contract for autoparts, car sales plummeted too as interest rates went through the roof. Even the company's one great ray of hope, a major contract to supply Xerox with plastic housings for its office equipment, caused trouble as Camoplast struggled to correct start-up problems with the new products. With a debt/equity ratio close to infinity, Camoplast had no room to manoeuvre and teetered on the edge of bankruptcy less than six months after it was formed.

When Carpentier first approached the Royal Bank to finance his leveraged buyout, he had given them a professional, exhaustive business plan. The bank manager spent an afternoon with Carpentier examining his numbers and explaining her analysis of the loan. When she left, she promised an answer within three weeks. True to her word, she delivered $8 million within the agreed time. Now, six months later, Carpentier had to go back for another $500,000, armed with a new plan to take account of the sorry first six months. To his great surprise, the bank accepted his projections, agreeing to provide the extra financing, provided Camoplast contributed some extra money itself. Carpentier shook down his receivables, met the bank's target and received his second loan. In the following four years, results came in remarkably close to that revised plan. Sales doubled to $40 million and the company paid off debt as fast as it could, reducing the debt/equity ratio to 0.84 by 1986.

Naturally, the route to the targets identified in Carpentier's plan bore no resemblance to the plan's projections. A third of the company's sales in 1982 had come from Runyband, which retreaded tires for trucks. Camoplast was banking on this operation to provide some balance to the slump in sales of snowmobile components, but it was not to be. Because Runyband was much smaller than its main competitor, an American-owned firm, Carpentier realized he could never increase sales to improve his economies of scale. Instead, he went to his competitor and offered to sell Runyband. He told his competitors they could kill Runyband, but that no one would make any money at it. The offer was accepted. Although Carpentier lost a significant chunk of his revenues, he turned a lot of receivables and inventory into cash and soon rode the recovery in the auto business to pick up the slack.

It's taken its toll. Carpentier's face is battle-scarred, and he looks much older than his 45 years. But he is enjoying the fruits of his Herculean struggles in 1981 and 1982. By 1988, annual sales had reached $60 million. The same year, after only five years in the business, he became president of the Automobile Parts Manufacturing Association, proud of the high ranking for quality bestowed on him by the auto manufacturers. Utterly without pretension, he has a tiny, utilitarian office stuck away in a corner of the plant in Kingsbury, a village in the Eastern Townships of Quebec.

Like most entrepreneurs, he has a great sense of fun and tremendous energy. An avid jogger, he had to hang up his running shoes because of tendonitis and is frustrated because he hasn't found a suitable replacement yet. He is sensitive, acutely aware of his own role in the company and the roles of all the people who work for him. He has acquired the entrepreneurial proclivity for tight cost control and a deep concern for detail in every corner of his operation. However, he hasn't lost all his big-company training, particularly in his approach to planning.

Each division in Camoplast produces two plans a year. In the first half of the year, they update their three-year plans and in the second they prepare their operating plans for the following year. The general managers of each division are entirely responsible for their own plans. "We've forced our managers to learn their markets, their market share and so on," says Carpentier. "Head office just approves or rejects their plans."

At the beginning of each planning cycle, Carpentier sets the scene with a comprehensive survey of the company's situation. (All employees, without exception, are told what the company's sales and profits are in each division.) To give them a conceptual framework for the firm's opportunities and problems, Carpentier usually brings in a well-known scholar who gives a speech on a subject Carpentier feels his key managers need to think about. The focus can be on anything, broad or narrow, and has included industrial labour relations, portfolio theory for multi-division companies and new concepts of management.

Carpentier's input into these plans is informal, mainly through the monthly operational meetings with each of his general managers. He also monitors the plans closely. "If something goes off track, the manager has to do a contingency plan," he says. "It's tough. If someone tells us he won't meet plan, it's not very friendly. We tell him, 'You've been dreaming once—if you dream again, you won't be working with us.'" He expects plans to be adjusted repeatedly, but each change has a base to build on, each new plan is the starting point for its successor.

Slightly more than half the entrepreneurs in this study use full-scale planning. However, the proportion rises to 66% in firms more than 20 years old, compared to slightly more than 40% in firms aged between six and 20 years (see Appendix C, Table 14.3). Almost two-thirds of the youngest firms also use full-scale planning, but this is probably a tribute to the growing influence of bankers and investors, who insist on a full-scale plan from start-ups seeking financing.

It would appear that once the start-ups survive their critical first five years, they drop the full plans in favour of project planning or direction setting. They then return to the fold of full planners in their more mature years. It's possible that the current crop of young businesses may stick to the full-scale planning their investors have demanded, even when the investors have lost their hold over them, but it's too early to tell. The more specific approach of project planning and goal setting does make sense for businesses growing strongly.

Oscar Grubert of Champs Food Systems in Winnipeg has watched the entrepreneurs who have changed the way they plan. He himself did so as his firm grew, and he's helped many young entrepreneurs follow his example along the way. "There are different stages," he says. "The entrepreneur doesn't start by writing down his plans. He starts in a simple, basic way. If he has the entrepreneurial spirit, the odds are he doesn't have an organized plan. He comes across an idea, seizes it, uses good common sense and some finance to start the idea. Planning comes much later, unless they're MBA grads who really apply the principles they learned at business school. But I've come across very few who've started that way. When you get to the size that you can no longer operate with pure gut feel, then you've got to make that transition to boardroom strategy. We made that size when we got to $25 million."

Not all entrepreneurs can handle this change. Goal-setters seem to be about the same proportion of the entrepreneurs in this book regardless of how long they've been in business. And direction-setters, though uncommon among firms less than five years old, seem to occupy a consistent share of firms once they've passed five years (see Appendix C, Table 14.3).

## VISION

An entrepreneur's vision transcends all planning types and stretches far beyond the scope of long-term planning. It is the dream that fundamentally drives the entrepreneur and is the (sometimes) hidden agenda in every strategic plan. It is rarely a drive to achieve a quantitative goal. It is more likely to be a dream of attaining a certain size within an industry or community, or the achievement of a particular standard of performance, or a desire for a certain role in society.

Greig Clark of College Pro Painters has built his business to annual sales of $36 million in 1986. He has a branch in every city in English Canada with more than 20,000 inhabitants. He has more than 550 student franchisees who supervise an army of 5,000 painters who canvass every home in their neighbourhoods. Clark has built an extraordinary business by channelling the energy of his student workers. It is a remarkable challenge, because, of course, they have so little experience, and he has to deal with continual turnover as they leave to find regular jobs.

His secret has been to develop top-flight management skills in his managers. An intense young man, Clark was already a walking encyclopaedia on business skills by the time he reached 30. Almost skinny, he radiates high energy, probing people incessantly, sucking out of them any information he senses may be useful to him. He has developed a sophisticated planning system, based on a study of just about every book and article published on the subject. But the plan is not his vision.

Clark dreams of building an organization that will combine the open-mindedness, enthusiasm and energy of young people with the discipline and self-knowledge of much older, experienced businesspeople. He wants to build a management machine that will be able to master whatever challenge it turns its hand to. "My vision," he says, "is to be a truly great organization that delivers the best value in any market it's in. I want to provide the best training in the world for youth."

He is assembling his knowledge-base about the motivation and training of young people by experimenting and studying fanatically. He has developed an elaborate model of what constitutes competence in each level of management at College Pro, and he encourages managers to advance their careers by acquiring the appropriate expertise. "Patience is a wonderful virtue," he says. "Take time to season someone, do it properly and you get wonderful results. The focus is to build a superb team. I call it the SDR strategy—select, develop and reward. Especially the development. That's our competitive advantage."

A vision is often a critical element in the urge to plan. Almost two-thirds of the entrepreneurs who have a vision for their businesses are full-scale planners, while only a third of those who don't have a vision are full-scale planners.

## THE NON-PLANNERS

Four of the entrepreneurs in this book don't plan at all. It doesn't seem to have hurt them much so far, even if their average growth rate in annual sales is slower than the rest of the entrepreneurs. Their progress, moreover, is sometimes closer to a ride on a roller coaster than a steam engine. One of them, Abram Dyck of Saskatoon Fresh Pack Potatoes, which sells more than $3 million worth of perogies and potatoes across Canada and in the U.S., has never planned anything in his life: "Everything we've done, we didn't plan. We're like water in the spring."

He's not exaggerating. Dyck has had devastating failures that would have defeated most people, but he has remarkable equanimity and an indomitable resilience which inures him to life's vicissitudes. He feels no urge to plan, even though it terrifies some of his family. The only goal Dyck will admit to is passing on to his family a profitable business that will enable them to earn a good living—and he seems to be successful enough now that he will achieve that goal.

Another genuine non-planner is Joe Shannon of Atlantic Corporation. He ran the government-owned Cape Breton Development Corp. (Devco) for 13 months in 1984-85, so he knows all about planning, especially big-business planning. He doesn't like what he saw. He runs a lean shop and he can turn on a dime. Because he's more nimble than Dyck—he has diversified to insure himself against cyclical downturns—his progress has not been a roller coaster ride. With his superb business sense, he attracts opportunities like a magnet. "If something occurs to me as a good business, I look up the names in the Yellow Pages and ask them if they want to sell." Enough of them say yes that he figures he can do without planning.

All he will concede is that as he gets bigger and more spread out, he has to communicate more. He doesn't have systematic strategic plans for any of his various subsidiaries, and he will sell any of them if someone offers him a good enough price or if he can't make it as profitable as he would like. "We don't brainstorm," he says. "I deal with the managers of my businesses individually. I get input from them and then I decide. It's all in my head." He has no blueprint for change, but his strategy of no strategy has worked like a charm for him.

# CHAPTER 15

# THE TRICKS OF EFFECTIVE PLANNING

*"It's surprising how 90% of our blue-sky objectives are achieved. The only thing you need is to want something and it will happen! Even the most crazy things. We don't know how, but it happens."*
— Claude Lessard of Cossette Communication-Marketing

There's more to planning than the plan. The way each type of planning is prepared can have a big impact on how it's used. This chapter explores three planning techniques:

- *The process of planning.* Some entrepreneurs invite the full participation of their employees in setting their goals and strategies. This means sometimes abandoning their own preferences if there's a strong consensus among their employees. Others seek input from their employees, but make all the strategic decisions themselves. And some do it entirely on their own.
- *Planning style.* There are strategic plans, which map out a route, and opportunistic plans, which map out a goal.
- *Time frames for plans.* The deadlines for objectives and the horizon of the overall plan give each plan a unique perspective.

## THE PROCESS OF PLANNING

### Participatory planners
Entrepreneurs have a reputation as individualists who don't

share much information with their employees or give them much rope in setting strategic directions. In fact, most of them do share information with their employees and encourage them to participate to some degree in formulating their plans. If this does nothing else, it secures a commitment from the employees to strive for the goals they helped create.

Guylaine Saucier of the Saucier Group inherited the family business in 1975 when her father died. It had a sawmill and logging operation, with annual sales of $17 million, which was an impressive achievement considering her father and his partner only started the firm in 1966. At the time, Guylaine, a chartered accountant and the oldest of six children then aged 12 to 29, had been working with her father for four years.

The family was nervous about asking Guylaine to take over, but she was the only one with any experience in the company. They need not have worried. Twelve years later, in 1987, sales had risen to $85 million, and the company was doing just fine after Saucier had stick-handled it through some rough patches that had hurt a lot of other companies in the industry. (She had to sell the company, however, in 1988 to avoid being squeezed by the rationalization of the industry.)

Strangers might be excused for finding the family's nervousness understandable. To look at her, Saucier seems too fragile to cope with the rough and tumble world of the forest industry. She is a beautiful woman, with fine features and a petite figure, clad in elegantly tailored dresses. She speaks in a very quiet voice, almost diffidently, surrounded by women, in offices decorated in peach and grey. When she takes coffee, the service is sterling silver coffee pots and delicate bone china. But she knows how to handle herself and the men with whom she deals outside the office. She smiles gently at the way doors open for her because she's a woman, then moves with a flair that leaves them all gasping. One of her more effective habits is arriving at meetings in her company helicopter.

One suspects she takes quiet joy in surprising people, which she has done for most of her career. She has mastered the intricacies of her industry, having served on the forest products committee in the free-trade consultations, and is widely respected by the business community. She served as president of the Quebec Forest Industries Association and of the Quebec Chamber of Commerce. Her passion, however, is strategic planning. When she talks about it, she comes alive. She sees her vision as one of her major strengths. "I can see what's coming," she says. "I'm well informed. I can foretell the shocks."

She developed an elaborate process to integrate her planning into the company's operations. In the fall, she takes her top 11 executives to a meeting away from the office. It could last half a day or two, but there is no agenda, and no documents. "We put everything on the table," she says. It's not structured, but a direction usually emerges, which she articulates for them. Then the executives all prepare their three-year plans separately, consulting only with Saucier. In November, they have another meeting at which the separate plans are integrated into a unified plan. Saucier then presents the result to her board in January. The busy time in that industry is the summer, so her schedule means that the plan for the following year is in place before everyone gets too busy to plan.

She says she had to use participatory planning when she first took charge at 29, but she's kept the system, because it works so well for her. Participatory planners are not always this structured, however. Ian Sharp of I.P. Sharp Associates allows the strategic direction of his firm to evolve in casual exchanges of information with employees, customers and competitors. "There's no way of knowing where the sense of direction comes from," he says. "We don't go to the mountain and examine our navels. It grows out of conversations, what you read, customer reactions."

The secret of his success is that he keeps in close touch with those employees who are developing applications he thinks might be important to the future of his company. He doesn't hesitate to spend time with them, wherever they are, if they are working on something he thinks has potential. "Things feed on each other. We might get into a certain application and find our technology is suited to it. So we'll extend it to other areas and industries. It's important to be aware and to be able to extrapolate."

### Planners who accept input only

Doreen Braverman of The Flag Shop doesn't believe in market surveys, because people don't know they're going to buy a flag until they buy one. She does, however, conduct one market survey a year to a select and unusually well informed group of just three people—the managers of each of the divisions of The Flag Shop. The managers fill in a form five pages long, detailing who their customers and competitors are. They profile their competitors and suppliers. They assess their own operations, looking at their locations and new ideas for product lines.

Braverman stretches this process out over six months. "They have to keep thinking all year long," she says. Braverman herself is the fountainhead of ideas. She keeps a whole drawer in a filing cabinet stuffed with clippings, notes and reminders, which contain enough ideas to keep her going for years, all filed by the applications she has in mind for them. She also has regular brainstorming meetings with her staff. By the time she's finished, she and her managers have a pretty clear idea of what they could do, if the circumstances were right.

Braverman has acquired a high profile in the business community. Tall and self-possessed, she has a calm and balanced approach to life, powered by her prodigious energy. Beyond running her $2¼-million business with an iron fist, she gives speeches all over B.C., promoting the interests of small business. She has been on the national board of the Canadian Chamber of Commerce, and she was instrumental in resuscitating the Kitsilano Chamber of Commerce in Vancouver. In her "spare" time, she attended night school at Simon Fraser University, where she earned her MBA.

Despite her range of activities, Braverman is a model for how to run a tight ship. She gets weekly sales reports from her managers and monthly reviews on progress against the annual plan. Her plans are all her own. When she has aired all her and her managers' ideas, she calls a meeting with her board, all of whom are outsiders. They then hear her view of the world and give her their input. Finally, she sets her mission for the following three years and puts in the annual budgets to fit. "Most of the time I do what I think is best," she says. "But I do listen. I know where I want to go. I make myself articulate that, and draft reasonable steps to get there."

### Solo planners

Paul Abildgaard of Nanton Water is a solo planner. He is also almost a caricature of the stereotypical entrepreneur. A big, rugged man who works hard and plays hard, he's game for anything. He is both fearless and fearsome. Fearless because he'll take on any challenge and any competitor. Fearsome because his willpower sweeps all before him. He is used to getting his own way, and he likes to make all the decisions for everyone within earshot. He's also canny, because he knows and understands his own limitations. He is a fascinating and attractive cowboy entrepreneur, a larger-than-life Dane living in Alberta, who makes other Albertans seem like tame easterners.

He does nothing in half measures. When he was courting his wife Elinor in Denmark as a young man, she happened to mention in passing that she liked chickens. The next day, a truckload of 200 chickens arrived. Friends know better than to express a wish when Abildgaard is feeling good. He doesn't spoil his children, though. He gave them an allowance of 10¢ a week and encouraged them to work in the summers to build their finances. They had all bought houses by the time they were 18. Father paid the down payment, but they had to figure out how to finance the mortgage payments. They all became millionaires.

Abildgaard is the King of the Good Deal. He left his native land for Canada at age 27 after he had conquered the world of food packing in Denmark. He crammed two degrees into three years at university, one in biology and one in commerce, at a time when it was unusual to have degrees in different disciplines. He joined a packing firm and became general manager of one of the largest packing plants in the country at the age of 24. But he found Europe constricting, so he moved to Hamilton, where he used his expertise to build a successful packing business. He then sold the business to Burns Foods at a considerable profit and moved out west. After dabbling for 15 years, he finally jumped back into business in 1981 when he started Nanton Water, which bottles carbonated water in competition with the likes of Perrier.

At 56 years old, Abildgaard shows no physical signs of living life as fully as he does. He's put on a bit of weight, but he has the enthusiasm and drive of a 30-year-old. He once called in one of his sons and told him he'd bought a piece of land nearby and wanted the son to put up a building on the site. The son asked, naturally enough, what kind of building his father had in mind

and was told, "I don't know yet, just put one up." Abildgaard
had found out the land was going for a ridiculously low price,
so he bought it, not knowing which of several potential projects
he would use it for. He collects projects in his mind the way
some people collect exotic cars. When he chances on an
extraordinary bargain to give one of his projects an unbeatable
edge, he wheels it out and starts it up.

On that occasion, he heard soon after he bought the land that
Burns Foods was closing down one of its plants and auctioning
off the machinery. He went along and bought a meatball machine for $2,000. It was missing a head, however, so he went to
one of the plants owned by Swift Canadian and asked them if
they'd be interested in selling him a meatball machine, because
he had another customer who wanted one. "If I had told them
what I was really going to do with it, the price would have gone
straight through the roof," he says. It so happened they had a
machine, and it happened to have a spare head, so he then had
two meatball machines for about $5,000. If he had bought them
new, they would have cost $50,000. That put him back in the
packing business, in the building his son put up on his new
plot of land.

He used the same techniques to start his brewery. He heard
a widow in Vancouver wanted to sell the brewing equipment
her late husband had bought in England for $2 million. He
found out she badly wanted to sell and offered to buy it for 10%
of its value. She accepted and Abildgaard was in the beer
business, brewing Appaloosa beer for the Albertan and U.S.
markets. His next project is to start a ship-building factory on
the Albertan prairie—80-foot yachts made from a steel frame
inside an oak hull. He has the building (bought cheaply,
naturally). All he needs now is the time, which he hopes to find
once he's got his breeding herd of 28 thoroughbred racing
horses, sired by a son of Northern Dancer, settled down on the
200-acre farm he recently bought.

Abildgaard stores his strategies in his head and no one
knows what he's planning. "All strategies come from me," he
says. "I never get any strategic ideas from anyone else." He
develops his strategies until they are fully formed, then waits
for the right circumstances to appear. He might wait 20 years,

and tell no one, then start a new business on a day's notice. He's always ready, even if some of the people around him find it hard to keep up.

The degree to which entrepreneurs invite their employees to participate in the planning process depends a great deal on whom they consider to be the main source of ideas in their firms. Only a quarter of the participatory planners consider themselves to be the idea people, compared to almost all (92%) of the solo planners. About three-quarters of entrepreneurs who seek input from employees, but make all the strategic decisions themselves, feel they are the main source of ideas. Not surprisingly, the entrepreneurs who prefer to plan alone rarely use full-scale plans (see Appendix C, Table 15.1). That would be too much work.

## PLANNING STYLE

The planning type that entrepreneurs use is a measure of what kinds of goals they set for themselves. But they also have different styles of planning, which are a measure of how they approach the task of setting goals. There are two styles adopted by the entrepreneurs in this book: opportunistic and strategic.

### Opportunistic planning style

When these entrepreneurs make plans, they don't try and anticipate the kinds of opportunities they should exploit to achieve their goals. They build into their plans flexibility on the specific initiatives and projects that will advance their goals. They leave decisions on these opportunities to their own judgement when and if the opportunities emerge.

Marcel Dutil of Canam Manac is an avid planner. He aims at annual growth of 20% on the bottom line. He tells his managers he is not concerned how they get there—if it takes a growth in sales of 30%, "that's their problem." He also aims at a market share of 25% in any market he's in. He achieved that share in the Canadian market for steel joists some time ago, and now he's aiming to repeat the performance in the U.S. He measures these goals over five-year periods, so that his managers can accommodate bad years. All they have to do is double their profits every five years. When they have bad years, Dutil expects them to increase their market share and eliminate competitors, even if they don't meet his standards on the bottom line.

Dutil now has subsidiaries in construction steel, trailers, office furniture and in Noverco, the holding company for Gaz Métropolitain, a gas utility with annual sales of more than $1 billion. He bought Noverco because he was acutely aware of the vulnerability of his annual earnings in the highly cyclical construction industry. In 1986, when he was interviewed for this book, he hadn't bought Noverco yet. He knew, however, that he had to stabilize his cyclical earnings and was looking for another leg to his business. He was considering life insurance companies, trust companies and a service business, among others.

He didn't much mind what industry it would be in, as his main criteria for buying were stability of earnings and management in place. In his acquisitions in the steel and office furniture business, he had found that incompatible management cultures caused him a lot of grief. He learned that the best solution was to send one of his top Quebeckers to manage a new plant, so that he could be assured the right culture would be built into the firm. If he was entering a whole new industry, however, that wasn't an option, so he had to be comfortable with the management. In the end, none of the financial institutions came up for sale at a price he considered reasonable, but Noverco did. In a classically opportunistic planning style, he bought it because it fitted his criteria.

### Strategic planning style
This is the more popular planning style among successful entrepreneurs—two-thirds of the people in this book have a strategic style. These people like to map out the route to their ultimate goal. The timing and exact nature of the opportunities that will be exploited on the path toward the goal may not be known in advance, but the intent is to stick to initiatives that fit specific parameters. This doesn't mean, however, that unanticipated or unexpected opportunities are ignored. Seizing the right opportunities is critical to the success of any venture. Strategic planners are just a little more fussy than opportunis-

tic planners about the context of any opportunities they will exploit.

John Gillespie knows exactly how he is going to achieve his objectives. The principal objective is straightforward—to be number one in any market he enters. To reach that goal, he analyzes the market exhaustively, assesses the competition, determines the factors that will offer the greatest chance of success and then goes after it with every ounce of willpower he can muster. When he and his partner, Michael Overs, decided to expand Pizza Pizza into another city, they discussed at some length which one they should try first. They eventually rejected Vancouver (too volatile), Montreal (too unfamiliar), Calgary (they were concerned about consumer bias against an eastern company) and decided on Ottawa. With a population of about 800,000, Ottawa is virtually recession-proof because of its civil servants. Its French-speaking residents would offer them a test-market for Montreal, and its retail market is well developed. Gillespie avoids markets where there isn't much competition because that means the retail market is under-developed and he doesn't want to waste time doing missionary work.

Having selected Ottawa, Gillespie lined up financial backing from H.J. Heinz of Canada (Pizza Pizza invested very little apart from the partners' time and expertise). Then Gillespie went to Ottawa to develop his strategic plan. He walked the streets of Ottawa, watching the traffic flows and noting the better potential sites for outlets. He also studied all the retail and merchandising statistics, of course, and mapped out the competitors' stores. Finally, he went to the real estate agents and started acquiring sites. Only then was he ready to start selling franchises and pumping up the advertising. Ottawa was tough, because there weren't a lot of good locations available, but, by the end of its first year, Pizza Pizza scored higher than any of its competitors for customer recognition.

The distinction between strategic and opportunistic planning styles is quite different from the distinction between opportunity grabbers and creators. It would seem logical that entrepreneurs with an opportunistic style would be opportunity grabbers who avoid full-scale plans, just as it would seem logical that entrepreneurs with a strategic style would be full-scale planners who create their own opportunities. That's true for most of the entrepreneurs in this study (see Appendix C, Table 15.2), but more than a third defy the apparent logic—and illustrate the important differences between the two concepts.

Jack Donald has a strategic style but is an opportunity grabber. When he detects a gap in his conglomerate's portfolio of companies, he doesn't just go out and buy a company to fill the hole. He will wait as long as he has to, until a buying opportunity, at the right price, comes his way. In January, 1986, Donald's Parkland Industries was almost an integrated oil company. He had service stations, drilling rigs and producing properties, but nothing to turn the crude oil into gas. It wasn't a priority because he had a good working relationship with the major companies. Then the majors' refineries stopped negotiating prices independently with the gasoline retailers and switched to a rack pricing system, in which they controlled the margins.

He saw red. "It made me do more long-term planning," he said later that year. "I'm going to go into refining, either by leasing space in an existing refinery or buying one." But not at any price. Donald stalks his prey. "If I decided 'this is the year to buy X', I'd pay 50% more than it's worth. But if I wait till someone wants to sell, I'll pay what the assets are worth." For all of 1986, he devoured every annual report he could lay his hands on, combing them for signs of weakness. Less than two years later, he closed a deal with Shell to buy its refinery in Bowden, Alberta. Although he had to work hard to ferret out what was available, he still sees himself as capitalizing on current opportunities at any one point of time rather than creating his own opportunities.

At the other extreme, opportunity creators can plan opportunistically. They may have complete confidence in their ability to create opportunities but decide not to specify what kinds of opportunities to plan for. They would set goals that do not depend on the type of opportunity to be exploited. Marcel Dutil does this. Like Donald, he won't pay more for a company than he thinks it's worth, but, unlike Donald, he is committed to growth above all else, even if that means he has to forego expansions in the directions he would prefer. If one avenue is closed to him in his search for that growth, he will explore another and then another, until he finds one that suits his growth objectives. He can switch, without any concern, from looking for a life insurance or trust company to buying a gas utility. He creates his own opportunities, even if he's not fussy about the industry his opportunity happens to be in.

## TIME FRAMES FOR STRATEGIC PLANS

A plan that doesn't trigger action is nothing more than a wish list. Someone has to believe in the plan and turn its ideas into concrete actions. The magic ingredient that turns people into believers, empowering them to make a plan come alive, is a sense of urgency.

All successful entrepreneurs have a sense of urgency. It can come from anywhere, from great ambition as much as from imminent failure. Most of all, competitive pressures have a way of bringing into focus the dangers of procrastination. Sometimes this sense of urgency can be artificially created by imposing deadlines on initiatives, thereby forcing actions that might otherwise have been delayed until it was too late. This is where the time frames of strategic plans become important.

Deadlines can be a powerful tool, but they must be properly set. Too easy a deadline kills the sense of urgency; too demanding a deadline has the same effect, because it kills the deadline's credibility. With this caveat, putting deadlines on all the key parts of a strategic plan delivers two important benefits. Estimating the time it will take to achieve an objective weeds out the projects that would take too long to be economically feasible; and attaching time frames to projects permits priorities to be set realistically.

Deadlines are not always appropriate, however. If a plan depends to a significant degree on external circumstances that the entrepreneurs feel they don't control, it would be futile for them to put a time frame on their plans. A person like Paul Abildgaard implements his plans only when he finds someone willing to sell the equipment he needs at an absurdly low price, so he cannot give himself a deadline, because he cannot predict when a deal like that will materialize. Other people who plan projects can decide easily when they will start a project, but find it impossible to estimate how long it will take, so they can't set deadlines either.

The project planners and direction-setters in this book are generally wary of putting time frames on their plans (see Appendix C, Table 13.1). The goal-setters are a different matter—almost 90% of them have deadlines, largely because the simplicity of their goals lend themselves to target dates. And slightly more of the full-scale planners have specific deadlines in their plans. In some cases, they have no choice, because their industries operate with long lead times. Aerospace companies, for example, cannot survive if they aren't looking ten or more years down the road for themselves, and for their competitors, customers and suppliers. And real estate developers have to base their plans on absorption rates and building plans stretching five or ten years into the future.

Claude Lessard of Cossette Communication-Marketing is perhaps the most enthusiastic planner of all. He sees his firm's strategic planning as the characteristic that distinguishes it from the many advertising agencies against which it competes. Its five-year plan covers everything: overall corporate objectives; the firm's product, employees and clients; and organizational development. In 1985, Cossette set itself the target of increasing its billings from $50 million to $200 million within five years. It achieved its target by 1989. "It's surprising," he says, "how 90% of our blue-sky objectives are achieved. The only thing you need is to want something and it will happen! Even the most crazy things. We don't know how, but it happens."

Cossette had to start its next plan earlier than expected. Lessard now anticipates broadening its scope to become a North American company. He projects billings will increase to $350 million in 1994 in Canada, where Cossette is already the largest domestically owned advertising agency. Cossette will also diversify out of advertising, giving it some countercyclical strength and building alliances with strong partners in other industries.

Lessard and five partners paid their boss, the owner of Cossette, $30,000 for the agency in 1971, when it was still small and they could not agree with him on how to make the agency grow. The firm was located in Quebec City, a backwater in the advertising industry, but that didn't restrict the dreams of its young new owners. Over the next five years, the six partners built on their remarkably good chemistry to grow at a steady, if unspectacular rate, as they "matured their ideology." By 1976, the firm's clients started pushing them to become more adventurous. By this time, Lessard had assumed the leadership role, and he launched Cossette into a vigorous program of expansion, moving into Montreal and then, in 1982, into the Toronto market, where 70% of all advertising decisions in Canada are made.

Cossette's offices, in a converted old house on the prestigious Grande Allée, just outside the ramparts of old Quebec, are understated and littered with colourful but inexpensive pastel posters and prints. The house is airy and spacious, unencumbered by the weight of luxury. Lessard, who has an office to match the general decor, is a handsome man, slim, elegant and impeccably dressed. He shows almost no emotion, even when he's talking about planning, the subject dearest to his heart. His Cartesian mind revels in the complexity of the merger of separate strategic plans for each city, industry and client.

In the necessarily decentralized organization of an advertising agency, where local people make or break a national firm, his role seems to be finding a way to create a sense of unity among disparate and divergent parts. His principal tool in this task is the five-year plan and the planning process. By focussing on potential initiatives to achieve a target five years away, every part of the company can see its phenomenal growth in the context of the whole organization. It works. In an industry notorious for its fickleness, Cossette's managers in every city buy into the dream with a sense of urgency that has made it the fastest growing agency in Canada.

A year after Lessard put together his five-year plan in 1985, he said it would remain substantially unchanged until 1990, although he speculated at the time the tactics might change. He said the same thing in 1989 when the first plan was rendered obsolete and he had to build a new five-year plan. Although he says he'll review the plan every year, few of the people in Cossette expect the current strategic thrust to remain in place for much more than three years. Cossette's experience is typical of many firms that are finding the horizons of their plans too long. As the pace of change accelerates, it is becoming more difficult to make realistic plans.

There is, nonetheless, a strong argument for extending the horizons further out rather than shortening them. In *Innovation and Entrepreneurship*, Peter Drucker writes that he has found a consistent lag of 25 to 35 years from the time new knowledge becomes available to its acceptance in the marketplace. Many other trends can be forecast with confidence well into the future, such as demographics and 60-year economic cycles. And some trends—for example, the shift of manufacturing industries to lower-wage countries, the economics of energy or the impact of the computer—can be forecast, albeit with less certainty, at least ten years into the future.

Richard Prytula of Leigh Navigation Systems has a 20-year horizon. "You have your long-range scanners," he says. "It's never going to happen that way, but you've got to have a plan."

# CHAPTER 16

# A SENSE OF TIMING

*"Market timing is not all that important. Economic cycles change the price, but that's not really important either. There's always someone to say, 'It's not the right time.' What counts is a good product, a good reputation and good distribution."*
— Richard Bourbeau of Venmar

*"There are three major cycles in this industry. Your forecasts don't have to be right, but you have to be in shape for whatever is coming. You're a damn fool if you don't read the graphs constantly. You'll fall off the cliff."*
— Bob Lamond of Czar Resources

It wasn't exactly a run-of-the-mill day for the luckless federal cabinet minister. He had been pelted with a hail of dead chickens by a group of enraged Quebec chicken farmers, who were unhappy with the price their eggs were fetching on the free market. Across the continent that evening in the 1960s, in Calgary, Ed Davis watched their antics on TV and something clicked.

"It was a sign of social change," he says. Soon afterwards, in Montreal, he met a senior civil servant in the department that looked after agricultural marketing boards and asked him point blank if Ottawa was planning an egg marketing board. The bureaucrat declined to comment, so Davis knew right away that an egg marketing board was on its way. He went back to Calgary, made some contacts in the egg industry and bought de Witt & MacKenzie Farms Ltd., which was in trouble at the time. He knew nothing about the industry, so he hired a good manager and gave him a piece of the action.

The politicians didn't disappoint him. The marketing board was introduced shortly afterwards, and he immediately applied for additional quota. With a guaranteed customer, he built a new modern plant and created a vertically integrated operation that packed and distributed the eggs. Then he sat back and waited for the money to roll in.

Davis was 70 when he was first interviewed for this book, but even with his white hair, which looks almost incongruous against his tanned and youthful skin, he looked more like 55. Small and wiry, he possesses enormous energy. Whenever he can find the opportunity, he loves to go fishing or hiking in the foothills, and he still plays tennis three or four times a week. He's a devout contrarian, happiest when he's tilting against windmills. He loves to write essays on economic issues, which he passes around to the vast network of influential people he knows across the country. He has even written a book, called *An Economic System for Canada*, which he published himself.

He does not approve of marketing boards, but his sense of timing is exquisite. He is in the business of starting businesses. At last count, he had started 17 businesses (the egg farm was his twelfth) and, although not all of them have been successful, he has made "a few million." He says he would have made much more if he had stuck with one of his successful ones. "To make big money, you have to stay with something once it's flying, but I get bored out of my mind."

Davis concentrates on two types of business propositions. Class A opportunities, as he calls them, are situations where something new is happening. He almost never invests in a product that is already on the marketplace. Class B propositions exist because of a political situation. The egg farm was one, of course, but there were many others. "In the last two decades," he says, "there has often been more money in Class B than in Class A."

When he sold his egg farm seven years later, he got more for his quota than for the business itself. The marketing board was by then buckling under the inevitable political pressures of a regulated industry. To protect the smaller producers, it established a pricing and quota structure that ensured solvency for a 5,000-chicken operation. Davis had 31,750 chickens, so it was guaranteed to make money.

Not everyone pays as much attention to their timing as Davis. Mark Blumes of Mark's Work Wearhouse has seen sales of his company reach almost $200 million only 11 years after he started it, and he thinks timing is just not an issue. "If it's a good idea, we do it NOW," he says, "but in small enough quantities that it can't hurt us."

Every year, he starts a new "book" which he fills with "visions" and "discussion papers." The visions are concepts for new products, and the discussion papers are his detailed assessments of concepts that have progressed to the point where they are ready to be tested. "My role is to pass ownership," he says, "to get someone to own a project." Once people take ownership of ideas, they are then responsible for developing them until they are on the shelves. There is no timing. Blumes wants those products in his stores in the shortest possible time.

He subscribes to the mud-against-the-wall theory. He is bursting with ideas and was for a long time the main contributor to the "book," although he's trying to encourage others to join in. He sees his job as ensuring that enough good ideas make it through the screening process that there is a steady flow of new products into his stores. He then lets the market decide which ones are right. "If it's wrong, do something else. If it's a good idea, do it. The pressure of results will push the cream to the top."

He's a large man, who hides his sharp brain with an exaggerated folksy manner. Dressed in his blue jeans and running shoes, he certainly doesn't project the image of a man running a mid-sized growth company. He tries to maintain a casual, first-name relationship with all his 1,200 employees, but it doesn't work as well as it did when the company was smaller, so he is devising systems to give him the contact he used to enjoy first-hand. He treats the development of his employees in the same way that he treats new products. "I don't believe in the interview process," he says. "I prefer to test them in a role and give them a chance." That makes for some fantastic opportunities for employees who are prepared to grab the brass ring, but it also entails a high turnover.

The entrepreneurs in this book are evenly split between the views of Davis and Blumes on the importance of timing. Of the ones who think it's not important, some subscribe to Blumes's mud-against-the-wall theory, while others believe that things happen because they decide they're going to happen, not because the timing's right. These entrepreneurs have honed their willpower to achieve whatever they set out to achieve. Lawrence Bloomberg of First Marathon Securities, for example, says, "When we went into business in 1979, people said the outlook's not good, maybe you shouldn't do it. But it's always the right time to go into business. Timing is only that you're there and you decide to do something. We do it because we do it."

The other half of the entrepreneurs in this book support the view of timing espoused by Davis. It's important to distinguish between strategy (the decision *what* to do) and timing (*when* to do it). Although some factors are common to both, the context is quite different.

## THE CARE AND CONTROL OF TIMING

Joe Shannon is highly sensitive to timing in his incessant search for opportunities. "I have three or four files open all the time," he says. If he sees an interesting situation, he might buy a company within weeks. Or sell one of his companies. But he also knows how to lie in wait. He eyed the fishery industry in the Maritimes from the time the government proclaimed its sovereignty over the oceans up to a 200-mile limit. "I've been thinking about it for ten years," he said in 1986. "First the big companies wouldn't let you in. They went hogwild. Then they went broke. Then the government got in. Now it's going to be good for six years or longer." Two years later, he found his fishery investment, but on the day he closed the sale, he was offered such an outrageously high price for it, he flipped it that evening.

Shannon is unusual in having an active as well as a passive sense of timing. The entrepreneurs with a passive sense of timing generally know which opportunity they would like to exploit and are prepared to wait for the circumstances to evolve until they are ripe for their project. They may, like Shannon, nurse a private dream for years until they feel the conditions are right. The ones with an active sense of timing don't like waiting. They are seldom committed to any particular opportunity. Good timing for them is picking the project that has the best chance of succeeding today. Tomorrow, another one will work better. It's a mentality of opportunism. "It's a decision to be alert," says François Vachon of Cartem. "You've got to react to situations. If you haven't thought already about an acquisition, you can't decide when one comes your way. Timing is not really a factor. We're looking for something and if the price is right, we go."

Among the people who think timing is important, two-thirds also believe, like Davis, that they can control the timing to make their ventures successful. The rest believe, like Frank Stronach, that good timing is a matter of luck. "It's important to be in the right place at the right time with the right ingredients. When I started, I did not choose this industry. Fate has blown me into this field."

## SPURS TO ACTION

Entrepreneurs invariably ascribe their sense of timing to intuition or gut instinct, mostly because they have never tried to articulate the process of timing. That's entirely understandable, because there are so many factors that influence timing. The decision to embark on a significant initiative in business should involve a considered assessment of the product itself, the market for it, the capabilities of the team producing and delivering it, the financial support required to bring it to profitability and the capacity of the entrepreneur to give the leadership to pull the venture through its difficult early stages.

If entrepreneurs analyzed the impact of all these factors on their decisions, they would never make a move. Instead, most of them decide to act on the basis of a single, particular facet of the complex decision, usually the facet that contains the entrepreneurs' peculiar strength, the one that gives them their competitive edge. If that special factor is right for a project to be started, the project can take shape in an entrepreneur's mind and all the other factors will be dealt with, one way or another, as effectively as possible. The factors that prompt action are the underpinnings of timing. They are the initiating factors.

Half the entrepreneurs in this study base all their timing decisions on a single initiating factor. The rest have a second string to their bow. That doesn't mean they consider both factors, just that they base some of their timing decisions on one and some on the other. Overall, the most common initiating factor is the sheer willpower of the entrepreneur who sees a goal and goes for it, regardless of market, financial or economic conditions. The other popular factors are market conditions and having the right people to make it happen.

| Initiating factor | Percent of entrepreneurs who base their timing decisions on each factor |
|---|---|
| *External factors* | |
| Market conditions | 33% |
| Economic and social cycles | 12% |
| *Internal factors* | |
| Entrepreneurial willpower | 38% |
| People | 29% |
| Financing | 11% |
| *Combined factors* | |
| Strategic fit | 17% |
| Technology | 6% |

Combined factors balance external situations and internal capabilities. Strategic fits prompt action to take advantage of a window of opportunity to close deals that fill perceived gaps in the business or offer avenues for expansion through once-in-a-lifetime situations.

More than half the entrepreneurs who believe that the good ideas for their businesses come from people other than themselves base their timing on people versus only a sixth of those who believe they are the source of most of the ideas for their business.

### Cycles

In the bloodbath of the 1981-82 recession, Serge Racine of Shermag, in his scholarly way, applied to his furniture company the economic principles he taught at university in the U.S. and in Sherbrooke. He loved the recession. "Our big expansion was during those years," he says. "The companies were cheap. In the past 72 years, there have been 12 cycles. If there's a crisis, there's prosperity on the way. You've got to be counter-cyclical." When he bought his plant in Disraeli (his fifth acquisition) toward the end of 1982, he estimated the machinery alone was worth more than $6 million. He offered $400,000 for it and discovered there was $150,000 worth of lumber on the site, plus he got a grant from the Quebec government for $200,000. "Now," he says, with just a touch of satisfaction, "it's worth $78 million."

Allied to the economic cycles, there are broad psychological cycles too. Don Watt of the Watt Group read those right in the 1970s: "From October, 1973 to 1981, the developed countries wanted consumers to trade down. In the early 1970s, we were ahead of everyone in anticipating the middle class was going to find new ways to shop. It was warehouses with style." His client, Loblaws, cleaned up with its No Frills supermarkets. "When Reagan came in, he boosted the US$ and we started trading up, putting more quality into products." Loblaws introduced President's Choice, its house brand, in a wide variety of goods, and cleaned up again. "The next step," he said in 1987, "is inflation and high interest rates. Consumers will trade down again. That's bad for durable goods." Before it came to that, however, Watt helped Loblaws ride another consumer wave by introducing environmentally-friendly "green" products.

Entrepreneurs themselves go through cycles. It's a common pattern for them to lead their companies through a spurt of manic growth, then shut down while they consolidate and regain a measure of control. Then they get bored and start the whole cycle again. Products have life cycles, too, starting with the high-priced, low volumes of a new product and maturing to the low-priced, high volumes of a big business.

Industries also have regular cycles that can be predicted with a degree of certainty. Bob Lamond of Czar Resources was one of the superstars in the oil patch when it was booming in the 1970s. He was also one of the entrepreneurs who was badly overextended when the bottom fell out of the market. He hung in, however, and gave a virtuoso performance adjusting to radically changed conditions. He squeezed every ounce of fat out of Czar, restructuring it and laying off two-thirds of the staff, including the president, until he brought its breakeven point to a level that allowed Czar to stay in business in the terrible markets that have prevailed for most of the 1980s.

Lamond thinks a lot about cycles. He writes essays to himself, a kind of private Ph.D. to educate himself and keep his eye focussed on where he's going. He has a probing mind and a wide range of interests, including a passion for military strategy. He loves to keep in touch with journalists and has two large files of clippings in his office. In one he keeps all the articles that described him in heroic terms; in the other all those that pilloried him for his excesses. Small and gregarious, he has a Scottish accent as strong as the day in 1965, when he arrived in Canada to work for Imperial Oil as a geologist. He's more a businessman than a geologist now, however. "I've become very interested in business as such," he says. "It's like being a gene splicer."

He takes his industry graphs seriously. "There are three major cycles in this industry," he says. "The basic exploration cycle of ten years, the U.S. market activity of four to five years and the annual climate cycle. Your forecasts don't have to be right, but you have to be in shape for whatever is coming. You're a damn fool if you don't read the graphs constantly. You'll fall off the cliff."

Lamond had a brilliant career as a geologist before he turned his mind to business. He didn't stay long with Imperial Oil, however, because he found big companies stifling. Three years after he arrived in Canada, Lamond started his first business and enjoyed a meteoric rise to fame and fortune. His major innovation was bringing German money into the Calgary oil patch. He was so successful, Czar became cash-driven, as he puts it. "We had to beat investors off with a big stick." When the crash came in 1981, he was caught off guard with his practice of financing his drilling programs after the work was performed. To compound matters, he approved $25 million of exploration spending, unfinanced, after the federal government introduced the National Energy Program, which devastated the industry. That $25 million quickly became $35 million with interest, because he had neglected to lock in the interest rates on his bank loans. With a debt load of $70 million, Czar looked like a basket case, but Lamond's restructuring convinced the bank to exchange $30 million of its loans for common shares and warrants in 1987, giving the company a new lease on life.

Besides the financial restructuring, the major reason for Czar's survival was Lamond's ability to find markets for his natural gas when other companies couldn't. He pioneered direct sales to industrial companies. Sales peaked in 1982 at $16 million, but they didn't go much below $15 million in the following seven years, and the company stayed in business. Lamond is ready for the recovery. "In the next upturn," he says, "I can build a medium-sized company which I run myself, or go into the delegation process and grow really big. I haven't decided what I'll do yet."

### Markets

The market is critical to virtually all strategic decisions, but it is less often the key factor in timing. Mark Blumes is one person who never worries about market timing even though marketing is the most important discipline in his industry. Nevertheless, market timing is a critical factor for most businesses.

Jim Robinson of Petwa Canada spends 20% to 30% of his time looking for new ideas, although few ever make it into his product line-up. Petwa manufactures water treatment equipment, and, like many small companies, avoids jumping into a market that is already well enough established that big companies can do market surveys on them. It's already too late then. "Most of our situations we get into before the market's there," he says. "We try to push the market rather than follow it. The timing is, 'Is the market able to absorb this new product?'" Robinson has a simple way of finding out. He goes calling on the organizations to which he would sell the product. "I look at the enthusiasm of people off whom I bounce the ideas." He talks only to the top people. " Middle management is no good—they're unrealistic."

Another example of market timing is the hotel industry, where good timing is notoriously elusive. Bill Pattison of Delta Hotels says that his industry is the thermometer of the economy (as opposed to the barometer). When things are tough, it hits hoteliers first. That's hard enough to deal with. However, the other major influence on the bottom line is the number of beds available in a market. The decision to build or buy a hotel in a city where there is reasonable equilibrium between demand and supply can be destroyed in a matter of months by other hoteliers deciding to go into the same market. In his understated way, Pattison comments, "The knowledge of what our competitors are doing is key."

### Entrepreneurial willpower

Richard Bourbeau is the president and biggest shareholder in Venmar, which makes residential ventilation equipment in the backwater town of Drummondville, halfway between Montreal and Quebec City. Bourbeau and his partner, Jacques Morrissette, bought Venmar in 1977, when its only asset was a good idea. In the following 11 years, they built it to sales of $34 million, with its products in stores from coast to coast.

"When we started Venmar, there was nothing," he says. "There was no market. The second oil crisis in 1979 opened it up, but market timing is not all that important. Economic cycles change the price, but that's not really important either. There's always someone to say, 'It's not the right time.' What counts is a good product, a good reputation and good distribution." He might have added a determined leader.

A lot of the credit for Venmar's success goes to the tall and cool Bourbeau, a young man in a big hurry. Before he took off on the acquisition trail to build his sales quickly, he spent years building the executive team that forms the base of his operations now. He won't say where he wants to take his company, but the scale is continental. "I want to build something that will last, like GM or Ford. I like building. I feel I have the capacity to do much more than I'm doing now." His ambition is matched by his matter-of-fact expression of a self-confidence that can only be described as awesome. "I was always ahead," he says. "If I get interested in something, I have to be the best. If I couldn't be first, I'd do something else. It's in me. It's the way I am. I'm a leader and entrepreneur. They smell it, even if they don't say it."

His tightly controlled zeal is never far below the surface. He is not a warm man, his interest in people being strongly skewed toward their potential to contribute to the invincible team he knows he has to build to achieve his goals. He is highly focussed and precise, wasting few words and less time. Although he accepts the burden of making himself available to the media because Venmar is now a public company, he clearly derives no pleasure from the exposure—he could spend the time more productively on the job. Having decided in his late 30s that he doesn't have a lot of time left to achieve his goals, he accelerated his growth targets, taking the company public and buying two competing firms with double the sales of Venmar.

Venmar has grown because Bourbeau has decided to make it grow. And it's grown according to his personal timetable. His inner power drives his timing. Maestros also often base their timing on the whims of their particular expertise. With their marvellous skills, they take initiatives when it seems right for the long-term development of their product. It is not always a happy basis for timing, but it does work.

### People

Many entrepreneurs, like Mark Blumes of Mark's Work Wearhouse, let people determine their timing. Michael de Pencier of Key Publishers recently bought Trans Canada Press, a small company distributing business books. His timing was simple. "Roy is really interested in the business, so we got into it." Roy is Roy MacLaren, former president of CB Media, which is owned 30% each by MacLaren, Key Publishers and Maclean Hunter, with the remaining 10% in the hands of Alexander Ross, CB Media's peripatetic and brilliant vice president and editorial director. CB Media publishes *Canadian Business* and *Small Business Magazine.*

De Pencier has made decisions this way for years, building a small publishing empire with annual sales of $30 million in 1986. His technique has its unhappy moments, though. Ross thought a magazine about energy was a great idea in 1980, so de Pencier put up the money and Ross went to Calgary to be close to the action. He was just in time to get crushed by the collapse of the Albertan economy, and it cost both men a lot of money.

De Pencier is a people person. He has a bookish, slightly absentminded look about him, but that's not his personality. When he's interested and engaged, he's gregarious and radiates a powerful personal warmth. He clearly enjoys people and loves to see them succeed. In fact, he structures his whole business that way, sharing ownership in his many companies with the chief operating people, so that their success makes money for them and him.

He has created an environment in which people can express their talents with complete freedom. He draws people into his ambit by allowing them into his sanctum, where they either figure out the culture and find themselves a niche consistent with the overall objectives of Key Publishers, or they drift away. It's worked well for him.

Marcel Dutil of Canam Manac has also built his business empire with a sense of timing that depends heavily on people. "My team has to be ready," he says. "When you start a company, you push your people. After you get to a certain size, they push you. The head of the Missouri plant is a Beauceron. He thinks I'm getting old, because we have delayed the opening of our Florida plant until I find the right people. Sometimes I push, sometimes I brake."

### Financing
Although it is central to the health and, of course, the survival of a business, financing is seldom an initiating factor in timing decisions. It is far more often a factor that stops ventures than starts them. However, it can also be an initiating factor when entrepreneurs buy assets so cheaply that it makes a previously uneconomic project viable.

Paul Abildgaard of Nanton Water is one example of an entrepreneur who moves on a business idea when he finds an opportunity to buy a key component of the project at a price so low that it gives the business an unbeatable edge against the competition. Others allow the price of an acquisition to make their decisions for them. They establish criteria for return on their investment and if the price meets those criteria, they buy. If it doesn't, they walk away.

### Strategic fit
Sometimes a deal comes along that provides an opportunity to fill a gaping hole in a firm's product-line or structure. No matter what the difficulties are in financing, staffing or marketing it, it's a deal that has to be closed because the chance may not come again.

Guylaine Saucier of The Saucier Group was suffering from

uncertain supplies of wood for her plant that makes studs for construction. "I'd been looking for several years for a way to increase our wood supply," she says. "I didn't know how to, but that was the aim. Then a logging company got into trouble in 1984 and I bought it. Sometimes it's so important for the company, you just have to do it. We'd just had a recession, it was expensive and it was political (two cabinet ministers were involved). But we found the finance, and everyone worked weekends to close the deal without ever being asked."

## Technology

Technology is perhaps the easiest of the timing factors to understand, because it claims so many victims of bad timing. The acquisition of technology is very expensive in the pioneer stage. It's relatively cheap, however, when it has been developed but is still six months away from being introduced to the market. Once it's in the market, it becomes expensive again because its profit potential is proven. Finally, it becomes cheap again when the next generation of technology is being developed and it has a limited life span.

Perspectives of the price of technology change with the size of a firm. Once a firm grows to a reasonable size, it can worry less about the price. Its marketing clout would normally allow it to depreciate the cost of the technology over a large number of sales, as the Japanese have shown so competently. However, the technology must be state of the art, preferably very close to the time it was introduced to the market. Otherwise, the life span of the product is too short to pay for the cost of the technology.

## RESTRAINING FACTORS

Timing decisions are not all decisions to go ahead. Decisions to abort a project are often critical to the survival of businesses. The considerations that influence these decisions are restraining factors, the most common of which is financing. For any young business, still struggling to make it through the start-up phase, lack of capital is a particularly familiar problem, but it's true for established firms too. Other initiating factors can be restrainers as well, the next most common being people. Without the right people to head up a new project, it is often better not to do it at all.

Petwa's Jim Robinson has perfected his system of rating restraining factors. Whenever he is assessing a new venture, he puts it through his test of seven barriers. If the venture scores low, he will pursue it further by consulting with his partner Ken Heuchert, or, if he doesn't know the industry well, with experts in the field. If it scores high, he drops it immediately. The seven barriers are:

1. The number of competitors. If there are no competitors, you give it a low score, unless the total score is very low, in which case competitors can come in easily, so you score it high on this item. (This is a market factor.)
2. The size of the building. (This is financing.)
3. The number of people needed to run it. (This is a people factor, which also touches on the entrepreneur's available time.)
4. Skills requirements. (People.)
5. Capital requirements. (Financing.)
6. Manufacturing operation or selling only. (Entrepreneur's time.)
7. Breadth of the market. (Market.)

## THE EVOLUTION OF A SENSE OF TIMING

Of course, a small, young firm doesn't approach timing decisions the same way an established firm does. The smallest firms are overwhelmingly influenced by the market situation and entrepreneurial willpower in their timing decisions, and hardly at all by people (see Appendix C, Table 16.1). By contrast, the bigger entrepreneurial firms tend to base their timing on cycles, people and strategic fits to a far greater degree. Entrepreneurial willpower and the market are more rare in their sense of timing. Medium-sized firms depend disproportionately on entrepreneurial willpower, largely because so many of them are in the critical phase of rapid transition from small to large firms.

# EPILOGUE

It's an exaggeration to say that anyone can succeed as an entrepreneur, but it can be argued that anyone can *learn* to do so. The catch is that it takes enormous determination and verve, as the stories in this book so vividly demonstrate. Potential entrepreneurs everywhere agonize over whether they have what it takes to survive the initiation process. The good news in this book is that they can do it. The bad news is that they won't get much help. Succeeding as an entrepreneur is a very personal challenge.

The education of entrepreneurs comes at two levels. The first is the technical knowledge required of all businesspeople—the skills that contribute to competence. A successful entrepreneur needs to have a good understanding of the full range of business skills, including an understanding of financial statements, the basics of motivational skills, the principles of marketing, the main laws applying to business affairs and much, much more. These skills relate purely to learning facts that can be absorbed by anyone who is prepared to apply himself or herself to the task. The necessary knowledge is available in university courses, in countless good books, and, most of all, in the day-to-day experiences of running a firm.

The second level of skills needed to be a successful entrepreneur is more complex, because it touches on how entrepreneurs influence their environment and how they respond to the situations they encounter. These skills are not based on facts but on character, and it's much more difficult to learn them. In fact, many people who deal with entrepreneurs believe they cannot be learned. They believe that entrepreneurs are born, not made, and that they will succeed only if they have the right combination of "unlearnable" attributes such as leadership skills and integrity. In many cases, they are right. Failed entrepreneurs invariably suffer from shortfalls in their skills at this level. However, the successful entrepreneurs in this book conclusively debunk this theory. Many of them do not have the unlearnable skills deemed to be necessary. They have found ways to adapt themselves to their environment to achieve the results they want.

The entrepreneurs in this book, like their counterparts everywhere, possess every kind of personality imaginable. The difference is they know how to marry their own skills with the environment they choose for themselves. They know their own strengths and weaknesses so well that they can build on the former and compensate for the latter. By applying their own skills or by motivating others to provide them on their behalf, they find the necessary market niches, take the necessary risks, provide the necessary leadership, and design the necessary plans of action. In the end, their personalities are not important, because they succeed by responding appropriately to the situations they face.

The most striking thing about them is that they have found relatively few patterns of behaviour that are effective in any given situation. There are only five styles of leadership, four types of planning and three perceptions of risk. Yet there is sufficient range in these patterns to accommodate any and every personality. They all have unique approaches to entrepreneuring. In every element of entrepreneurship, the people who succeed are those who pick the style or approach that best suits themselves.

For some people, being an entrepreneur is a natural expression of their personality. For others (at least half the people in this book), success is a product of a tremendous desire to be an entrepreneur allied to an indefatigable determination to find a way to apply their own attributes to the challenges they have chosen. Either way, they are fascinating people, all the more so for the responsibility they bear in a modern economy struggling to adapt to rapid change.

As I said at the beginning of this book, it has been a privilege travelling from one coast of Canada to the other to learn about their businesses, their hopes, their dreams and their fears. I hope readers will have drawn from this book as much inspiration as I myself drew from the individuals who people it.

# THE 100 ENTREPRENEURS

The names and companies of the entrepreneurs interviewed for this book are shown below. The company names were accurate when the interviews were conducted between mid-1986 and mid-1987. In several cases, the entrepreneurs are no longer with the company mentioned or the company has failed. Further details about the entrepreneurs and their companies are in Appendix B, which summarizes their vital statistics.

| NAME | COMPANY | CITY |
|---|---|---|
| *Newfoundland* | | |
| 1 Harold Duffett | Standard Manufacturing | St. John's |
| *Nova Scotia* | | |
| 2 John Bragg | Oxford Frozen Foods | Oxford |
| 3 John Currie | Internav | Sydney |
| 4 John Lindsay | J.W. Lindsay Enterprises | Dartmouth |
| 5 Tom Murdoch | Keelson Electronic Marketing | Halifax |
| 6 Ken Rowe | IMP Group | Halifax |
| 7 Joe Shannon | Atlantic Corporation | Port Hawkesbury |
| *New Brunswick* | | |
| 8 Rick DesBrisay | Sumner's | Moncton |
| 9 George Jenkins | Process Technology | Oromocto |
| 10 Joe Landry | Cape Bald Packers | Cap-Pelé |
| *Quebec* | | |
| 11 Pierre Boivin | Norvinca Inc. | St. Laurent |
| 12 Richard Bourbeau | Venmar | Drummondville |
| 13 Francine Brulé | Les Agences Francine Brulé | Montreal |
| 14 Normand Carpentier | Camoplast | Kingsbury |
| 15 Germain Courchesne | Industries Aston | St. Léonard d'Aston |
| 16 Jean-Guy Dionne | Textiles Dionne | Ste. Foy |
| 17 Marcel Dutil | Le Groupe Canam Manac | St. Georges |
| 18 Bernard Faucher | Communications Voir | Montreal |

| 19 | Michel Gaucher | Socanav | Montreal |
| 20 | Michel Gendreau | Garaga | St. Georges |
| 21 | Jean-Luc Giroux | Gentec | Ste. Foy |
| 22 | Michel Lapointe | DAP Electronics | Vanier |
| 23 | Claude Lessard | Cossette Communication -Marketing | Quebec City |
| 24 | Benoit Métivier | IPL | St. Damien |
| 25 | Phil O'Brien | Devencore | Montreal |
| 26 | Jean Pouliot | CFCF/ Quatre Saisons | Montreal |
| 27 | Richard Prytula | Leigh Navigation Systems | Pte. Claire |
| 28 | Serge Racine | Shermag | Sherbrooke |
| 29 | Guylaine Saucier | Saucier Group | Laval |
| 30 | François Vachon | Cartem | Ste. Marie |

*Ontario*

| 31 | Lawrence Bloomberg | First Marathon Securities | Toronto |
| 32 | Jim Brickman | Brick Brewery | Waterloo |
| 33 | Rod Bryden | Kinburn Corp. | Ottawa |
| 34 | John Bulloch | Canadian Federation of Independent Business | Toronto |
| 35 | Dave Campbell | CMQ Communications | Toronto |
| 36 | Steve Chepa | Dicon Systems | North York |
| 37 | Greig Clark | College Pro Painters | Toronto |
| 38 | Mike Cowpland | Corel Systems | Ottawa |
| 39 | Michael de Pencier | Key Publishers | Toronto |
| 40 | Jim Egan | Egan Visual | Woodbridge |
| 41 | Diana Ferguson | Berwick Ferguson Payroll | Toronto |
| 42 | Harvey Gellman | Gellman Hayward & Partners | Toronto |
| 43 | John Gillespie | Pizza Pizza | Toronto |
| 44 | Walter Hachborn | Home Hardware Stores | St. Jacob's |
| 45 | Ron Hume | The Hume Group | Toronto |
| 46 | Johnny Lombardi | CHIN Radio/TV International | Toronto |
| 47 | Mary Macdonald | Venture Economics (Canada) | Toronto |
| 48 | Karl Magid | Lulu's Roadhouse | Kitchener |
| 49 | Jim MacKenzie | Molly Maid Home Care Services | Toronto |
| 50 | Jim McKinney | Stephenson's Rent-All | Rexdale |
| 51 | Jim Neill | Metro Toronto News | Scarborough |
| 52 | Peter Oliver | Oliver's | Toronto |
| 53 | Walter Oster | The Whaler's Group | Toronto |
| 54 | Bill Pattison | Delta Hotels | Toronto |
| 55 | Jarvis Peacock | Jarvis Design & Display | Ottawa |
| 56 | Alan Perlmutter | Micro Cooking Centres | London |
| 57 | Anna Porter | Key Porter Books | Toronto |
| 58 | Mike Potter | Cognos | Ottawa |
| 59 | Clive Raymond | National Business Systems | Mississauga |
| 60 | Des Rice | Turf Management Systems | Mississauga |
| 61 | Chris Rudge | Bedford House | Toronto |
| 62 | John Seltzer | GBB Associates | Toronto |

| 63 | Ian Sharp | I.P. Sharp Associates | Toronto |
| 64 | Mike Simmons | Air Star | Mississauga |
| 65 | Vern Simpson | Swift Sure Courier | Oakville |
| 66 | Dave Steele | Three Buoys Houseboat Vacations | Toronto |
| 67 | Frank Stronach | Magna International | Markham |
| 68 | Tom Vincent | ETA Suites | Toronto |
| 69 | Don Watt | The Watt Group | Toronto |
| 70 | Kingsley Ward | Pharmapak | Scarborough |

*Manitoba*

| 71 | Richard Andison | Powell Equipment | Winnipeg |
| 72 | Sheldon Berney | Reliance Products | Winnipeg |
| 73 | John Buhler | Farm King Allied | Winnipeg |
| 74 | Oscar Grubert | Champs Food Systems | Winnipeg |
| 75 | Carol Johnson | Pace Setter Swim & Gym Wear | Winnipeg |
| 76 | Richard Kroft | Tryton Investments | Winnipeg |

*Saskatchewan*

| 77 | Abram Dyck | Saskatoon Fresh Pack Potatoes | Saskatoon |
| 78 | Jim Figley | Spectron Computer | Saskatoon |
| 79 | Albert McElwee | Linnvale Steel | Saskatoon |
| 80 | Terry Summach | Flexi-Coil | Saskatoon |
| 81 | Jim Yuell | Prairie Chemical Industries | Saskatoon |

*Alberta*

| 82 | Paul Abildgaard | Nanton Water | Nanton |
| 83 | Mark Blumes | Mark's Work Wearhouse | Calgary |
| 84 | Don Cormie | Principal Group | Edmonton |
| 85 | Ed Davis | Systems Investments | Calgary |
| 86 | Jack Donald | Parkland Industries | Red Deer |
| 87 | Bob Lamond | Czar Resources | Calgary |
| 88 | Lou MacEachern | Servpro/Fortune Industries | Calgary |
| 89 | Rob Peters | Peters & Co. | Calgary |
| 90 | Jim Robinson | Petwa Canada | Calgary |

*B.C.*

| 91 | Ramona Beauchamp | Ramona Beauchamp Int'nl | Vancouver |
| 92 | Doreen Braverman | The Flag Shop | Vancouver |
| 93 | Mike Brown | Ventures West Technologies | Vancouver |
| 94 | Chris Corbett | Interscience Industries | Victoria |
| 95 | Klaus Deering | Glenayre Electronics | Vancouver |
| 96 | Helmut Eppich | Ebco Industries/Epic Data | Richmond |
| 97 | Gail Gabel | Anderaa Instruments Ltd. and Meteor Communications | Victoria |
| 98 | Jim Pattison | The Jim Pattison Group | Vancouver |
| 99 | Basil Peters and Peter van der Gracht | Nexus Engineering | Burnaby |
| 100 | Jack Wilson | RSI Robotic Systems Int'nl | Sidney |

# WHO THE ENTREPRENEURS ARE AND WHAT THEY DO

| Genesis | |
| --- | --- |
| Founders | 68% |
| Acquirers | 26% |
| Inheritors | 6% |
| Total | 100% |

Genesis refers to whether the entrepreneur is a founder, or acquired the business or inherited it. Where a person owns several businesses, the start-up, acquisition or inheritance of the first business is what counts. A founder may have bought many businesses once he or she got started, but is a founder because the first one was started from scratch. In the same way, a person who inherited a business, sold it and bought another is counted as having inherited the business.

| Age of entrepreneurs | |
| --- | --- |
| Less than 30 | 3% |
| 30-39 | 22% |
| 40-49 | 35% |
| 50-59 | 29% |
| 60-69 | 10% |
| 70 or more | 1% |
| TOTAL | 100% |

# Number of businesses owned by the entrepreneurs, by industry classification:

| | Principal Business | All Businesses | |
|---|---|---|---|
| | # | # | % |
| Primary | 0 | 10 | 4 |
| Mining | 1 | 5 | 2 |
| Manufacturing | 45 | 91 | 39 |
| Food | 5 | 9 | 4 |
| Tobacco | 0 | 0 | 0 |
| Rubber & plastics | 3 | 6 | 2 |
| Leather | 0 | 0 | 0 |
| Textiles | 1 | 2 | 1 |
| Knitting mills | 0 | 0 | 0 |
| Clothing | 1 | 3 | 1 |
| Wood products | 1 | 2 | 1 |
| Furniture & fixtures | 2 | 4 | 2 |
| Paper & allied | 1 | 3 | 1 |
| Printing & publishing | 6 | 8 | 3 |
| Primary metal | 0 | 1 | 0 |
| Metal fabricating | 6 | 10 | 4 |
| Machinery | 4 | 6 | 3 |
| Transportation equipment | 1 | 9 | 4 |
| Electrical products | 9 | 15 | 6 |
| Non-metallic minerals | 0 | 1 | 0 |
| Petroleum & coal | 0 | 1 | 0 |
| Chemicals | 2 | 5 | 2 |
| Miscellaneous | 3 | 6 | 3 |
| Construction | 0 | 5 | 2 |
| Transport./Commun./Util. | 6 | 19 | 8 |
| Wholesale trade | 8 | 14 | 6 |
| Retail trade | 5 | 14 | 6 |
| Finance, Insurance, Real est. | 7 | 21 | 9 |
| Services | 28 | 54 | 24 |
| Education | 0 | 1 | 0 |
| Health | 0 | 1 | 0 |
| Religious | 0 | 0 | 0 |
| Amusement & recreation | 3 | 4 | 2 |
| Services to business | 13 | 25 | 11 |
| Personal | 0 | 0 | 0 |
| Accommodation & food | 6 | 13 | 6 |
| Miscellaneous | 6 | 10 | 4 |
| TOTAL | 100 | 233 | 100 |

The business or businesses of each entrepreneur were coded by three-digit 1970 SIC numbers. Between them, the 100 entrepreneurs ran 233 businesses. This excludes investments (property, for example, that was not administered by the entrepreneurs themselves).

### Size of Businesses

| | |
|---|---|
| Very small | 4% |
| Small | 35% |
| Medium | 38% |
| Large | 17% |
| Very large | 6% |
| Total | 100% |

Size was determined primarily on the basis of the number of employees, although annual sales were also considered. Where the sales figures and the employee figures put the firm in different size categories, the number of employees generally prevails. The approximate limits of the size categories are as follows:

| Size | Number of employees | Annual Sales |
|---|---|---|
| Very small | less than 10 employees | less than $2 million |
| Small | 11 to 99 employees | $2 to $10 million |
| Medium | 100 to 499 employees | $10 to $50 million |
| Large | 500 to 2,499 employees | $50 to $250 million |
| Very large | more than 2,500 employees | more than $250 million |

### Number of years that the entrepreneur has owned the principal business

| | |
|---|---|
| 0-5 years | 25% |
| 6-10 years | 28% |
| 11-15 years | 19% |
| 16-20 years | 10% |
| 21 + years | 18% |
| Total | 100% |

The years that the business has been owned is the period that the entrepreneurs have owned what are now their principal businesses. Sometimes the original business is still owned by the entrepreneur, but the current principal business was acquired or started more recently; in this case the years of ownership refer to the current principal business.

# STATISTICAL TABLES

## PART 1 ENTREPRENEURS AND ENTREPRENEURSHIP

### Table 3.1
**Degree of ownership and personal financial exposure**
Percentage distribution within categories of ownership control
of the personal financial exposure of entrepreneurs

| OWNERSHIP CATEGORY | PERSONAL FINANCIAL EXPOSURE | | |
| --- | --- | --- | --- |
| | *Little or none* | *Moderate* | *Full* |
| Control | 4% | 25% | 71% |
| Control with a partner | 17% | — | 83% |
| Management control | 18% | 44% | 38% |
| No control | 67% | 33% | — |
| All | 14% | 29% | 57% |

### Table 3.2
**Entrepreneurial strengths**

| *Entrepreneurial characteristic* | *Percent of entrepreneurs claiming to have the characteristic* |
| --- | --- |
| 1 Inner power | 44 % |
| Business judgement | 44 |
| 3 Perseverance | 36 |
| 4 Motivation skills | 34 |
| 5 Idea generator | 24 |
| 6 Technical skills | 20 |
| 7 Personal values | 19 |
| 8 Marketing skills | 17 |
| 9 Decisiveness | 17 |
| 10 Empathy | 15 |

| 11 | Conceptual facility | 14 |
|----|---------------------|-----|
| 12 | Ownership | 12 |
| 13 | Enthusiasm | 9 |
| 14 | Committed to quality | 4 |
|    | Perfectionist | 4 |
|    | Administrative skills | 4 |
| 17 | Financial expertise | 3 |
|    | Sense of humour | 3 |
| 19 | Luck | 1 |

These entrepreneurial strengths can be grouped in three major categories:

| | |
|---|---|
| Leadership skills: | *Charismatic leadership* — inner power, personal values, enthusiasm; *Dynamic leadership* — perseverance, decisiveness; *Cerebral leadership* — conceptual ability, idea generation, commitment to quality; *Ownership leadership* |
| Competence skills: | Business judgement, technical skills, marketing skills, and, much less frequently, perfectionism, administrative and financial skills. |
| People-management skills: | Motivation and empathy. |

**Table 4.1**
**The genesis of entrepreneurs and their source of ideas**
Distribution of where the ideas come from for each genesis of entrepreneurs

| SOURCE OF IDEAS | GENESIS | | |
|---|---|---|---|
| | *Founders* | *Acquirers* | *Inheritors* |
| Entrepreneur | 70% | 50% | 17% |
| Others* | 12% | 38% | 83% |
| Entrepreneur and others | 18% | 12% | — |
| All | 100% | 100% | 100% |

*Mostly employees, but some from outside the firm.

## Table 7.1
## Entrepreneurial motivation

| Entrepreneurial motivation | | Percentage of entrepreneurs claiming to have this motivation |
|---|---|---|
| 1 | Having fun | 44 % |
| 2 | Building a lasting organization | 34 |
| 3 | Money | 33 |
| 4 | Winning in business | 29 |
| 5 | Recognition | 26 |
| 6 | Sense of accomplishment | 23 |
| 7 | Seeing people fulfill their potential | 21 |
| 8 | The challenge | 14 |
| 9 | Improving the world in some way | 12 |
| 10 | Problem solving | 10 |
| | Producing a top-quality product | 10 |
| 12 | Meeting interesting people | 9 |
| 13 | Independence | 8 |
| | Power | 8 |
| 14 | Proving a point to doubters | 7 |
| 15 | Creativity | 6 |
| 16 | Helping the family | 4 |

# PART II   LEADERSHIP

## Table 10.1
## Leadership styles and skills
Percentage of entrepreneurs in each leadership style
who have the leadership skills shown

| LEADERSHIP SKILLS | LEADERSHIP STYLES | | | | | |
|---|---|---|---|---|---|---|
| | Solo | Osmosis | Managerial | System | Figurehead | Average |
| **Cerebral** | | | | | | |
| Conceptual | — | 19% | 10% | 17% | 18% | 13% |
| Ideas | 30% | 29% | 17% | — | 55% | 24% |
| Quality | 20% | 3% | 3% | — | — | 4% |
| **Dynamic** | | | | | | |
| Perseverance | 40% | 35% | 47% | — | 36% | 36% |
| Decisiveness | — | 26% | 20% | 17% | 9% | 17% |
| **Charismatic** | | | | | | |
| Inner power | 80% | 32% | 47% | 67% | 18% | 41% |
| Values | 20% | 13% | 20% | 33% | 27% | 18% |
| Enthusiasm | 20% | 6% | 10% | 17% | — | 9% |

### Table 12.1
### Criteria for hiring employees

| Characteristic | Percent responding |
|---|---|
| 1  Appropriate experience | 44 % |
| 2  A good attitude | 42 |
|    Compatibility with existing employees | 42 |
| 4  Ambition | 30 |
| 5  Good character | 29 |
| 6  Initiative | 27 |
| 7  Good judgement | 21 |
| 8  People skills | 16 |
| 9  Hard worker | 13 |
| 10  Willingness to grow | 10 |
| 11  Conscious of quality | 9 |
| 12  Decisiveness | 8 |
| 13  Educational background | 7 |
|    Personality for the job | 7 |
| 15  Sense of humour | 3 |
| 16  Creativity | 2 |
|    Reading habits | |

The criteria shown above encompass many different wordings. A sample of them follows:

1  Appropriate experience, track record, training, skills, reputation.
2  Good attitude, enthusiasm, loves the job, commitment, energy, motivation, passion, tries hard, interested.
3  Compatibility with existing employees, team player, fits in, loyalty, takes orders.
4  Ambition, aggressive, self-starter, drive, dynamic.
5  Character, integrity, ethical, honesty.
6  Initiative, not yes-men, able to defend their ideas.
7  Judgement, intelligence, common sense.
8  People skills, empathy, congenial.
10  Willing to grow, flexible, handles failure openly.
12  Decisive, practical, gets things done.

**Table 12.2**
**Theory Q\* and Theory K\* — team players and individualists**
Percentage of Theory Q or Theory K entrepreneurs
who say they look for the employees who have the traits shown

| Desired trait in employees | Theory Q | Theory K | Both and neither |
|---|---|---|---|
| Ambition | 53% | 4% | 28% |
| Compatibility | 71% | 8% | 39% |
| Experience | 76% | 4% | 44% |
| Attitude | 13% | 73% | 67% |
| Judgement | 13% | 42% | 11% |
| Initiative | 16% | 42% | 33% |
| Number of entrepreneurs | 38 | 26 | 18 |

\* Theory Q entrepreneurs weight the characteristics they seek in their employees toward ambition, compatibility with existing employees and experience. Theory K entrepreneurs weight their preferences toward a good attitude, judgement and initiative.

**Table 12.3**
**Organizational structures and firm size**
Distribution of organizational structures by size of firm

| STRUCTURE | FIRM SIZE | | | | | |
|---|---|---|---|---|---|---|
| | Very large % | Large % | Medium % | Small % | Very small % | Total % |
| Ad hoc | 0 | 15 | 24 | 53 | 9 | 100 |
| Decentralized | 18 | 14 | 39 | 29 | 0 | 100 |
| Structured | 3 | 25 | 50 | 22 | 0 | 100 |
| All companies | 6 | 17 | 38 | 35 | 4 | 100 |

**Table 12.4**
**Leader styles and how they make decisions**
Distribution of decision-making styles
within each leadership style

LEADERSHIP STYLE

| DECISION STYLE | Solo | Osmosis | Managerial | System | Figurehead |
|---|---|---|---|---|---|
| Solo | 59% | 9% | — | — | — |
| Input/solo | 33% | 22% | 13% | — | — |
| Tight delegation | 8% | 38% | 48% | 33% | 8% |
| Consensus | — | 12% | 19% | 33% | 8% |
| Loose delegation | — | 3% | 13% | 33% | 8% |
| Targeted | — | 16% | 7% | — | 76% |
| Total | 100% | 100% | 100% | 100% | 100% |

# PART III   STRATEGY

**Table 13.1**
**Planning types, showing their time frames and how many are written**

| Planning type | Distribution of entrepreneurs | % that have a time frame | % that are written |
|---|---|---|---|
| | % | % | % |
| Project plans | 24 | 38 | 50 |
| Goal-setting | 8 | 88 | 17 |
| Direction-setting | 11 | 45 | 28 |
| Full-scale plans | 53 | 91 | 98 |
| No plan at all | 4 | — | — |
| Average | | 70 | 65 |

**Table 14.1**
**Type of planning used by the seven types of entrepreneur**

TYPE OF PLANNING

| TYPE OF ENTREPRENEUR | Project plans | Goal-setting | Direction-setting | Full-scale plan | No plan | Total |
|---|---|---|---|---|---|---|
| Startup artists | 8 | 0 | 0 | 2 | 0 | 3 |
| Deal-makers | 0 | 25 | 0 | 0 | 25 | 3 |
| Maestros | 17 | 38 | 9 | 13 | 25 | 16 |
| Niche players | 58 | 25 | 64 | 35 | 25 | 43 |
| Supermanagers | 4 | 0 | 9 | 6 | 0 | 5 |
| Conglomerateurs | 0 | 0 | 0 | 10 | 25 | 6 |
| Visionaries | 12 | 12 | 18 | 38 | 0 | 24 |
| Total | 100 | 100 | 100 | 100 | 100 | 100 |

**Table 14.2**
**Influence of approach to opportunity on planning type**
Distribution within each planning type
of opportunity approach

PLANNING TYPE

| OPPORTUNITY APPROACH | Project plans % | Goal-setting % | Direction-setting % | Full-scale plan % | No plan % | Total % |
|---|---|---|---|---|---|---|
| Creators | 46 | 38 | 36 | 63 | 0 | 52 |
| Grabbers | 46 | 50 | 55 | 29 | 100 | 40 |
| Combined | 8 | 12 | 9 | 8 | 0 | 8 |
| Total | 100 | 100 | 100 | 100 | 100 | 100 |

**Table 14.3**
**Planning type by number of years that the owner**
**has owned the business**

| PLANNING TYPE | NUMBER OF YEARS OF OWNERSHIP | | | | |
|---|---|---|---|---|---|
| | 0-5 | 6-10 | 11-15 | 16-20 | 21+ |
| | % | % | % | % | % |
| Project plans | 21 | 36 | 22 | 30 | 11 |
| Goal-setting | 8 | 11 | 6 | 10 | 6 |
| Direction-setting | 4 | 11 | 22 | 10 | 11 |
| Full-scale plans | 63 | 42 | 44 | 40 | 66 |
| No plan | 4 | — | 6 | 10 | 6 |
| Total | 100 | 100 | 100 | 100 | 100 |

**Table 15.1**
**Employee involvement in each planning type**

| EMPLOYEE INVOLVEMENT | PLANNING TYPE | | | | | |
|---|---|---|---|---|---|---|
| | Project plans | Goal-setting | Direction-setting | Full-scale plan | No plan | Total |
| | % | % | % | % | % | % |
| Participatory | 30 | 0 | 64 | 45 | 0 | 38 |
| Input only | 33 | 37 | 27 | 43 | 0 | 36 |
| Solo | 33 | 63 | 9 | 12 | 100 | 24 |
| Don't know | 4 | 0 | 0 | 0 | 0 | 2 |
| All | 100 | 100 | 100 | 100 | 100 | 100 |

**Table 15.2**
**Distribution between opportunistic/strategic planning styles**
**and opportunity grabbers/creators**

| | Opportunistic planners | Strategic planners |
|---|---|---|
| | % | % |
| Opportunity grabbers | 20 | 20 |
| Opportunity creators | 11 | 41 |
| Combined | 2 | 6 |
| Total | 33 | 67 |

**Table 16.1**
**Initiating factors for timing used by each size of firm**
Percentage of firms within each size group
that use the initiating factors shown

FIRM SIZE

| INITIATING FACTORS | All firms | Very small | Small | Medium | Large | Very large |
|---|---|---|---|---|---|---|
| | % | % | % | % | % | % |
| Cycles | 12 | 12 | 6 | 9 | 14 | 57 |
| Market | 33 | 62 | 33 | 34 | 14 | 14 |
| Entrepreneur | 38 | 50 | 33 | 51 | 21 | 14 |
| People | 29 | 12 | 24 | 26 | 50 | 43 |
| Financing | 11 | 0 | 12 | 14 | 7 | 14 |
| Strategic fit | 17 | 0 | 15 | 17 | 29 | 29 |
| Technology | 6 | 0 | 12 | 3 | 7 | 9 |
| Number of firms | 98 | 8 | 33 | 36 | 14 | 7 |

# INDEX